FOR DIANA

VERGIL'S Aeneid

HERO 🌿 WAR 🌿 HUMANITY

Translated by
G. B. Cobbold

Bolchazy-Carducci Publishers, Inc.
Mundelein, Illinois USA

Editor: Laurie Haight Keenan
Contributing Editor: L. Dale Griffith
Cover Design & Typography: Adam Phillip Velez
Cartography: Margaret W. Pearce
Cover & Other Illustrations: © Thom Kapheim, All rights reserved

Vergil's Aeneid
Hero • War • Humanity

Translated by G. B. Cobbold

Bolchazy-Carducci Publishers, Inc.
1570 Baskin Road
Mundelein, Illinois 60060
www.bolchazy.com

Printed in the United States of America
2014
by United Graphics

ISBN 978-0-86516-596-0

Library of Congress Cataloging-in-Publication Data

Virgil.
 [Aeneis. English]
 Vergil's Aeneid : hero, war, humanity / G.B. Cobbold, translator.
     p. cm.
 Summary: "A prose translation of Vergil's Aeneid with new illustrations and
informational appendices"--Provided by publisher.
 Includes bibliographical references and index.
 ISBN 0-86516-596-3 (pbk. : alk. paper)
 1. Epic poetry, Latin--Translations into English. 2. Aeneas (Legendary character)
3. Legends--Rome. I. Cobbold, G. B. II. Title.

PA6807.A5C57 2005
873'.01--dc22

                                                                              2005004513

Contents

ACKNOWLEDGMENTS

I am extremely grateful to Stephanie Quinn, who, during the early drafts of this translation, offered crucial comments and advice, and to Dale Griffith, who spotted ambiguities with an eagle eye for detail and made many rough places smooth. Adam Velez' design of the completed work is both ingenious and elegant, and certainly contributes to the overarching vision of Lou and Marie Bolchazy, that the ancient classics must and can be made accessible to a wider world than the scholars' dusty libraries. But above all I would like to thank Laurie Haight Keenan, who with inexhaustible patience and good humor guided the whole work *ab ovo usque ad malum.*

NOTES ON THE TRANSLATION

Everybody takes for granted that, in an ideal world, it would be preferable to read a work of literature in the original language rather than in a translation. No translation can imitate the peculiar music of the "out of" language, and so some aesthetic or emotional effect must be lost in any "into" version. The *Aeneid* is, of course, no exception: regardless of their meaning, the words and phrases of Vergil's Latin do not *sound* like English, and Latin sentences are not put together in the same way as English; they cannot therefore strike the ear or the heart in exactly the same way. The subtleties of Latin allow effects and emphases unachievable in English; and such devices as alliteration or assonance or onomatopoeia can at best be only approximately reproduced. Moreover, the rhythms of the *Aeneid's* verse are characteristically Latin, even though its meter is the same dactylic hexameter* that Vergil's model Homer had used in Greek. Vergil uses the hexameter (which is unfitted to English) both because it comfortably fits the natural rhythms of Latin speech, and because its flexibility allows him to echo any variation of pace and mood in the progress of his narrative. And he uses it inimitably: Tennyson said that, as Vergil wrote it, it was "the stateliest measure ever moulded by the hand of man."

* Six metrical feet: each of the first four can be either a spondee (two long syllables) or a dactyl (one long syllable followed by two short). The fifth foot is always a dactyl, the last a spondee.

But for all the difficulties, if the *Aeneid* continues to be worth reading, it is better to read it in translation than not at all. Ever since Latin ceased to be generally spoken in Europe, the *Aeneid* has been translated and re-translated, always with new insights and interpretations, just as new productions of Sophocles or Shakespeare or Moliere or Ibsen are mounted at regular intervals, and old movies are remade. Every day's headlines demonstrate that ancient history and ancient literature are certainly worthy of careful attention. Nothing that happens today has not already happened in the past, and there is no tale that has not been told before.

The backdrop to the *Aeneid* is the Trojan war, the long conflict between the Greeks and the Asian city of Troy, which had been fought in a murky past but was made famous by Homer's epic poems, the *Iliad* and the *Odyssey*. The war had begun when three goddesses, Juno, Minerva and Venus (Hera, Athena and Aphrodite to the Greeks) became involved in an argument: which of them was the most beautiful? Jupiter (Zeus), the king of the gods, asked Paris, the son of king Priam of Troy, to adjudicate, and Paris chose Venus, the goddess of love, as the winner.

Juno, a sore loser of the beauty contest, never forgave Paris. But Venus made him a present of Helen, the most beautiful woman in the world, and he brought her home to Troy. Helen, however, was already married to Menelaus, king of Sparta, who, along with his brother, Agamemnon of Mycenae, raised an expeditionary force from all the cities of Greece in order to capture Helen back. Supported by Juno, the Greeks laid siege to the city and after ten years sacked it. Most of its men were executed, and the women and children were distributed among the senior Greek officers as concubines and slaves.

Aeneas, the son of Venus and the hero of the *Aeneid*, was a Trojan warrior who fought bravely in the war but was remarkable because of a prophecy recorded in the *Iliad* that he would one day "rule the Trojans, and after him his sons and grandsons for ever." (*Iliad* XX.307). In the *Aeneid*—an epic poem commissioned in 25 BCE by the emperor Augustus—Vergil re-works, modifies and elaborates on the tradition that had arisen from this prophecy, the tradition that Aeneas had made his way from his home in Troy to Latium in Italy, where his descendants had been the first founders of Rome. Into his account of Aeneas' exploits in the past, Vergil ingeniously weaves references to the Romans' even more splendid achievements still to come. Aeneas is guided, for example, by the prophecies of various gods and soothsayers. He meets with the spirits of unborn Roman heroes. When he lands in Italy he is given a guided tour of what will eventually be the site of Rome. And Venus gives him a new shield, on which are inlaid a series of historical scenes, from the city's future founding by Romulus and Remus to the victory of Actium, which had, a few years before (31 BCE), confirmed Augustus' position as the first Roman emperor.

But just as the *Iliad* and the *Odyssey* are not primarily about the Trojan war, the *Aeneid* is not primarily a retelling of the legends of Rome's earliest beginnings or an exercise in nostalgia and patriotic encouragement. It would not have survived for more than two thousand years if that were all it was. Like the *Iliad*, it illustrates the eternally frustrating paradox of war: that we can be intoxicated by its glory and excitement, and at the same time cast into despair by its futility. Like the *Odyssey*, it celebrates a universal human toughness and ingenuity under the most daunting circumstances, an ability to live a life of grace under the most intense of pressures. And like all good stories, the story of the *Aeneid*—complete with adventures on the high seas, passion, battles, romance, magic and even some comic relief—turns on the complexities of human character. Aeneas' god-fearing constancy is tested by everyone, friend or foe, mortal or immortal, that he meets, and what he does, along with what they do in response to him, evokes the pity and terror that Aristotle suggested were the correct response to tragedy. Although everyone in the *Aeneid* has different and distinctive traits or motivations, there is an underlying unity in their membership of a single circle of loss.

Families lose their homes, warriors lose their illusions, lovers lose their loves, wives lose their husbands, fathers lose their sons—until, at the very end, we are left to wonder whether Aeneas himself, just as he is about to win the whole world, will lose his own soul.

In choosing to put the *Aeneid* into prose, I have assumed—since an epic is above all a story—that for some modern readers at least the plot will be paramount. Nowadays our epics come to us in novels or movies or sports: novels and movies and sports have trained many of us to want to know first and foremost what will happen next, and how it will all come out in the end. Narrative in verse is not part of today's idiom, but a prose reincarnation of Aeneas certainly deserves to be born into the twenty-first century.

My hope, then, in this version is to engage readers immediately with Aeneas' dangers and difficulties, and in his persistent moral dilemma—Do I do what I want or what I ought?—without the risk of their being distanced by any conventions of versification, or by any turn of phrase that might be seen as awkward or old-fashioned. I have tried to use language that is up-to-date without being colloquial, that preserves the dignity and leisured flow traditionally associated with epic, and that at the same time maintains the speed and energy appropriate to a captivating story.

I have certainly not intended to provide a crib or crutch for Latin students—though perhaps those who are making a detailed scrutiny of selected passages may find it useful as a summary of the entire work. Nor do I propose to make a contribution to Vergilian scholarship—though it is pleasing to imagine that perhaps some scholars may see something here that they have not seen before. I have assumed no previous knowledge of Roman history or politics, and no experience of Latin. But above all else I have attempted to sweep away any perceived difficulty in the fact that the *Aeneid* was originally written in a foreign language a very long time ago, and to present it as a novel.

In the search for a novelistic tone, however, I have constantly had to pick my way between the Scylla of too "free" a version (which might result in an inaccurate reflection of the original), and the Charybdis of a literal one (which risks clumsiness or even incomprehensibility). Latin diction tends to be compressed, even laconic, and I have had constantly to ask myself: How much is lost if the tightness of the Latin is rendered into an English phrase that has been, in the search for elegance and clarity, loosened and expanded?

For example: it may universally be admitted that the literal decoding of the famous *sunt lacrimae rerum* (I.462) into "There are tears of things" is not particularly useful in putting across what the phrase nevertheless quite clearly *means*. Does "We live in a sad world" (which does not contain any of the actual words of the Latin) sufficiently put across both Vergil's intent and his tone? At I.291, during his revelation of the future greatness of the Romans, Jupiter says: *aspera tum positis mitescent saecula bellis* (literally, "Then, wars having been put aside, they will soften the harsh times"). A purist might protest (rightly) that "There will be no more fighting. Those who have made war will make peace" is not what Vergil wrote. But I would counter that it does represent, in the style of translation that I have chosen, what he perhaps intended.

In the second instance, another question arises: how closely should one keep to Latin sentence structure? For all the compactness of each subordinate phrase or clause, Latin sentences as a whole—including Vergil's—are very often long and tortuous, as a result of certain characteristics of Latin syntax that tend to be avoided in modern English. So on many occasions, including the one just quoted, I have broken the original sentence up into two or three English ones. The purpose, as ever, has been to bring out more clearly what I have been bold enough to suppose is Vergil's meaning, and at the same time to make the English narrative line livelier and easier to follow. I have also, more rarely, transposed the order of lines or sentences in an attempt to achieve a more coherent sense.

The most glaring example is the switching, for a better dramatic impact, of the descriptions of Turnus and Camilla at the end of Book VII. In two passages (VI.601–623 and X.660–665), the shifts have the support of ancient editors.

Other changes have been made with respect to the specific traditions of the epic style that Vergil echoes directly from the Homeric epic, but that will today mean little to anyone except scholars. In the comparatively small world of ancient Greece or Rome, where everyone grew up surrounded by the same common forest of myths and legends, references to people now considered obscure might perhaps have been significant. Today it seems better to obey the standard instruction given to modern writers of fiction: "Don't name your minor characters." So from time to time I have omitted proper names, as in the roster of the sea-gods at V.823 ff., or in the battle scenes (e.g. X.569 ff. and X.702 ff.). Nor have I represented the epic custom of using variants of the names of certain gods or heroes or places: the non-specialist reader will only be confused if Venus is at one moment Cytherea and at another Acidalia, in allusion to the places where she was particularly worshipped; or if Achilles is sometimes Peliades after his father or Aeachides after his grandfather; or if Italy becomes Ausonia or Oenotria. (In two thousand years, who will recognize "Ike" and "Dubya" and the "Bronx Bombers," or know where to find "The Smoke" or "The Big Apple"?)

I have not dealt consistently with the epithets that are in ancient epic attached to proper names like a signature tune, such that Aeneas is routinely "pious," Achates "faithful," and other warriors either "fierce" or "strong"; similarly walls are usually and unhelpfully "high," trees are "tall" and altars "sacred." If I have not omitted these epithets altogether, I have translated them slightly differently, according to the context, on each occasion that they occur.

On the other hand I have put in a few words here and there that Vergil did not write. Any ancient reader's cultural literacy would have allowed him to know all that he needed to know about any person or place that Vergil might mention. But I have justified in adding a word or a very brief phrase of explanation where extra information seemed crucial to a clear understanding, and if nothing else in order to avoid an annoying footnote. For instance, when Vergil in the opening lines says that Juno loves "Carthage more than anywhere else on earth, more even than Samos," I have thought it fair to attach to Samos the label "where she was born." Examples of other glosses built into the text are included in the description of the heroes of Roman history whom Aeneas meets in VI.756 ff., and to the incidents that Vulcan depicts on Aeneas' new shield (VIII.626 f.). There is more information, if it is required, in Appendix V: "The Main Characters."

There are three places where, in imitation of the Catalog of the Ships in the second book of the *Iliad*, Vergil has made formal lists—of the competitors in the boat-race (V.115 ff.), of the Italian commanders who come to support Turnus (VII.647 ff.) and of Aeneas' Etruscan allies (X.164 ff.). Here, in order to avoid a long repetitive sequence of conjunctions, I have used anachronistic bullets.

Vergil—again following the convention established by the epic tradition—frequently uses the second person in order to address directly either his Muse (e.g. V.840) in order to ask for extra inspiration, or a character (e.g. V.40, X.186) in order to warn him of danger or sympathize with his predicament. In the first instance I have substituted this convention for another, by having the author speak directly to the reader ("What was the cause of his difficulties...?" or "Who could write an epic to describe...?"); and in the second I have simply reverted to the normal narrative third person.

A distinctive feature of the *Aeneid,* common also in the *Iliad* and the *Odyssey*, is the frequent use of simile, where one action or situation is compared to another—a surprise attack, for example, may be likened to a wolf pouncing on its prey, or an intransigent leader to a tree battered by a storm. Vergil's similes, much too vivid and effective to be modified

THE LIFE OF VERGIL

Vergil (Publius Vergilius Maro) was born in northern Italy in 70 BCE. At the age of about seventeen he left home and went to Rome to study rhetoric in order to become a lawyer, but he soon gave up law in favor first of philosophy and then of writing poetry. His first published work was the *Eclogues*, a pastiche of Greek songs about country life. Then came the *Georgics*, a long poem on agriculture in praise of the indefatigable labor of Roman farmers and the beauty of the Italian landscape, which was written during the painful civil wars that brought the Roman republic to an end. Vergil read the *Georgics* to the new emperor Octavian (not be re-named Augustus for a year or two yet), who was so pleased that he commissioned Vergil to write an epic poem which would celebrate Rome throughout her entire history.

Vergil began his Roman epic, the *Aeneid*, about 25 BCE. The first draft was finished when he died in 19 BCE, exhausted and unsatisfied with what he had written; he claimed that another three years was needed for revision and polishing. On his deathbed he asked that the manuscript be destroyed, but the emperor ignored him and ordered its immediate publication, just as it was; and it is in that form that the *Aeneid* has survived.

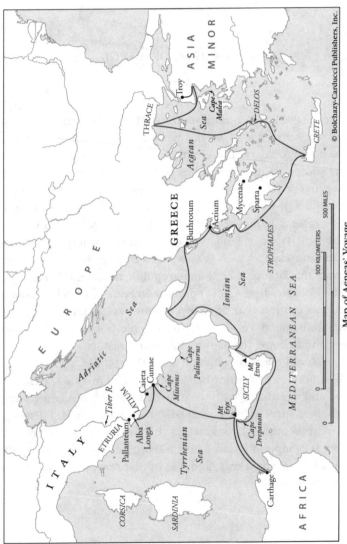

Map of Aeneas' Voyage

© Bolchazy-Carducci Publishers, Inc.

BOOK I
A Shipwreck and a Rescue

Why Juno hates the Trojans

This is a story of a war—and the story of a warrior, the first of the fugitives from Troy to make his way to Italy. Constantly driven off course by fate, or by the power of the gods, and harassed by Juno's relentless anger, he came ashore at last in Latium—but even there a long and bitter conflict lay ahead of him before he could establish a city and a home for his ancestral gods. But his descendants would be the founding fathers of Alba Longa, and one day they would build the walls of everlasting Rome.

What was the cause of all his trials? This man was famous for his obedience to the gods, so what had he done to offend Juno, the queen of the gods? Why did she make him suffer so much, and put so many obstacles in his way? Is a desire for vengeance a mark of the immortals?

Many years before, colonists from Tyre in Phoenicia had come to Libya and founded an aggressive, prosperous city that they called Carthage; it lies a long way from Italy, due south from the mouth of the river Tiber. It was well known that Juno favored Carthage more than anywhere else on earth, more even than Samos where she was born; and in Carthage she kept her armor and her chariot. The Carthaginians were very dear to her, and she hoped and prayed that they would become very powerful. But she had also heard what the fates had in fact decided: that the descendants of this man from Troy would one day govern a proud empire of their own, and that they would invade Libya, and that her beloved Carthage would fall.

And so Juno was uneasy. She could not forget the Trojan war: she had fought against Troy in support of the Greeks, and she could not put her old hostility out of her mind. She still remembered the judgment that Paris had given against her, and how he had been unmoved by her beauty; she was still jealous of the Trojan prince Ganymede, who had been kidnapped by Jupiter and then rewarded with special honors. And now there were these Trojans who had survived Achilles' attacks and escaped from Troy. And so for many years she had kept them far away from Latium; and instead she had let them be blown about on the high seas, lost and out of sight of land. But they had patiently endured, and it was that endurance that made their descendants, the Romans, what they are today.

The Trojan fleet is scattered by storm at sea

Sicily had fallen below the southern horizon. With sails spread to a following wind and spray flying at their bows, the Trojan ships headed cheerfully for the open sea.

"Am I to be compelled always to abandon my plans?" muttered Juno to herself, as usual harboring her hatred inside her. "Will I ever be able to prevent Aeneas from reaching Italy? The fates will not allow me, I suppose. But why not? When Ajax raped Cassandra, Minerva was offended by his sacrilege and burned his entire fleet and drowned all their crews. She whipped up the waves and scattered his ships; she threw one of Jupiter's thunderbolts and trapped Ajax in a whirlwind of flames; and when he was dying she impaled him on the spike of a rock. All that—for just one man? But on the other hand *I* have been at war for years with an entire race, and I am the queen of the gods, the sister and the wife of Jupiter. Is there no one left who brings offerings to *my* altars or prays to *me?*"

Still seething, still indignant, she flew to the birthplace of storms, the island of Aeolia, where the angry south winds are bred. Here King Aeolus keeps all the tangled gales reined

in, chained up, imprisoned—but even though they are shut inside their rock, you can still hear them grumbling. Up on his throne, he soothes their wild spirits with his scepter, and tempers their anger. He has to hold them constantly in check; if he did not, they would whirl in confusion over sea and land and sky, and hurtle incoherently through the air. The thought of that always has Jupiter worried: so he has hidden them in a dim cave and piled a huge mountain on top of them all, with Aeolus in charge of them. Aeolus knows how to let them loose or hold them in—but he may only act on Jupiter's command.

Juno approached Aeolus very politely. She said: "I have come to you because the father of gods and men allows you to smooth the waves or to raise the winds. A race of people whom I hate is now crossing the Tyrrhenian Sea. Even though they have been defeated, they are heading north for Italy from Sicily, carrying their family gods with them from Troy. Now—how would you like to have Deiopea, the loveliest of my fourteen lovely nymphs, as your wife? I will arrange for her to come live with you forever, and make you the father of a splendid family, if you will blast those Trojans with a gale, swamp their ships, sink them, scatter them and pitch their bodies into the sea."

"Your wish is my command," said Aeolus. "After all, it is you who have given me, with Jupiter's approval, whatever authority I have. It is with your permission that I sit and feast with the gods, and my power over clouds and storms derives from you alone."

He took aim with his spear and drove it into the side of his hollow mountain. He opened up a space, and the winds came bursting out, whirling and twisting, like soldiers through a

breach in a wall. South, east and west, they tumbled in a maelstrom of squall-bursts, sweeping enormous rollers toward the coast. Sailors shouted. Rigging whined. Clouds blotted out the daylight. Night lay low and black over the sea. On one side of the sky the lightning flashed and crackled, and on the other side the thunder answered. Everywhere the sailors looked, they saw lurking death.

Aeneas' limbs were weak and shivering, but he lifted his hands to the gods: "My friends who died at Troy, before their fathers' eyes and in defense of the city walls, were three times—no, four times—luckier than I," he groaned. "Diomedes, you were the strongest of the Greeks: why could I not have spat up my life on your sword, back on the plains of Troy where Hector was transfixed by Achilles' spear, where the river Simois washed away the bodies of all those gallant men—shields and helmets and all?"

A screaming squall from the north interrupted him, splitting sails and lifting the crests of waves far overhead. Oars were snapped off, the bows wrenched around: his ship lay broadside on to the wind, and a great weight of water flooded on board. Some sailors were swept upward on the surges; others could look directly down to see surf breaking on sand. A southerly gust took three ships and smashed them onto a jagged reef far out at sea and just below the surface—rocks that the Italians call the Altars. Three more, driven from the deep water into treacherous shallows, went aground. Sand piled up around them, and stopped them from floating off. A colossal sea broke over the stern of one ship, manned by Lycians under Orontes, and Aeneas could do nothing but watch as a whirlpool spun her around three times before it sucked her down. Orontes was swept overboard, while the heads of a few swimmers showed briefly in the eddies, among tackle and planks and treasure brought from Troy. Other captains—Ilioneus and Achates and Abas and the elderly Aletes—were in trouble, too. Their ships' ribs were cracking apart: they took in water and broke up.

Neptune calms the storm

Neptune, the god of the sea, was livid when he became aware of the roaring waves and the whole ocean turned inside out. But he did not lose his temper; he lifted his head above the ocean's surface and from far away he observed Aeneas' fleet scattered and all his Trojans overwhelmed by tangled water and sky. And Juno's part in it—her anger and her secret approach to Aeolus—did not escape him either. He called the winds to come before him.

"How have you come to be so sure of yourselves, you winds? How dare you stir up earth and sky without my express permission? I have a good mind to... but first I must calm the storm that you have caused. Next time you will pay for what you do with a much harsher punishment. For now, disperse—and give this message to King Aeolus: tell him that I alone hold the trident that represents command of the sea. I have all the power, and he has none. If he fancies himself as a tyrant, he can rule all he wants in the cave where you live. He is nothing but your jailer."

Imagine a riot: people are milling restlessly about, a mindless mob. Madness grips them. Stones are thrown. Bonfires are lit. But if one man of authority and responsibility stands up, they will listen quietly; with words alone, one man can control their passions and soften their hearts.

In this same way Neptune made the winds die down, and blew away the clouds that Aeolus had gathered, and brought back the sun, while his nymph Cymothoe and his son Triton heaved and hauled until the ships slid off the reef. With a single motion of his trident he laid bare the great sandbank, and at his glance the tumbled waters fell back from it, flat and smooth. And then he turned away his horses' heads and gave them free

rein. The light wheels of his chariot skimmed the tops of the waves as he drove away across a clearing sky.

Landing at Libya; Aeneas comforts the survivors

Aeneas' men were exhausted. The nearest land now was the coast of Libya, and there they found an inlet, carved rough and deep by the action of the sea. An island lay across the entrance, and offered good shelter behind it, while on both sides enormous threatening cliffs, dappled with leaves and sinister shadows, rose steeply to the sky. An overhang hid the opening of a cave where nymphs lived: there were fresh springs inside and benches carved from the living rock. Far down below, the water lay so safe and still that there was no need of lines to hold the weary ships, no need of anchors.

Aeneas counted his ships: of his whole fleet, seven were left. The Trojans disembarked, eager to feel solid earth under their feet again. They made their way up the beach and stretched their salt-soaked limbs on the sand. The first to get a fire going was Achates: he collected some dry leaves for tinder,

and struck sparks onto them from a flint, until they burned
with a steady flame. Then, tired though they were, the Trojans
fetched their cooking gear and the wet grain from the ships,
and got ready to dry it out over the fire and grind it on a rock.

While they were working, Aeneas climbed the cliff and
looked out over the sea for any sign of the other Trojan ships
or their captains—for Antheus or Capys or Caicus, always high
up on his poop-deck. Nothing. But inland he spotted three
wandering stags, conspicuous by their antlers, which spread
out like branches; and behind them a whole herd grazing in
a valley. His friend Achates was as usual carrying a bow and
arrows; Aeneas took them from him, and brought down the
three leading stags. Then he shot at the rest of the herd as they
crowded through the woods, and did not
stop until he had seven animals down on
the ground, one for each ship.

Down at the harbor again, he shared
his kill with his companions, and divided
up the casks of wine that the king of Sic-
ily, Acestes, had given them as they left
his court. Then he tried to comfort his
gloomy crews:

"My friends—you all know what has
happened to us in our travels. You have
suffered worse misfortunes than this:
you escaped the fury of the monster
Scylla when you passed by her cavernous

cliffs; and you avoid-
ed the rocks that the
giant Cyclopes threw
at you. The gods will
bring you out of this
as well. Don't think
about it any more; put
your fear and sadness
behind you. One day,

perhaps, you will be able to look back even on this disaster and take some pleasure from the memory of it. But for now, whatever may happen to us, whatever crisis is yet to come, keep in mind only that we must still press on to Latium. The fates have made it clear that, once there, we can settle in peace. And that is where—we may be sure of it—the city of Troy will rise once more. Be strong: keep up your spirits by thinking of happier times ahead."

Even though inside he felt sick and helpless, he put on a brave face and kept his anxiety to himself, while his Trojans prepared their meal. They stripped the skin from the animals' ribs and scooped out the entrails. Some of them cut up the meat into chunks and impaled it still quivering on wooden skewers, others arranged the cooking pots on the beach or attended to the fire. With food, they got back their strength, and they lay back on the grass and enjoyed the feeling of stomachs full of old wine and venison. And when they had eaten all they could, and had pushed back from the tables, they reclaimed their lost friends in conversation, switching always between hope and fear.

"Might they still be alive?"

"Are they in danger?"

"Do you think they could hear us, if we called out to them?"

"What about Orontes?" asked Aeneas sadly. "He was always so full of energy. And what has happened to Amycus? And poor Lycus? Can Gyas and Cloanthus be dead? They both seemed indestructible."

Aeneas' mother Venus complains to Jupiter about Aeneas' treatment by Juno; Jupiter foretells Rome's future power

And now it was the end of the day. From far above them, Jupiter was looking down at the sail-flecked sea and the shore and the men who lived on the land. Over Libya he paused, and Venus approached him, her eyes bright with tears:

"My lord," she said. "Both men and gods live in awe of your thunderbolts;

you will rule forever. What is it that my son Aeneas has done now? And what can his Trojans have done? They have undergone so much already, but because they are making for Italy, a landing anywhere is forbidden them. Did you not promise me that one day—far off in the future—the Trojans will be reborn in Italy as Romans? They would govern an empire, you said, that would include every land and every sea, all to be bound by Roman law. What has happened to make you change your mind? I have weighed one fate against another, and I have helped them survive the capture of Troy and its sad destruction. But ill fortune dogs them still, and still they are pursued by trouble. When in your omnipotence will you set a limit to their sufferings? After all, you let Priam's son Antenor make his way through the Greek lines out of Troy, and escape to the jagged coast of Illyria, and then travel in safety to Italy. And you guided him at last to a place where a river bursts out noisily from inside a mountain and floods the fields before it flows through nine channels into the sea—and there he has founded a town. Its inhabitants are still referred to as Trojans, and he has hung Trojan weapons on its walls. Now he lives there quietly and undisturbed. But *we*—Aeneas and I—are your children, and you have granted to us a place on Mount Olympus. Are we now to be betrayed because of the anger of just one goddess? How can it be right that he has lost his ships, and is kept away forever from the shore of Italy? Is this how his piety is to be rewarded, and my authority upheld?"

The father of gods and men smiled at her—the same look that he uses to calm stormy skies—and he kissed his daughter gently. "Don't be afraid," he said. "My plan for your children has not been altered, and my mind has not been changed. You will see them establish their own town, exactly as I have promised. They will fortify it and call it Lavinium, and later you will introduce the high-hearted Aeneas into heaven. If I explain the secrets of Aeneas' future, you will perhaps be less distraught. He is to fight a great war in Italy and overcome a dangerous enemy; through it all he will keep his people safe and he will teach them to be good. Once his enemies have been defeated, he will rule in Latium for three summers and three winters. And then his boy Ascanius, also called Julus, or Ilus—from Ilium, Troy's other name—will rule through the changes and chances of thirty more years. He will move his capital from Lavinium to a new stronghold at Alba Longa, and in Alba Longa kings descended from him will rule for three hundred years until Rhea Silvia, a priestess-queen, gives birth to twins, whose father will be Mars.

"One of those twins, Romulus, will proudly wear a yellow wolf-skin in honor of the wolf who brought him up, and he will build new walls strong enough to resist any attack. Into their shelter he will welcome a people that he will call, after himself, the Romans. For them there will be no limits of time or space. My mind is made up: I have ordained for them an empire without end. And then fierce Juno, who now intimidates the sea and land and sky, will think kindlier thoughts. She and I will love those Romans. Arrayed in their togas, they will be the masters of the world.

"And then, when many generations have passed, it will turn out that these reborn Trojans will conquer Greece: the capitals of Achilles and Agamemnon will submit to them. And then will come Caesar's turn—Julius Caesar, named after the great Julus. To both east and west, only the ocean will bound his empire, and his fame will soar to the stars. He will be weighted down with plunder from the Orient, and you will be free to receive him into heaven, where he too will be approached with prayer. There will be no more fighting. Those who have made war will make peace. Romulus and his brother Remus will give them their laws, in the name of Integrity and the goddess of the hearth. The doors of the temple of war will be closed tight and bolted firm; and Rage, the god who despises the gods, will be forced to sit inside, his terrifying weapons at his feet, his hands lashed behind his back and held by a hundred knots of bronze, cursing horribly from his bloody mouth."

When he had finished, Jupiter sent his messenger Mercury down to the earth. His instructions were to make sure that the new city of Carthage and all its people would welcome the Trojans, and that Carthage's Queen Dido would not turn them away out of ignorance of what was fated for them. Mercury flew through the empty air, the rhythm of his wings like the oars of a ship, and hovered above the Libyan shore. He did exactly what he was told: the Carthaginians put aside their hostility to strangers, and their queen in particular prepared to welcome the Trojans with an easy mind and a kindly heart.

Venus in disguise tells Aeneas the history of Carthage's foundation

Meanwhile, always conscious of his duty, Aeneas had spent the night in thought. At the first comforting glimmer of dawn he decided to explore this strange country where the storm had cast him up, and to bring detailed information back to his companions. Who lived here? Were there men—he saw no signs of cultivation—or only wild animals? He made sure that the ships were hidden in the rustling shadows beneath an overhang; and then he and Achates, each of them holding at the ready a broad-bladed spear, set out together.

Deep in the woods, Aeneas' mother Venus met them; she was in disguise, and from her expression and her clothes and her armor she might have been taken for a Spartan girl, or a princess of Thrace who rides harder and faster than the river Hebrus. She had slung a useful-looking bow across her shoulder and allowed her hair to blow loose in the wind; her legs were bare and her skirts were knotted up above her knees.

"Excuse me," she said. "Could you tell me if you've seen one of my sisters around here? She would be wearing a quiver, and a spotted lynx-skin? Or perhaps you've heard her shouting? She might be on the track of one of those wild boars—you know how they are, all spit and spray."

And her son said to her: "I haven't seen or heard any of them. But you're not a girl, are you? You don't have the face of a mortal, or a human voice. You're a goddess, aren't you? Are you the sister of Apollo, or related to the nymphs? Good luck to you anyway, whoever you are. Perhaps you can help us? We were caught in a great storm, and we've been shipwrecked. We don't know who lives here or what the country is like. Can you tell us where on earth we are, where we have fetched up? May we offer you a sacrifice?"

"Please, no," answered Venus. "You don't have to sacrifice to me. This is just the way that Tyrian girls dress; we always carry a quiver and wear these red hunting boots. We're descendants of King Agenor. The land around here is called Libya— the local people are a fierce and warlike lot—but you're actually in Phoenician territory. Our queen is Dido, and she came here from Tyre after she was forced to take refuge from her brother. The story of the injury that he did her, and everything that happened after that, is a long one. But I'll cut it short.

"Dido's husband was called Sychaeus. He was the richest landowner in Phoenicia, and he was madly in love with her, poor thing. Her father had given her to him in marriage when she was still a virgin, and all the omens were excellent. But her brother Pygmalion, the king of Tyre, was a very evil man, worse than anyone else in the city. Pygmalion and Sychaeus quarreled. The godless Pygmalion, who thought of nothing except money, caught Sychaeus by surprise when he was at prayer. He killed him, of course without a thought for his sister Dido's love. She became sick with grief for her dear lost husband, but for a long time Pygmalion was able to keep his crime secret, and, by telling her all sorts of wicked lies, he deceived her into hoping that he was still alive. But Sychaeus' body had not been buried, and his ghost, marvelously pale, appeared to Dido in a dream. He showed her the stab wounds in his chest, and told her how he had been murdered in his own house. And then he urged her: 'Get out as fast as you can. Leave the country. I'll show you a place where a hoard of treasure was buried long ago: who knows how much gold and silver there is, but it will help you on your journey.'

"Dido was convinced. She gathered up what she needed, and collected companions who either hated the vicious tyrant or were terrified of him. A woman acting all on her own, she arranged for some ships, which by chance she discovered ready to sail, to be stolen and loaded with the gold that had belonged to the greedy Pygmalion. Together they put out to sea, and landed here: you can see that construction has already begun on the great walls of our new city—its name is Carthage—and its citadel. We called the citadel Byrsa (from the Greek word for "bull") because we bought for the site as much land as could be marked out by the hide of a bull torn into strips. And now: who are you? Where have you come from and where are you trying to go?"

When she asked these questions, Aeneas sighed, and brought up his answer from deep in his heart. "If I were to start at the beginning and you had the time to hear the whole story of our troubles, evening would have swept away the sunlight from Olympus long before I was done. My name is Aeneas, and I am a servant of the gods. I am well-known in heaven because I rescued my family gods from the hands of the enemy, and I carry them with me still. I'm trying to get to Italy from Troy—you've heard of Troy, of course—to find a race of men who are sprung from Jupiter. My mother—she's a goddess—showed me the way, and I followed wherever my fate led me and put out from Troy with twenty ships. A storm caught us and blew us about all over the sea; and now by sheer chance it has cast us up here, in Libya. Of my ships, seven have managed to survive, and even they are badly damaged. So here

I am, wandering in this uninhabited country, with all my possessions gone, an exile from Europe and from Asia."

Venus would not let him say any more about his trials. "Whoever you are," she interrupted him, "you are not entirely unloved by the gods. At least you're still alive, and you have safely arrived at Carthage. So now go on, and make your way to the palace of Queen Dido. I can tell you now—unless my parents deceived me when they taught me the art of foreseeing the future—that the rest of your companions have arrived here too, and the rest of your fleet has been brought safely to shore by a change of wind. Look at that line of twelve swans, calling gaily to each other. They were scattered by an eagle of Jupiter's that swooped down on them out of a clear sky, and they have just recovered their formation. Now you can see

them looking for a place to land—in fact I think that they have already spotted one. Together they call and play about the sky, and their steady wings are bringing them home. Your ships and their crews are just like them—they have either already entered port or they're approaching the estuary under full sail. Come on now, and follow the path wherever it leads."

She turned her head away. The nape of her neck, gleaming like a rose in bloom, and the wonderful scent that wafted from her hair, made him think that she must be a goddess. And when he saw her walk, with her skirt swirling now around her ankles, he was in no doubt. He recognized her as his mother Venus, and as she faded away he called after her.

"Why do you confuse me with disguises? How unkind you are. Why can't we hold each other's hands? Why can't you talk to me in your normal voice?"

He was still grumbling as he set off towards the city; but Venus surrounded him and Achates with a mist, and wrapped them in a cloud, so that no one could see them or touch them or delay them or ask them what they wanted. And she herself departed to her home in Paphos; a temple is dedicated to her there, and Arabian incense, mingled with the scent of fresh garlands, burns on a hundred altars.

Aeneas views Carthage, still under construction

Aeneas and Achates came at last to the top of a hill, whose summit overlooked the city below. Aeneas was impressed by the immense scale of the buildings, and by the gateways and paved streets in a place where a short while before there had been nothing but huts—and also by all the noise. The Carthaginians were working tirelessly: they were tracing out the line of the outer walls, and bringing up stones by hand to lay them in course after course for the citadel. For each structure one team chose the site, another plowed a furrow to mark out its outline. Vast excavation projects were under way as well: they were dredging a channel in the harbor; and at the same time they were sinking deep foundations for a theater and cutting out huge columns from the rock, from which the backdrop would be suspended during performances. And they were also drafting a constitution; they were electing magistrates and a council of elders, who had been blessed by the gods.

It was like looking at a swarm of bees in the sunlight
of early summer, busy in the fields among the flowers:
the young ones, as soon as they are grown to full size,
cram the liquid honey into the cells and pack them
with nectar, and as new arrivals come up, they relieve
them of their loads, or organize themselves to keep
the drones away from the bustling hive—and all of it
in a perfumed haze of thyme from the honey.

"I envy these people," said Aeneas, looking out over the rooftops, "and the way their walls are going up so fast." Still hidden in his magic cloud, he went down and mingled with them. Nobody could see him.

Aeneas, clouded in invisibility, enters Carthage and explores Juno's temple

In the middle of the city there was a grove of delightful shade-trees. Here, when the Carthaginians first arrived from Tyre, battered by their stormy voyage, Juno had showed them a place to dig; and they had found the head of a war-horse, which they had taken as an omen foreshadowing success in war and eternal prosperity. And here Dido had laid out a great temple for Juno: already, among all the lavish fittings, the goddess' presence was clearly felt. A flight of bronze steps led up to the entrance, bronze encased the beams, and the doors creaked open on bronze hinges.

In the temple Aeneas made a discovery that for the first time lifted his spirits a little: perhaps a break in his luck was coming and he could dare to hope for safety. He had decided to wait for the queen in the grove, and to while away the time, he had walked inside. He was admiring the workmanship, and the attention to detail, and wondering what the future of this city would be—and then, on the wall, he saw a fresco illustrating all the various battles that had been fought under the walls of Troy, the war whose fame had now spread all over the world. He saw Priam and Agamemnon and Menelaus and Achilles, whose wrath had so affected both sides.

"Achates," he said, standing still before the painting with tears in his eyes, "is there any place on earth where no one has heard of our misery? Look at Priam—even here he is recognized and remembered. We live in a sad world; whatever we do must touch a universal heart. So don't be afraid any more—if we are already familiar to these people, we may very well be safe here."

Although it was only a painting, the scenes affected him deeply, and his sighs gave way to sobbing that he could not stop. He saw the fighting around the citadel: the Greeks fleeing as the young Trojans attacked, and then the Trojans falling back before Achilles in his plumed helmet, who was charging at them in his chariot. Not far off, he recognized through his tears the snowy canvas of Rhesus' tents, and the bloodthirsty Greek warrior Diomedes surprising Rhesus as he slept. Rhesus' men were slaughtered and his fine horses were spirited away before they could graze any more in Trojan fields or drink any more from the Xanthus river. In another scene Troilus, poor boy, had lost his weapons and was in flight. He had never had any chance against Achilles, and now he was lying on his back in his empty chariot, still hanging on to the reins while his horses bolted. His neck was broken, and his hair was trailing on the ground; his spear, upside down, scored a

line in the mud. Meanwhile Trojan women were coming humbly to the temple of Minerva with their hair loose, beating their breasts in mourning. They were bringing a new robe to the goddess, but she would not support their cause; she had turned away her face and kept her eyes on the ground. And there was Achilles, dragging Hector three times around the walls of Troy, ready to ransom his corpse. A groan came shuddering up from the depths of Aeneas' heart as he saw his old friend's chariot, and his plundered armor and his dead body—and Priam, reaching out helplessly to touch it with his hand. Next he found himself, fighting hand to hand with the leaders of the Greeks, as well as the exotic native troops of Memnon, the emperor of Ethiopia. And there was a contingent of Amazons, carrying their crescent-shaped shields. The fiery Penthesilea led them, a warrior-queen conspicuous among so many thousands of soldiers; she had one breast uncovered and a golden belt, a woman who dared to fight with men.

Aeneas sees Dido for the first time

The painting was so absorbing that Aeneas could not take his eyes from it or move away. He was still standing there when a crowd of young men came into the temple, escorting Dido, their beautiful queen. Can you picture Diana, and the dancing nymphs who cluster around her in their thousands on the banks of the Eurotas river, or on the mountain-ridge of Delos where she was born? Can you tell how happy her mother Latona is to see her there, even though she says nothing? Diana is the tallest of all the goddesses, with a quiver always slung across her shoulder—and Dido, surrounded by her cheerful courtiers and protected by her guards, had exactly the same air about her, as she eagerly carried out her plans for her kingdom's future. Settled on her throne under the arched vault of the temple roof, at the entrance to Juno's shrine, she interpreted laws, handed down judgments, and allocated tasks, either dividing them out evenly among her people or drawing lots.

The rest of Aeneas' companions appear

And then suddenly, pushing through the crowd, came Antheus and Sergestus and brave Cloanthus, and with them many others of the Trojans whom Aeneas had last seen scattered and carried away by the whirling storm. He had thought that they were lost, and when he saw them again now, he and Achates were overcome with both fear and joy. They badly wanted to greet their friends, but there was a mystery here that unsettled them. So they remained wrapped in their dark cloud and whispered to each other: "What happened to them? Where have they left their ships? How did they get here? There's someone here from each of the lost ships: they must have come to the temple to look for help."

The Trojans assembled before Dido's throne. When she had given them permission to speak, Ilioneus began with quiet confidence: "Your majesty, you have founded your new city under the protection of Jupiter, and your subjects, guided by the reins of your law, are rightly proud. We are from Troy. A storm has blown us far off course, and now we need your help. We beg you, do not destroy our ships. Spare our lives—we are a god-fearing people—and listen closely to what we have to say. We have not come to lay waste to the land of Libya. We have not come to kill or steal or plunder—such intentions hardly belong to a people who have just been beaten in a war. Our destination is an ancient land of fighters and farmers that they used to call Oenotria—Hesperia, in Greek—but I believe that now they have renamed it Italy, after a legendary king. We were well on our way there, but with the rising of Orion we were caught by high seas and vicious southerly gales. We were blown into a jumble of shoals, with waves breaking over our heads, and we could not extricate ourselves.

"A few of us managed to swim ashore. But once on the beach, we were still not safe. Your people attacked us and forbade us to land. How could they do that? Only savages would allow such a custom. If you are afraid of armed men, or even if you despise the whole human race, at least you should hope for gods who know the difference between what is right and wrong. Our leader was Aeneas; no one was fairer and more god-fearing than he was, and no one was more distinguished in war. If the fates have spared him, if he is still alive and is not lying among the shades in the cruel underworld, then we have nothing to be afraid of—and you should not be ashamed to treat us as he would treat you. You are familiar with Sicily? Their famous king Acestes is of Trojan blood: the people there are friendly to us, and they support us. If it is fated that we are not to reach Italy safely, and if Aeneas has been drowned— even his son Ascanius has lost hope for him, I think—then at least allow us to head back towards Sicily, where we just came from. We can settle there and Acestes can be our king. But if it is in fact the will of the gods that we should meet our leader and our companions again, and that we should find peace in Italy and Latium, then give us your permission to haul our damaged ships up onto the beach, so that we can replace their timbers from your woods and repair our oars."

Dido welcomes Aeneas' companions

The other Trojans murmured their agreement with what Ilioneus had said. Dido nodded to them, and answered briefly: "Put all uneasiness out of your minds, you Trojans. Don't be afraid. Life is not easy here, and our kingdom is very new. This is why we have to take such precautions and guard our frontiers closely. Who has not heard of the race of Aeneas, and the city of Troy, and the courage of her warriors, and the conflagration that brought the war to its end? We Carthaginians are not as uncivilized as you think; we are not entirely unknown to Apollo. Whether you choose to go to Italy, or to the fields of Sicily and King Acestes, I will help you on your way and I will give you supplies. Or perhaps you might wish to settle here in this kingdom, with me? If so, then beach your ships. You're welcome in this city that I am building, and I will make no distinction between your people and mine. I only wish that Aeneas himself had arrived on that same wind that brought you to us. I will send search parties along the coast, and I will order them to look for him in the farthest parts of my country, in case he has been cast ashore, or is lost in the woods or in some distant village."

Achates and Aeneas listened excitedly, longing to break out of their cloud. "Don't you think now that everything is going to turn out well after all?" said Achates. "The fleet is safe, and all our people. Only one man is missing, and we saw him drown ourselves. But everything else is just as your mother told us."

Aeneas is magically revealed to all

And at that very moment the cloud that had kept them invisible split apart; as it faded away into the air, it left Aeneas shimmering in the light that Venus herself had wafted over him. It fell on his face and shoulders and made him look like a god: his hair shone, his skin glowed with youth, and delight sparkled in his eyes. On him lay the glory that an artist might lend to an ivory statue, the shimmer of gold set in silver or marble from Paros.

There was a moment of astonished silence, and then he addressed the queen: "I am the man you're searching for—and yes, I've come safely ashore. I am Aeneas of Troy. You are the only one who has felt pity for the unspeakable horrors that our city has suffered, and you have made us welcome in yours. Since we escaped from the Greeks, we have met with every possible disaster by land and sea. Like the rest of the Trojans, who by now are scattered all over the world, we have lost everything—even the power to thank you as you should be thanked. If the gods have any respect for the humans who revere them, if they have any sense of justice, or any under-standing of what is right, they will, I trust, bring you the re-wards that you deserve. What admirable parents, what happy century, have produced you? As long as the rivers run in their beds, as long as the shadows shift across the mountain valleys, as long as the heavens keep the stars alight, I will praise you, and honor you and keep your name alive, wherever I may be." And he put his right arm round Ilioneus' shoulder and his left round Serestus'; and after them he embraced all the rest, fin-ishing with Gyas and Cloanthus.

Queen Dido was amazed, first at Aeneas' sudden appear-ance and then at his report of his misfortunes: "Who has been bringing all these dangers and difficulties on you? You are, after all, the son of a goddess. What power has brought you to our desert shores? Your father is Anchises of Troy, isn't he? He's a mortal; but your mother is Venus—she gave birth to you by the river Simois. I remember when Teucer, a Greek king, visited Phoenicia. He had been driven out of his own country and was looking for my father's help in establishing a new capital. My father had been campaigning in Cyprus, and he had just brought it under his control. Since that time I have been well aware of your story and the story of Troy, and of the kings of Greece. Teucer thought very highly of the Trojans, although he was once their enemy, and he liked to think that he was himself descended from them. So now, come inside. Circumstances very similar to yours have brought me here; the fates have afflicted me with the same kind of troubles as you, but they have let me settle at last in this country. Since then, my own misfortunes have taught me that I must help anyone else in trouble."

She put her memories aside, and ordered honors to be paid to the gods in their temples. To the Trojans still at the shore, she sent, as gifts to celebrate a day of good omen, twenty bulls and a hundred boars and a hundred fat lambs with their mothers. Meanwhile she led Aeneas into her palace, where all was luxury and magnificence. In the central hall a feast was laid out for them, and there were tapestries skillfully embroidered with royal purple, and on the tables there were silver and gold vessels, chased with complicated designs that illustrated the deeds of Dido's forefathers and the history of the Phoenicians from their earliest beginnings.

Aeneas, however, could not stop worrying about his son, and was anxious to have news of him. So he sent off Achates to the ships.

"Go quickly to Ascanius. Tell him what has happened, and bring him back here with you. And fetch gifts for the queen, chosen from the treasure that we saved from the ruins of Troy: the robe stiff with gold thread, and the veil interwoven with yellow acanthus, which Helen used to wear—the one her mother Leda gave her, which she brought from Mycenae when she came to Troy for her illegal wedding to Paris. And also bring the scepter that belonged to King Priam's oldest daughter, and her pearl necklace, and her jeweled crown." Achates hurried away.

Venus plans for Dido to fall in love with Aeneas

But Venus mistrusted the Carthaginians. She suspected them of double-talk, and the vengeance of Juno was never far from her mind. At dusk all her fears returned, and her mind became busy with

a new stratagem: she would trans-
form her son Cupid into the ex-
act likeness of Ascanius, so that
it would be him that Dido would
see bringing the gifts from the
ships. Then Dido would be set
on fire with love, and love would
burn through her bones. Venus
therefore gave instructions to the
winged spirit of Love itself.

"Cupid, my child, my strength, my power, the only one
who can laugh at the thunderbolts that the giant Typhoeus
made for Jupiter: I come to you begging for your divine assis-
tance. You and I have often grieved for your brother Aeneas,
and you are well aware that he has been blown by storms to
every country in the world, because Juno hates him so bitterly.
Now Dido has him in her clutches; she is tempting him with
the most alluring invitations. Juno is encouraging her—for
what purpose I am not sure—but certainly she will not let
this crucial opportunity go by. But I intend to act first: I will
ensnare Dido myself. I will make her fall so madly in love with
Aeneas that she will always be in my power, and none of the
immortals will be able to shift her allegiance from me. Now
listen: this is what you have to do. I am worried about Asca-
nius: he is now preparing to go to Carthage at his father's sum-
mons, carrying gifts rescued from the sea and from the ruins
of Troy. But I will spirit him away in his sleep to the island of
Cythera, or to the mountain on Cyprus where I have a temple,
to prevent him from finding out my trick or interfering with
it. And you—for just one night—must magically take on Asca-
nius' form. You must, in fact, become him. Excited by the feast
and by the wine, Dido will keep you by her side. She will put
her arms around you and kiss you—and you must breathe into
her your secret fire and deceive her with its poison."

And so she trickled a peaceful calm into Ascanius' limbs.
She held him close, and lifted him away to a valley high in

the mountains of Cyprus, where fragrant marjoram enfolded him among flowers and shadows. At the same moment Cupid was obeying his mother's commands: he took off his wings and assumed Ascanius' jaunty way of walking; and then, with Achates leading the way, he made his way to Carthage with the royal gifts.

The other young men of Troy were already assembling in the banquet hall. On her throne in the center Queen Dido was ablaze with gold, and beside her Aeneas leaned back on a sofa spread with purple. Slaves brought bread in baskets, and poured water on their hands, and offered napkins. Behind the scenes, it took fifty women to prepare the food and to maintain the fire on the altars, and a hundred others, with an equal number of men, to bring the dishes to the table and place drinking-cups before the guests. Crowds of Carthaginians, too, came in and were invited to lie down among the embroidered cushions. They admired the robe that Aeneas had sent, and the veil interwoven with yellow acanthus; they admired too the boy who brought the gifts, with Ascanius' voice but a face like a god's. The queen in particular could not take her eyes off him. Poor woman, she did not suspect the disaster that stood over her, and she was entranced by the boy and his gifts. First he put his arms around the unsuspecting Aeneas, paying the respects of a dutiful son to his father; and then he came up to Dido. She stared, and sighed, and embraced him: she never knew that it was a god who was taking hold of her heart, a god who was beginning, little by little, to blot out the memory of Sychaeus. Always obedient to Venus' commands, Cupid was preparing to turn a spirit long given over to melancholy towards a livelier love.

At a banquet, Dido toasts the Trojans and asks to hear Aeneas' story

As the conversation died down, the slaves removed the tables and brought in great mixing bowls and garlanded cups. Then the talk broke out again, and the voices echoed back from the ceiling. Lamps were lit and suspended on golden cords, so that their darting flames could drive away the night. The queen had her own cup brought to her and filled. It was heavy with gold and jewels, and her father and his children had always used it.

She called for silence. "Jupiter," she said, "they say that it is you who make the laws that govern hosts and guests. Let this be a day of good fortune for the people of Carthage and for those who have come from Troy, a day for future generations to remember. Bacchus and Juno, bring us health and happiness; and you, my people, make our visitors welcome."

She poured a libation to the gods, and took the first sip. Then she smiled at Aeneas at her side, telling him that now it was his turn. He drank deeply, burying his lips in the froth below the golden rim, and passed the cup on, while

long-haired Iopas, a student of the giant Atlas, strummed on his golden lyre. He sang of the origin of men and beasts, of rain and lightning, and of the stars—Arcturus, the rainy Hyades, the big and little Bears. He sang of the wandering moon and the toiling sun: how in winter it dips early into the sea, and stretches out the evenings in summer. Both the Carthaginians and Trojans applauded loudly, but still poor Dido, with distant thoughts of love racing in her head, kept the conversation going late into the night. She asked Aeneas endless questions about Priam and Hector and the rest: "What were the weapons that Memnon, the son of the dawn, brought with him? What were Diomedes' horses like? What sort of a man was Achilles?"

And finally she said: "Tell me from the beginning the story of the Greek trick that caused the fall of Troy. And what about yourself? For seven years you have been at sea, and away from home. I want to know everything about your travels and adventures."

Book II

The Wooden Horse

Aeneas tells how the Greeks sailed away and left behind a wooden horse

Everyone sat silent and attentive. At last Aeneas spoke.

"Dido, you are asking me to tell you what should really not be told at all: You want to know how the Greeks overthrew the city of Troy—a city that was once so splendid and now is only to be mourned. I saw all the terrible things that happened and was involved in many of them myself. My mind still shudders at the memory of it all, and tries to shut out the pain—and I dare say that even the toughest Greek soldiers would not be able to hold back their tears if they had to talk about it now. In any case the night is already nearly done. It's damp, and the stars are going out, and it's time to go to bed. But if you really want to hear a brief account of Troy's last agonies, and to know what we did there, then I will tell you.

"The war had broken the spirit of the Greek leaders; the fates, they felt, had abandoned them. Time was running out. So under Minerva's eye they built a horse as high as a mountain, made of pinewood planks. It was to be an offering to ensure their safe return to Greece—or that at least was the story that they put out. But in fact they selected soldiers by lot and secretly shut them up inside the dark cavern of its belly, squeezed tightly in together and fully armed.

"Offshore, in sight of Troy, lies the island of Tenedos. In Priam's day it was famous, a prosperous place, but now it is known only for a bay that provides an anchorage—and not a very safe one at that. The Greeks sailed away behind the island and camped on an empty beach. But we thought that they were gone for good, and had returned home to Mycenae—and so we were freed from our long ordeal. We opened the gates and took great pleasure in going to see the deserted shore and the site of the Greek camp with no one about. 'This was where the Thessalians were stationed,' we said; 'this was Achilles' post; the fleet was anchored here, and here there was a battle.' And then we saw the horse: many people were in awe of Minerva's fatal gift, and amazed at its size. Thymoetes was the first to suggest that it should be hauled inside the walls and placed in the citadel. Was he in on the plot? I don't know—maybe it was just that the fates put the idea into his head. But Capys, and others who were more cautious, said that the horse was a Greek trick and should be thrown into the sea or burned; or at any rate that holes should be bored in it so that the space inside it could be examined. For a while the people were of two minds, and both points of view had their supporters.

"Then the priest of Neptune, Laocoon, hurried down from the citadel with his attendants. He stood in front of the crowd and harangued us passionately. 'What's the matter with you?' he cried. 'You're all mad. Do you really believe that the enemy has left? Don't you understand that *anything* that a Greek brings to you is a trick of some sort? You know Ulysses' reputation, don't you? Either there are Greeks hidden inside this wooden creature, or it's a contrivance specially designed to breach the walls, to spy into our houses or even destroy the city. There's certainly *something* wrong. Don't trust this horse. Whatever it is, I'm afraid of the Greeks—especially when they come with gifts.' And he hurled a heavy spear into its side, where the animal's ribs were curved round its belly. The spear stuck, quivering, and where the belly had been hit, the hollow places inside echoed and echoed again. If the fates and our own minds had not been set against it, the Greeks' hiding place would have been laid wide open there and then—and Troy, and Priam's citadel, would be standing intact to this day.

Sinon, a secret agent, tries to persuade the Trojans to accept the horse

"But at that very moment some shepherds arrived, dragging along a young man with his hands tied behind his back. Excitedly they deposited him in front of King Priam. They didn't know who he was, but apparently he had surrendered to them of his own accord. But in fact it was all part of a plan to get the Greeks inside the city—a typical piece of Greek treachery. Small boys came rushing up to see the prisoner, and took turns at making fun of him. But he was a brave man: he was ready to die if he couldn't make his ruse succeed. Listen: in the story of his deviousness is a lesson about the behavior of all Greeks.

"The stranger stood before us unarmed. He looked steadily at the crowd around him and put the question to us straight: 'Where can I go? Walking or sailing, what does it matter? What country will take me in? What further indignity is there that I can suffer? There's no place for me among the Greeks, and now you Trojans hate me too. All you want is to see me punished and tortured.' At this, the hostile jeering and jostling stopped. We encouraged him to tell us where he was from and what he was doing. How could he make what was—for a prisoner—such an eloquent appeal?

"'Whatever the consequences,' he said, 'I'll tell you the whole story. First of all, I won't deny that I am a Greek: my name is Sinon. Fate has made me unlucky, but she won't be so ruthless as to make me a joker or a liar as well. You remember Palamedes? He was very famous in his time. Ulysses brought some false charge against him and had him put on trial (he was supposed to have been opposed to the war). He was innocent, but the Greeks had him executed—although of course, now that he's dead, they're sorry. I was a friend and a relation of Palamedes; at the very beginning of the war, my father, who was not at all well off, had sent me to serve with him. As long as his position was secure and while he still had influence with Menelaus and Agamemnon, I took on something of his reputation and distinction. But after Ulysses' envy and hatred got him killed—you know the story—nobody took notice of me any more. I was angry about the fate of my innocent friend, but stupidly I didn't keep my mouth shut. I said a lot of harsh and bitter things, and I swore that, if ever fate gave me the opportunity, or if ever I returned to Greece as a hero after the war, I would avenge Palamedes. And from that moment my troubles began. Ulysses came up with fresh charges, and circulated malicious half-truths about me, and deliberately threatened me with force. He frightened me, and gave me no peace, until with the help of the priest Calchas ... But why am I going on with this? It does me no good to put off what's going to happen to me. And I can hear you saying it: all these Greeks are the same. If that's all there is to it, punish me now. That's what Ulysses would want, and the Greek commanders would pay good money to see it happen.'

"Well, we still did not understand the depths of Greek cunning and treachery. So of course we were eager to find out more, and to find out exactly why he had come. So Sinon continued, trembling with fake apprehension: 'The Greeks were exhausted by the long war, and they wanted nothing more than to abandon the siege of Troy and go home. I only wish they had! But hard winter weather constantly kept them from sailing, and they did not like the look of the prevailing wind. And another thing: as soon as the wooden horse was put into place, the sky rumbled with thunderstorm after thunderstorm. We were puzzled, and sent someone to consult the oracle at Delphi. This is the grim report that he brought back:

With blood you came,
With blood you must return.
Fair winds for Troy were bought with a virgin's life;
And now a death must buy your passage home.

"'When the Greeks heard this, they were really scared and they felt icy shudders up and down their spines. What did the fates have in mind? What did the oracle mean? Yes, Agamemnon had sacrificed his daughter, and now someone else must be killed. But who? And at this point Ulysses pulled the prophet Calchas out of the crowd, and asked him straight out: "What is the will of the gods?" Already some people began to whisper that Ulysses was plotting mischief against me. They saw what was coming, but they said nothing out loud. Well, for ten days Calchas didn't utter a word. He stayed in his tent and refused to suggest anyone as a victim. But Ulysses pressed him and pressed him until he broke his silence and—it had all been pre-arranged, of course—announced *my* name. I was the one, said Calchas, who had been chosen to die. Everyone was happy now: the fate that each of them had feared for himself had fallen on somebody else. And so a day was fixed, the preparations were made. Grain was scattered on the altar, and salt over that, and wreaths were put on my head. But then I managed to break free from my chains. I ran off and hid all night in the reeds by a lake, planning to stay there until such time as the Greeks should set sail—if that was in fact what they intended to do. In any case, I have no hope of ever seeing my native land again, or my family. Probably the Greeks will search out my dear children or my beloved father and punish them because I fled. My family will have to pay for my mistake with their own deaths. By the gods above who alone know the truth, I beg you to believe my story and pity me. Even what I have already suffered I have not deserved.'

"His tears moved us: we had mercy on him and spared his life. Priam himself ordered his manacles and his chains to be taken off, and spoke to him kindly: 'Whoever you are, from now on you will be one of us. Forget the Greeks—they're gone. But still you must answer my questions. Why did they construct the horse? Whose idea was it? What do they want? Is it a matter of religion? Or is it designed for war?'

"And Sinon, slippery Greek that he was, lifted up his hands, now free from chains, to the sky. 'I call on the eternal stars, the unconquerable stars; I call on the altars and the knives that I have escaped; I call on the wreaths that I wore when I was a sacrificial victim. I call them all to witness that when I break the oaths that I swore to the Greeks, and when I reveal the Greeks' secrets, I am doing no wrong. I hate them, and I am no longer bound by their laws. And now that they are no longer a threat to you, I trust you to keep your promises to me. In return I will tell you the truth and repay my debt to you.

"'Throughout the war, the Greeks had always depended on Minerva's help to achieve what they hoped for and what they wanted. But Diomedes and Ulysses, the inventor of all mischief, came up with an audacious plan to break into Minerva's temple in Troy, assassinate her attendants and capture her statue. They tore her sacred image from its base, and with their bloodstained hands they stole the wreaths that had been dedicated to her. And from that very moment, the Greeks' luck changed, and success began to elude them. Their strength was broken, and Minerva turned away her face from them. But still she gave them unmistakable warnings: her statue had scarcely been deposited in the Greek camp when flames shot from its staring eyes, and salt sweat ran down its arms. And three times (can you believe it?) the goddess herself rose up from the earth, complete with her shield and spear. The prophet Calchas had no doubt as to what these omens meant: "Yet another voyage lies ahead of you," he said. "Your weapons will never destroy Troy until you have first sailed all the way back to Greece. Only in Greece can you recover your luck and the gods' goodwill, which once you carried with you in your ships." So now you understand what's going on. Yes, the Greeks are gone—on a following wind all the way back to Mycenae. But their comrades at home are gathering new weapons for them, and new images to worship; and then, when they're least expected, they will cross the sea again, and be back here once more.

"'And Calchas had one last piece of advice: to construct this horse to take the place of the statue that they stole, as penance for their dreadful sacrilege. He showed them how to fit its planks together, and told them to make it so high that it couldn't go through your gates or be taken inside your walls; it should represent a clear break, he said, from the old religious traditions of Troy. It is a gift for Minerva: and if you were to damage or destroy it (may the gods prevent such a thing!), then that would be the end of you—of you and of Priam's city. But if you carry the horse up into the city, then Asia will one day make war on the cities of Greece, and that would be the end of *us*—us and our children's children.'

"That, then, was Sinon's story—and a masterly piece of fiction it was. But we believed it. And that is how lies and fake tears were able to bring down the city that Diomedes and Achilles, and their thousand ships, could not capture in ten years of fighting.

Sinon's lies are supported by a terrifying phenomenon

"At that moment something even stranger, and much more frightening, happened, and caught us entirely by surprise. Just to talk about it makes me shudder. Out from behind Tenedos, over the flat calm of the sea, came two serpents. Side by side they swam toward the beach—necks held up straight, eyes glaring. The blood-colored crests on their heads showed up above the surface, the water swirling and curling down the length of their backs in trails of spray. They reached the land. Their hot eyes were swollen with fire and blood, and their flickering tongues hissed wet in their mouths. We went weak at the sight of them. We ran for cover. But still they came on, and headed for the altar, where Laocoon the priest was sacrificing, according to proper ritual, a great bull. First the snakes wound themselves around the bodies of his two children, opening their jaws wide over their poor little arms and legs. As he came rushing up to help them, his knife in his hand, they seized him too, coiling and coiling about him. They twisted twice around his waist, and twice around his neck; they reared their scaly backs above his head while he tried to untangle their knotted bodies. His

sacred wreath was soaked with blood and venom, and his screams echoed horribly. He bellowed exactly like the bull that was now trying to escape from the altar and to shake off the axe that was hanging from its neck. But the snakes slid away to the innermost part of the temple, right into the shrine of Minerva, and disappeared under the goddess' feet, behind the circle of her shield. We were overcome with panic all over again, and some people said that Laocoon deserved whatever he got. 'He should never have thrown his spear at the wooden horse,' they said. 'That was sacrilege.' And then: 'Take the horse up into the citadel. We must offer prayers to Minerva.'

The horse is dragged into the city

"We breached the walls and opened up a way through the fortifications. Everyone helped. We slid wheels under its feet and lashed ropes round its neck. With its armed offspring in its belly, the fatal creature passed through the gap in the walls. Boys and girls sang solemn songs, and hauled enthusiastically on the ropes. The horse entered the city, and glided menacingly toward its center—the center of Troy, our home and the home of our gods, strong behind its famous walls. We didn't care that four times on the threshold of the gate the horse had stuck, or that four times we had heard its belly give off a sound of clanking metal. We were blinded by our excitement, and simply worked all the harder to settle the ill-omened monster in its final position in our holy citadel. Priam's daughter Cassandra tried to tell us that a catastrophe was about to happen, but Apollo had ordained that the Trojans would never believe her. And so, idiots that we were, we hung festival garlands all over the city. It would turn out to be our last happy day.

"Meanwhile the light was fading and darkness came in over the sea, wrapping earth and sky and Greek deceit all in a cloud together. The Trojans, posted haphazardly on the walls, did not talk to each other; they were tired out, even dozing. And then the Greek fleet in quiet columns came out from behind Tenedos, returning to the shore they knew so well,

under the light of the gentle silent moon. On Agamemnon's ship a torch flared—and Sinon, protected by gods whose sense of justice is hard to understand, secretly loosened the bolts under the horse's belly. The soldiers inside, released into the open air, lowered a rope from the trapdoor and slid easily down: Thessandrus and Sthenelus and Ulysses, scowling as usual, and Acamas and Thoas and Achilles' son Pyrrhus and Machaon and Menelaus and Epeos, the horse's designer. They found the city drowsy, awash in wine. They killed the sentries, and opened the gates for their comrades, who came surging in to join them.

Aeneas is warned of the approaching disaster and leads the resistance

"It was that time of night when tired mortals first sink into sleep, sleep that slips over them as a welcome gift from the gods. I was dreaming of poor dead Hector: he appeared in front of me with tears streaming down his cheeks, just as he was when he was being dragged along by Achilles' horses, swollen ankles lashed together, blood and dust all over him. He wasn't the Hector I once knew, the Hector who had returned from battle decked out in the spoils of Achilles, or who had thrown firebrands at the Greek ships. This Hector's beard was filthy, his hair was stiff with blood, and he had been badly wounded. In my dream I spoke to him sadly: 'You were always the brightest hope of all the Trojans. What has kept you away from us? We have been waiting for you—where have you been? So many of your friends are dead. So much has happened to your exhausted people, and to your city. And now I see your face twisted in anger and your body cut to pieces. Why?' No reply: my complaints were answered only with a deep sigh. But then, urgently, he said to me: 'You cannot stay here, son of Venus. You must escape. Troy is in flames, the enemy occupy the walls. The city is doomed, and Priam has ruled it long enough. If it had been possible for anyone to defend the citadel, I might have done it. But now Troy relies on you to preserve its traditions and its gods. You must take them with you wherever you go, and far across the sea you must build new walls to keep them safe.' And in my dream I saw him coming out from Vesta's inner shrine, carrying in his own hands her sacred wreaths and her awful image and her eternal flame.

"I started awake. From the walls floated the sound of confused shouting. The house of my father Anchises was set back and sheltered by trees, but more and more clearly we could hear the clatter of arms and danger coming closer and closer. I climbed as far up the roof as I could, and stood there listening carefully. You know how a fire is driven by a gusting south wind through a field of wheat, or how a flash flood roars down from the mountains? The water spreads out over the crops or the furrows that the oxen have turned up, and uproots the trees on the steep sides of a valley. Well, you can think of me as a shepherd, caught by surprise, listening helplessly to the chaos from a high rock. Now at last it was obvious what had really happened and how the Greeks had fooled us. The mansion of Priam's son Deiphobus was on fire, and so was Ucalegon's next door; the straits of Sigeum were ablaze with reflected flames. Men shouted and trumpets called. I could hardly think, but I put on my armor anyway. There seemed little point in fighting, but something inside me urged me to call together a band of soldiers and meet them on the citadel. Rage, and the anticipation of a noble death, drove me on.

"At this moment Panthus, out of breath and out of his mind, appeared at my door. He was a priest of Apollo's temple on the citadel, and the son of a priest as well. He'd given the Greeks the slip, and he'd come away with his little grandson, carrying the consecrated vessels and our humiliated gods. 'Panthus, what's happening? Where can we make a stand?' He interrupted me with a groan: 'This is the end; there's no way out. The Trojan people, the city they've built, the great things they've done—all have come down to nothing. Jupiter in his cruelty has given everything away to the Greeks, and the Greeks have become the masters of a bonfire. The horse is inside the walls; armed men are swarming out of it. And Sinon is gloating among the flames. He has won his war. All those thousands of troops who once came from Mycenae are back here again. They're already inside the city—the gates are open—and the sentries are bewildered by the dark. There's hardly any resistance. They're blocking every street and alley with a line of drawn swords, and they're not afraid to die.'

"From Panthus' report it was clear what I had to do, and to inspire me the gods gave me a dour desire for vengeance. As I made my way towards the flames and the confused sounds of fighting and shouting, Rhipeus and a great warrior called Epytus joined me—they had caught sight of me in the moonlight. Hypanis and Dymas came with them, and young Coroebus: he was madly in love with Cassandra, and as Priam's future son-in-law he'd come to help the Trojans in the war. Poor fellow, he would have done better to listen to Cassandra's warnings.

"When I saw them all so eager to go into battle, I said to them: 'You can be as daring as you like—but it makes no

difference if your courage is to end in death. Do you under-
stand our situation? Even the gods who used to protect our
kingdom have fled from their shrines. The altars are deserted.
You want to save your city, but there's nothing left to save.
All you can do now is to die fighting. You won't find safety by
looking for it after you've already been beaten.'

Street fighting in Troy

"Our young men were already ex-
cited, and my words now served to make
them angry. From that moment, we were
like wolves prowling viciously in the night, so hungry that they

don't care what happens as long as
their cubs don't have to wait aban-
doned and unfed. We launched our-
selves against the enemy, thinking
nothing of death, and made straight
through the enfolding darkness to-
wards the center of the city.

"Who will ever be able to find words to tell of the horror
of that night? Who can ever mourn enough for our slaugh-
tered comrades? Our ancient city, powerful for so many years,
had fallen. The bodies of the dead were scattered everywhere,
through every street, in every house and sanctuary. But the
Trojans were not the only ones to die: we hadn't lost the will
to fight back even though we had been conquered, and so
our conquerors died too. On both sides there was sorrow and
slaughter and panic, and the specter of death glared at us all.

"The first Greeks we met were a patrol led by Androgeos.
He thought we were Greeks ourselves, and greeted us with
friendly words. 'Come along with us!' he called. 'Why do you
hesitate? Why the delay? Everyone else is up on the citadel,
plundering and setting fires. Have you only just this moment
come ashore?' But as soon as he didn't get the answer he ex-
pected, he realized that he had stumbled into the middle of
the enemy. He froze—and then he stopped talking and took
a step backwards. Like a man who unexpectedly treads on
a snake in the underbrush, and then recoils when it rears

angrily up at him and puffs up its blue-green throat, Androgeos ran away in terror when he recognized us. But we attacked his party and surrounded it; they were paralyzed with fear and had completely lost their bearings, and we killed them all. So in the beginning, luck was with us. Coroebus was overjoyed. 'Friends,' he said, 'Fortune has shown us the way here; we should do what she suggests. Why don't we exchange shields and put on their armor? All's fair in war: they can give up their weapons to us too.' He put Androgeos' crested helmet on his head, picked up his shield—it had a very conspicuous design on it—and strapped on his sword. And following his example Rhipeus and Dymas and all the young men started laughing and equipping themselves with whatever they could strip from the Greek corpses. Now, under the protection of gods that were not our own, we could mingle safely with the enemy, and we fought unrecognized through the night, sending many of them down to the underworld. Some of the Greeks ran back to their ships and the familiar shore; and a few, with all shame lost, climbed back into the wooden horse and cowered in its belly.

"When even the gods' intentions are unclear, no mortal is to be trusted. The next thing we saw was a girl being dragged by Greek soldiers out from the inner shrine of Minerva's temple. Her hair was flying loose, her hands were chained so that she couldn't stretch them out to the gods, and she was trying to implore them with her eyes alone. It was Cassandra—

and Coroebus went crazy. This was the girl he loved, and he couldn't stand to see her as a prisoner. He went after her, but he might as well have been committing suicide; and when we went with him, to where the fighting was at its fiercest, we were a target for spears being thrown from the roof of the temple. Because of the Greek armor that we were wearing, and the Greek crests that we had on our helmets, many of us were killed by our own side; and the Greeks who held Cassandra were infuriated at us because they thought that we were coming to rescue her from them. They let out a shout and came at us all together—Ajax and Agamemnon and Menelaus and all Phoenix' men. You know how the winds blow from all directions at once in a typhoon—west and south and east, riding the horses of the dawn? And how tree-trunks crack in the woods, and Nereus the sea-god, cloaked in foam and waving his trident, churns up the ocean from bottom to top? That's what it was like as we battled up and down the city through the murk and shadows of the night, confusing the Greeks with our disguise. But in the end they spotted that our shields and arms were phony, and our unfamiliar accent gave us away. We were outnumbered and overrun. Coroebus died (Peneleus killed him) at Minerva's altar. Rhipeus died: of all the men in Troy he was the most fair-minded, the most careful in coming to a decision (though apparently the gods didn't think so). Hypanis and Dymas died, stabbed by their own allies; and as for my dear Pantheus… for all his loyalty to Apollo, and his sacred wreath, he couldn't escape. I swear by the ashes of Troy, and the funeral fires of my friends, that at their end I never flinched from an enemy weapon, and I never hung back. If it had been my fate to die, I would certainly have died nobly.

The fighting reaches Priam's palace

"Iphitus and Pelias and I became separated from the rest (Iphitus was slowed down by old age, and Pelias had been badly wounded by Ulysses); and the uproar drew us towards Priam's palace. There was a colossal battle going on there, as if Mars himself had lost all restraint. By comparison it seemed that no one else was fighting or dying in the whole city. Under cover of their shields, the enemy were thudding at the gates with a battering ram, and our troops resisted them with drawn swords, massed shoulder to shoulder behind the doors. Some of the Greeks were climbing onto the roof; they had propped ladders against the walls, and, rung by rung, they were working their way up past the pillars alongside the entrance. With their left hands they held shields to protect themselves against arrows, and with their right hands they grabbed at the battlements. Above them the Trojans, seeing that the end was near, were ripping up roofing-tiles from the towers and the living quarters, and using them as weapons—they were even pulling down the gilded beams that our forefathers had intended only for decoration. I took courage from their example: the palace must be protected at all costs, and I gave the harried guards whatever relief and support I could.

"In peacetime, when Hector's wife, poor Andromache, made private visits to her parents-in-law, or when she brought her little boy Astyanax to see his grandfather, she used to enter the palace by a secret postern gate and a long winding passage. I went in by this same entrance and climbed up to the place where the Trojans were throwing their makeshift missiles down from the battlements. Right on the steepest part of the roof there was a tower; it seemed infinitely high, and from its top you could see the entire city, as well as the Greek ships and their camp. We hacked away at its base, prying the floorboards from the joists until the whole structure was off-balance; we wrenched it free and pushed it over. Down it went with a sudden roaring crash, square onto the Greek troops below. And as soon as others came to take their place, we pelted them with rocks and tiles and arrows.

Achilles' son Pyrrhus breaks in to the palace

"Right on the palace threshold, in the entrance hall, was Achilles' son Pyrrhus. His spear and his bronze helmet were polished bright as new, and he was prancing about in arrogant excitement.

He made me think of a snake that has stuffed itself
with damp grass and lain low under the frozen ground
through the winter; but once it has shed its old skin, it's
as alert as ever. Pulsing with new energy, it winds its
slippery back out into the sunshine and lifts its head,
and its triple-forked tongue flickers from its mouth.

With Pyrrhus were the young men who grew up with him on
Scyros, and his gigantic friend Periphas, and Automedon, who
used to be Achilles' armor-bearer and charioteer; they got as
near as they could to the palace and threw torches back at
the men on the rooftops. Pyrrhus himself was in the lead: he
tried to beat down the doors with his double-bladed axe, but
finally he tore them off their hinges. Then he hacked out an
oak beam and used it to smash down the wall, until the way
was clear and open to the private apartments of Priam and of
all his predecessors, and he could see the bodyguards posted
at the threshold. Cries and shouts filled every room; even the
stars might have heard the women's laments, and their howls
of pain and grief. They were wandering to and fro, clinging to
the doorposts in a daze and kissing them. But it would have
taken more than bolts or sentries to stop Pyrrhus. With all the
wild energy he had inherited from his father, he forced a way
in: under the assault of his battering ram; the hinges gave way
and the doors fell flat. Cutting to pieces anyone who resisted
them, the Greeks flooded in after him, like a river that has
crested above its banks, and pours implacably over plowland
and pasture, swirling away cattle and their stalls together.

"So there they were, intruding wherever they did not
destroy. I saw them with my own eyes: Pyrrhus, drunk with
killing, and Menelaus and Agamemnon—and in front of them
Queen Hecuba and the wives of all her sons. And I saw King
Priam too. He had lit fires on the altars, and now the altars were
wet with blood. And through fifty doorways, ornate with gold
captured in wars against barbarians, I saw the fifty marriage
beds where, we had hoped, his heirs would be conceived."

"And what happened to Priam in the end?"

Priam's family is cornered

"When he saw the city captured and fallen, and everything in ruins, and the enemy entering the most private rooms of the palace, he went to put on his armor. He hadn't used it for a long time and his old shoulders trembled under its weight; but he strapped on his sword-belt, and a sword that he was too weak to lift. He was determined to die in action. When Hecuba saw him decked out like a young warrior, she cried out: 'My poor husband, what has possessed you to take up your arms? Where can you be going?' She and her daughters have assembled—what else can they do?—in the central courtyard, open to the sky. There's an altar there, under an ancient laurel tree that speckles the household gods with its shadow, and they're crouching like a flock of doves fleeing from a thunderstorm, with their arms round the statues. 'You can't help now,' says Hecuba, 'and no one in your position could. Even if my Hector were still alive, it would make no difference. Stay here with us. The altar will protect us, and if not we'll die together.' And she drew the old man over to her, and settled him on his throne.

A horrific slaughter

"One of Priam's sons, Polites, had managed to avoid Pyrrhus' assault, and he had fled along the colonnade, dodging enemy soldiers in and out of the deserted rooms. He was badly wounded, but that wasn't enough for Pyrrhus, who caught up with him at last in the courtyard; he grabbed him and thrust at him with his spear. Polites fell. He died in a final rush of blood, with his parents looking on.

Priam, with death all round him, could not restrain his anger. 'If the gods in heaven can understand the difference between right and wrong', he burst out, 'they will punish you for what you have done, and give you the reward that you deserve. You have killed my son right in front of me—my face is splattered with his blood. How can you say that you are Achilles' son? He was my enemy too, but he did not treat me like this. He respected my word of honor and sent Hector's body back to me so that it could be properly buried, and he gave me a safe-conduct back to my city.' And the old king threw his spear. It did no damage, but hit futilely against Pyrrhus' shield, and stuck dangling from its boss.

'Now, Priam,' said Pyrrhus, 'you are going to die. You'll be able to make your own report to Achilles. Don't forget to tell him about the despicable things that I did—and how I disgraced my own father.'

"Then Pyrrhus caught the king by the hair with his left hand and dragged him, trembling and slipping in his own son's blood, up to the altar. With his right hand he flashed out his sword and drove it in as far as it would go. And that was the end of Priam. He had ruled gloriously over many peoples and countries in Asia, but in the end he was compelled to witness his own city in flames and his citadel in ruins. His body was thrown out to lie on the beach, his head torn from his shoulders—nothing but a corpse without a name.

"As for me—I was left standing still and silent in the middle of the horror. I could think only of my own dear father, because Priam, who had just taken his last breath, terribly wounded, right in front of me, was exactly his age. I also thought of my wife Creusa, left all alone. And what had happened to young Ascanius and my household? I looked round for my band of companions. Where were they? Exhausted? Run away? Dead? Overcome by fire? There was so much light by the glare of the flames that there was nowhere for anyone to hide.

Aeneas spots Helen

"So I was the only one left—and then, unexpectedly, I caught sight of Helen. She was flattened against the wall just inside the door of the temple of Vesta, saying nothing, unnoticed. She was terrified—first of the Trojans, who hated her because of the war and the destruction that she had caused; then of the Greeks, who were determined to punish her; and finally of her angry husband Menelaus, whom she had deserted. An affliction to her own country and an affliction to Troy, she had hidden herself away, and now she crouched by the altar, despised by everyone. I was angry. I wanted revenge for the destruction of my city and I wanted to make Helen pay for her treachery.

"'Is this woman to be allowed to return to Greece? Is she to go home safe to her husband and children, like a victorious queen, accompanied by a crowd of Trojan prisoners and Trojan slaves? With Priam killed? and Troy in flames? and the shore streaming with our blood? No! Is there any glory or honor in attacking a woman? Yes, if her wickedness is punished and a vicious career is ended. Is there any pleasure in anger? Yes, if the fire of my anger appeases the ashes of my friends.'

Venus tells Aeneas: look after your own family

"I ranted on, barely rationally, until my dear mother Venus appeared to me. She had never shown herself to me so clearly: there was some kind of aura about her in the clear night light, and she had taken the form in which she must appear to the other gods in heaven. She put her arm around me and then spoke gently to me: 'My dear son, your grief has driven you mad. You must control your fury. Have you forgotten me? And should you not be first considering where you have left your father Anchises, and whether Creusa is still alive? And what of your son? Greek troops are circling all around them, and, if I were not keeping them safe, they would by now have been swallowed up in flames or cut to pieces by the enemy's swords. Though you hate her and blame him, it is not Helen or Paris who have squandered the riches of Troy and brought the city down—it is the gods, the merciless gods. Your mortal vision is dulled by the cloud that lies dark and dank around you. You can only see the collapse of buildings, stone torn from stone in billowing smoke and dust. You don't understand that Neptune is using his great trident to pry apart the lowest courses of the walls and to tear up the whole city from its foundations. And relentless Juno, with her sword by her side, is holding open the Scaean gates and summoning her beloved Greeks from their ships. Can't you see, up on the roof of the citadel, the monstrous head of a Gorgon in the center of Minerva's shield, and the shining circle round it? The Greeks are brave and strong because Jupiter makes them so; and now Jupiter is encouraging the other gods to side against the Trojans. There is nothing for you here, my son; and no purpose in any further agony. Do not be afraid of my commands or refuse to do what I tell you. I will stay by you, and see you safe to your father's house.' And with that promise she vanished into thick shadow, where murky shapes—the supernatural enemies of Troy—were flickering.

"In a vision I thought I saw a mountain-top with an ancient ash tree on it; farmers were trying to uproot it, taking turns chopping at it with their axes. It leaned over at a sharper and sharper angle, and its leaves shivered, until with a last cracking groan it dragged up the wreckage of its own roots from the earth. Like that tree, the city now seemed lost, totally consumed in fire. As I went down to my father's house, some god opened a way for me through the flames and the enemy weapons. I arrived at his door unwounded—not even a scratch—and sought him out.

Aeneas pleads with his father to leave

"When I wanted to take him up into the hills, he refused. 'I have no wish to drag out my life in exile once the city is gone,' he said. 'But the rest of you—while you still have your youth, your energy, your strength—you should escape. If the gods had wanted to prolong my life, they would have preserved a place for me to live. It is enough that I have survived to see the city destroyed and captured. Leave my body here, say a prayer, and depart. I will find a way to die. The enemy will doubtless pity me—and then look to see what they can steal from me. And if they don't give me a funeral, I can easily bear even that. Ever since the time when Jupiter scorched me with the winds and fire of his thunderbolt, the gods have hated me—and I have hung on uselessly for a long time now.'

"Anchises was obstinate. He said the same things over and over again, and would not be moved. We were all—Creusa and Ascanius and I, and even my slaves—in tears, trying to persuade him not to pull us all down with him, not to give way to the threats of fate. But he would not listen, and did not stir from his seat. I was so miserable that I picked up my weapons again, only wanting to find death in battle. What good could come from any other plan, or any other turn of fortune?

"'Father', I said, 'do you really suppose that I will leave you here, and go away? Did you really suggest such an awful thing? Well: if you think that it pleases the gods that nothing should be left of such a great city, and if it makes you happy to add yourself and your family to the general ruin, the doors of death are open wide. Pyrrhus will soon be here, with Priam's blood all over him. He doesn't hesitate to kill sons in front of their fathers, and then to kill their fathers, even though they are at prayer. Dear mother, did you keep me safe from fire and wounds for this—that I should have to welcome enemies into my house, and see my father and my wife and my son covered in each other's blood?' I called my household to action: 'If we are to be defeated, let us at least spend our last day together in arms, fighting against the Greeks. We are all going to die, but we will make the enemy pay.'

"I strapped on my sword once more, and settled my shield on my left arm. I was on my way outside, standing on the threshold, when my wife threw herself at my feet. My son was with her. 'If you are going out to die,' she said, 'then take us with you. But if you believe that arms can do any good, use them first to guard our house. If you leave us behind, what will become of little Ascanius, and your father? And me? Am I not supposed to be your wife?'

An encouraging omen

Creusa did not care who heard her railing at me, or weeping. But then—how can I explain this?—we saw an amazing phenomenon. As we looked sadly down at Ascanius and held him between us, a quick point of light seemed to start up from the top of his head. A gentle flame stroked his hair—though it did not harm him—and licked about his temples. We were filled with panic, but as we tried to put out the magical fire by pouring water on Ascanius' hair, my father turned his face joyfully to the sky and lifted up his hands. 'Almighty Jupiter,' he cried, 'if supplication can sway you, look down at us; and if our piety deserves your favor, do this for me—give us a sign, and explain what this omen can mean.'

"The old man had barely finished his prayer, when there was a crash of thunder to our left, and a star dropped out of the darkness, trailing sparks like a torch, and flashed across the sky. We watched its bright glow dip over the rooftops, and we could clearly mark its path until it buried itself in the woods of Mount Ida. Its track left a long line of light through the trees, and they smoked in a sulphurous haze. My father was convinced. He stood up to address the gods, and to worship the star that they had sent.

"'Gods of my fathers, I will follow wherever you lead. Save my house, and save my grandson. The omen means that Troy is still under your protection, and we must hesitate no longer.' We could hear the crackling of the fire on the ramparts closer now, and waves of heat swept towards us. He turned to me: 'I have changed my mind, and I will not refuse to go with you any longer.'

Aeneas leaves the falling city; Creusa's fate

"'Come on, then, father,' I say. 'Put your arms around my neck. I will carry you on my shoulders, and think nothing of the weight. However events turn out, we will share both danger and prosperity: one fate will serve for us both. Young Ascanius can walk beside me, and Creusa will follow in our footsteps. And you slaves: listen closely. As you leave the town, you will see a burial mound and an ancient temple of Ceres, long abandoned. Nearby is an old cypress tree, which our forefathers have held sacred for many years. That's where we will meet, even though we go by separate routes. Father, you must carry the images of our household gods. I cannot touch them, because I am still defiled with war and death, and first I have to wash myself in running water.'

"Over my head and shoulders, on top of my tunic, I spread a yellow lion-skin; then I lifted up my father. Ascanius took my right hand and skipped along beside me, taking two steps to every one of mine. My wife was right behind us. The light had grown dim, and I kept alert, fearing equally for my burden and for my companion. Earlier in the day, a near miss from a spear, or a band of Greeks standing in my way, had not perturbed me in the least, but now I was startled by the slightest breeze, by the faintest sound. We were not far from the gates, and I was just assuming we had made it all the way in safety, when I thought I heard the sound of marching boots. 'Run, my boy, run,' said my father, peering through the dark. 'They're coming. I can see the sheen of their shields and the light glinting on their armor.' At this I became confused: some evil force or other agitated me, and I stopped paying attention to Creusa. I never spotted that she was missing; I never even looked back for her, till we came to the burial mound and Ceres' temple. And there we all met up safely—all except one. Something had happened to Creusa while we were taking a short cut, to avoid the crowded streets. She had slipped away—away from her companions, her son, her husband. Had she stopped? Had she wandered off the path? Had she sat down to rest? I don't know. But we never saw her again.

"In my panic, I blamed anyone and everyone: gods or men, who cared? I only knew that, in all the destruction, this was by far my most painful loss. And so I left Anchises and Ascanius and the family gods hidden with my friends in a dip in the mountainside, and I made my way back into the city, fully armed. Whatever the risk and whatever the danger, the least I could do was to go over all the ground again. I searched along the walls and by the gloomy gates that we had just passed through. I carefully retraced our steps. I looked everywhere through the night. In my head—horror. Outside—a terrifying silence. I went back home: had Creusa returned there, perhaps? But the Greeks had broken into my house, and occupied it, and set it on fire. The wind was whirling the greedy flames through the roof, and the heat flared up to meet the stars. I went to Priam's palace, to the citadel. In the empty colonnades, in the sanctuary of Juno, I saw Phoenix and Ulysses, who had been picked to stand guard over the plunder. Within a circle of frightened women and children, all the stolen temple-treasure of Troy had been piled up: altars, solid gold cups and vestments stripped from the priests.

Creusa's ghost foretells Aeneas' future

"It was risky to make any kind of noise, but I shouted Creusa's name up and down the streets, calling her again and again—all for nothing. I searched frantically, endlessly, house after house—and then I thought I saw a vague outline, a sort of shadow: surely this was her, though she seemed a little taller than I remembered. I didn't move: my hair stood on end and my voice stuck in my throat; but she tried to soothe me: 'Why are you racking yourself with such pain, my dearest husband? All this is the doing of the gods. It is not fated that I should come away with you; Jupiter will not allow it. You are going to have to endure a long exile and a voyage over a long waste of sea; but you will arrive at last in Italy, where the river Tiber flows gently between its lush fields. And there you will have a happy life; you are to marry a princess and become a king. So although you love me, you must not mourn for me. I am a woman of Troy and the daughter-in-law of Venus, and the mother of all the gods will never let me leave the city. I will never be taken as a prisoner to the country of Achilles or his father, or enter the house of any Greek woman as her slave. And now farewell—and whenever you embrace our son, think of me.' Through my tears I tried to answer, but she floated away from me. Three times I tried to grasp her; three times I almost had her in my arms, but her body was air, and faded away into air. She had become a breeze, an unremembered dream.

"So the night ended. As the dawn brightened on the ridges of Mount Ida, I returned to the rest of my family. I was amazed to discover that a number of newcomers had joined them—men and women and children, a crowd of unhappy refugees bringing with their possessions only a determination to escape. They would sail with me, they said, wherever I wanted to lead them: there was no hope of returning to Troy, because the Greeks had barricaded every gate. I agreed, and went on up into the hills, with my father once more upon my shoulders."

BOOK III

Omens, Monsters and Signs

Book III
Omens, Monsters and Signs

Search for a new Troy; the Trojans sail to Thrace...

"Asia and Priam's people had not deserved it, but the immortals had willed it: Troy had fallen. The whole city lay in smoking ruins, and we were exiles. The omens had told us that we should seek safety far away, in some deserted country. So we kept together and found ships on the coast nearby, where the mountains come down to the sea. Still we had no idea where the fates would take us, or where we would find a place to settle. It was early summer. My father Anchises told us that we should hoist our sails at the random whims of chance. There were tears in my eyes as I put out from the shore that I knew so well, and

left behind the plain where Troy used to stand. With my son and with my companions, carrying my own gods and the great gods of Olympus, I headed toward the open sea.

"We made our first landfall in Thrace, a flat and empty place, sacred to Mars. Its fierce king, Lycurgus, had been an ally of Troy in the old happy days, and he worshipped the same gods as we did. The fates gave me no particular sign, but on the curve of the shore I traced out a line for fortifications, and I decided to call the place after myself.

"In the hope of gaining their approval of my new city, I planned to make an offering to my mother Venus and the other gods, and to sacrifice a glossy bull to Jupiter on the beach. Nearby was a mound of earth, and on top of it a thicket of dogwood and myrtle, bristling with spiky branches. I wanted to cover my altar with leaves; so I tried to strip off some green shoots. I tugged at a sapling and then—it's hard to put this into words—a terrifying thing happened: drops of blood splashed out from its roots all over the ground. A cold horror quivered through me from head to foot, and my heart slowed. What was going on, hidden deep inside? I tried again, pulling at another tough branch. Another gush of blood. What had I done? I prayed to the nymphs of the country and to Mars himself, who looks after the Thracians' land, that there should be a favorable meaning hidden in what I had seen, a hopeful omen. Then I went up to the thicket again and made a third, and greater, effort to pull off a branch. I wedged myself on my knees in the

sand, and then, after another struggle—I really should not tell you what came next—a tear-muffled groan from deep in the mound, and a human voice sounding in my ears:

"'Aeneas, stop: you must honor the gods. This is a tomb—leave it alone, or your hands will be polluted. You must get away from this country; there is nothing here but cruelty and greed. You are from Troy—well, I am a Trojan too. My name is Polydorus. I am trapped beneath this tree: its roots are iron and its sap is blood and its branches are a tangle of spear-points.'

"What was I to do? I was frightened and I did not move. My hair stood on end and my voice stuck in my throat, for Polydorus was someone I used to know. He was one of poor Priam's sons, and some time ago Priam had secretly instructed him to seek asylum in Thrace. He was sent off in possession of a great deal of gold—insurance for Priam if Troy should not be strong enough to withstand the Greeks. And when Troy was lost and the city's luck finally ran out, the king of Thrace, abandoning the obligations of an ally, switched his loyalty to the winning side, to Agamemnon. He murdered Polydorus and seized his gold. In the grip of greed, a man will stop at nothing.

"After a while I stopped trembling, and went back to report to the heads of each family, and especially to my father. I told them what the gods had shown me, and I asked them what they thought. Everyone agreed that we should leave this sinister country where only treachery had welcomed us, and we should sail away before the southerly wind. But first we gave Polydorus a proper funeral: we heaped up a mound for

him, and our women let their hair down so that it fell loose around him, as they would have done at home. We built a sad altar to the spirits of the dead, draped it with blue pennants and evergreens, and placed on it shallow bowls of milk, still warm and frothy, and blood from the sacrifices. We laid Polydorus in his grave and solemnly sang our last farewells.

... and then to Delos...

"After that it looked safe to set sail. The winds were fair and light, and a gentle breeze, rustling in the rigging, urged us out to sea. My companions gathered round to haul our ships down to the water's edge. We moved out of the harbor, and the land and its settlements fell away behind us. It was a long voyage across the Aegean Sea, and we were tired when we came into the peaceful port of Delos, a lovely place sacred to the mother of the sea-nymphs and to Neptune. Once it was a moving island, drifting aimlessly from shore to shore, until Apollo fixed it in its position between Myconos and Gyaros, and made it fertile and safe from storms. Reverently, we disembarked. The king of Delos, who is also a priest of Apollo, came to meet us, with his head wreathed in sacred garlands of laurel. His name was Anius, and he had known Anchises for many years. We joined hands in friendship, and proceeded into his palace.

"I went up to the old stone temple: 'Grant us, lord Apollo, a home of our own. We are the only Trojans to have escaped the cruelty of Achilles and the Greeks: give us walls to protect us while we rest, and a city where we may settle—a second fortress, a second Troy. What guide should we follow? Where ought we to go? Where ought we to stay? Give us a sign—and let us read your will in our hearts.'

"Even before I had finished speaking, the whole temple, along with Apollo's laurel tree, began to shake. The entire

mountainside swayed, the doors of his shrine sprang open and his sacred cauldron let out a groan. We flattened ourselves on the ground—and then came Apollo's voice:

"'The Trojan race has never flinched from any difficulty. If you return to the place where your suc-

cess began, the earth that first gave birth to you will receive you once again. You must search out your ancient motherland.

Here the successors of Aeneas will rule a great empire—they and their children and the children of their children.'

"We shouted with joy—but we were still confused. All talking at once, we asked each other where this new capital was supposed to be. What did Apollo mean? Where did he intend us to end our wandering? Where was this place where we were to return?

... and then to Crete

"And then my father reminded us of our long history: 'Listen,' he told us, 'to what you need to know. Your origins lie in the middle of the sea, on the island of Crete, on the other Mount Ida, where Jupiter was born. Crete was prosperous and fertile then, a land of a hundred cities. From there—I'm sure this is how it happened—our ancestor Teucer came first to the shores of the Hellespont, and chose a site there for his new city. Troy did not yet exist, and the people lived in the valleys below the hill that would later become its citadel. It was then that our ancestors began our worship of the earth mother—the goddess Cybele, who came originally from Crete. From Crete she brought her nymphs with their crashing cymbals, and the lions that she harnesses to her chariot. Even the place in the woods, where her quiet and secret ceremonies are performed, is named after Ida on Crete. The gods' message is clear: we have our orders and we must follow them. We must go to Crete. Pray for a fair wind. It's not a long voyage—only three days, if Jupiter is with us.' And at once he prepared altars for the ritual sacrifices: a bull to Neptune, a bull to Apollo, a black sheep to Winter and a white one to the gentle west winds.

"Of course, we had all heard the stories: how the king of Crete was in exile and had abandoned his inheritance; how his enemies left his palace empty, and his cities in ruins; and how the island is now deserted. From Delos, then, we chose a course to Crete that would keep us always in sight of land— quickly past Naxos, where Bacchus' followers dance in the mountains; past green Donusa and Olearus and Paros' snow-covered peak; past the scattered islands of the Cyclades. The oarsmen encouraged each other to pull harder; and my companions urged them on.

"And so at last, with a rising wind behind us, we came smoothly to the land of our ancestors. Here I began eagerly to lay out walls for the city that we had prayed for. I named it Pergamea, after Pergamon, the citadel of Troy, and I told my people: 'All these fortifications you are building, all these houses—they have a name to be proud of. This is a place that you can once more call home.'

"Our ships were now safely ashore, and I was kept busy drawing up regulations for the distribution of farmland to the young men who wanted to get married and make a fresh start. But suddenly the air turned poisonous: the people sickened away, and the new year brought only death to the trees and crops. Happy lives turned unhappy; sick bodies dragged through sick fields. With the rising of the dog-star came drought: the grass dried up and the harvest came to nothing. My father advised me to sail all the way back to Delos, and consult Apollo's oracle again. We should beg for mercy, he said. 'Tell the god that you are worn out from not knowing when the end will come, or what relief you can look for, and where you should go next.'

Aeneas is urged by the gods to continue his journey

"Night. The world slept. And I thought that I saw the statues that I had rescued—the Olympian gods and my own household gods—come to life in the light of the full moon that was flooding brightly through my unshuttered windows. They crowded round me, speaking to me in gentle voices: 'We will tell you what Apollo will say to you, if you go again to Delos. He has sent us to you, even though you did not ask him. We have followed you and your companions out from the ashes of Troy. We have traveled with you in your ships over the sea. We promise you a glorious future: a city and an empire for your children's children yet to come, and great walls to protect a great new generation. So though your flight is exhausting, you must not give up—you must move on yet again.

"'This is not where Apollo means you to settle. Jupiter forbids you to stay here. But there is another country—a land with a long tradition of warriors and farmers. Its first inhabitants came from Arcadia in Greece; later it was ruled by Italus and took the name of Italy—though in Greek it is still called Hesperia. It was there in Italy where your own most distant forefathers, themselves the sons of Jupiter, were born—and it is there that you should settle us. Get up now, and pass this message to your father. You must make your way to Italy—Jupiter has determined that Crete is not for you.'

"I was amazed by what I saw and by what my gods said. And it was no dream, but rather the gods seemed to be actually

there in front of me, and their long hair could not hide the expressions on their faces. I felt a cold sweat trickling down my back. Quickly I left my bed to say a prayer and then to make an offering of undiluted wine at the altars. And then, when the ceremony was complete, I went confidently to Anchises to tell him what the gods had told me. He admitted then that his understanding of our people's origins was confused—two ancient stories had made for a single new mistake. 'My boy,' he said. 'You know all the prophecies about the end of Troy—but Cassandra was the only one to get it right. She knew what was coming. I remember now: she was always talking about Hesperia, and Italus' kingdom. But still—who would ever have believed that Trojans would one day find themselves in Italy? And who ever took any notice of Cassandra? But now we should listen more carefully to Apollo, and move on again to the better things that lie ahead.'

The decision to make for Italy

"We all were delighted to obey Anchises. We abandoned our settlement—all but a few who decided to stay—and we hoisted our sails to set out on yet another voyage. But as soon as we reached the open sea, and were out of sight of land—nothing to see but sky and water—a purple rain-cloud piled up overhead, bringing with it darkness and cold. The waves were steep, shadowed. A gale howled. It whipped the surface of the sea into an enormous whirling wedge that forced our ships apart. Through the rain, we couldn't see the daylight, and at night we could not see the stars; and if the clouds did part, lightning flickered in the spaces between them. We lost our heading and circled hopelessly, blindly. My navigator, Palinurus, could not get his bearings. And so for three black days and three starless nights we were lost, seeing nothing and knowing nothing. But on the fourth day we glimpsed land lifting at last on the horizon, and distant mountains, and a drift of smoke.

"The sails came down and we laid to the oars. Without rest the straining sailors cut through the waves, making the spray

fly across a sea that was blue once more, till we safely reached the Strophades, islands that lie out in the Ionian sea. Celaeno and the other harpies lived there; they had been driven away from the court of the king of Thrace, where they had polluted whatever he tried to eat. They are the cruelest of monsters, and no plague or divine vengeance ever emerged more dangerously from beyond the Styx, the river of hell. They are women, but they have the features of birds of prey; they are suffused with the stink of their own excrement; they have hooks for hands and their faces are always white with hunger.

A horrible adventure, and an important prophecy

"Here, then, we made our landing. Everywhere peaceful herds of cattle and goats were grazing. There was no one to look after them, so we began at once to hunt them down, calling on all the gods, including Jupiter, to grant us a share of this prize. Then we spread blankets on the curve of the beach and laid out a splendid feast. But all of a sudden the harpies are upon us, swooping down from the mountains in a  horrific clatter of beating wings. They seize our food and ruin everything that they touch. Their shrieks are as horrible as their stench, so we shift everything out of their reach. Under a rocky overhang we spread out our tables again, and light

 other fires on new altars. And again from all parts of the sky, from their dark hiding-places, the monsters scream and crowd down upon us, snatching at our meal with their clawed feet, and smearing it with their saliva.

"I told my companions to fetch their weapons to fight these frightful creatures off. And at once they did as I said, hiding

their swords and shields carefully in the long grass. And the next time that the harpies swooped down, calling to each other along the shore, Misenus was watching out for them from a cave on the hill. He gave a signal on his trumpet. My companions charged into action—this was a new kind of battle for them—and tried to fend off these disgusting seabirds. But their armored feathers made it impossible to hurt them; they simply soared up and away into the sky, leaving behind our food half-eaten and fouled by their droppings.

Another message from the gods

"Celaeno sat on the top of a high rock, a lonely prophet of doom. She croaked out a warning: 'Are you ready for your next campaign, you Trojans? You seem to be preparing not just to kill cattle this time, but to expel the innocent harpies from their native land. So listen to what I have to say, and fix it in your hearts: I am the greatest of the Furies, and I will tell you what Jupiter told Apollo and what Apollo told me. You have called on the winds to give you passage to Italy; and to Italy you shall go. The gods have decreed that you will make a safe landfall, and that you will found a city there. But first you must repay the injury you have done us by your slaughter of our cattle: you are not to start to build its walls until you are so hungry that you are compelled to eat not only your food but the very tables from which you eat.' And with those words she spread her wings and vanished into the woods.

"My men cannot move; Celaeno's sudden terrifying appearance has paralyzed them. They are listless, drained of energy. 'This is the time for prayers, not swords,' they say. 'We should make peace with these creatures. Who cares whether they are goddesses of vengeance, or just disgusting birds?' And on the beach my father Anchises stretches out his hands to Olympus and promises due honors to the gods: 'Do not threaten us—we are always obedient to your commands. Keep us safe and free from harm.' At his order, we cast off our ships, and let loose the sheets. Our sails fill with a following south wind, and we slice through the whitecaps.

"Palinurus had plotted our course past wooded Zacynthus and Dulichium and Same and Neritos with its rocky shore. We flew by the cliffs of Ithaca, Laertes' kingdom, and we cursed the island, because cruel Ulysses had been born there. Soon we caught sight of the cloud-covered mountains of Leucas; and on the mainland, at Actium, we saw the temple of Apollo, the god that all sailors fear. We were tired now, and so we came ashore to explore the small town below. We dropped anchors from our bows and hauled our ships' sterns up onto the beach.

"After making this landing, which we had not expected, we lit fires on altars, made sacrifices to Jupiter and held games in the Trojan fashion. My companions stripped and oiled their bodies for the traditional wrestling matches, delighted to be safely away from hostile Greek territory. But meanwhile summer had faded, and the bitter north winds of winter whipped up the seas. In the temple portico I hung a shield of beaten bronze, which had once belonged to Abas, a Greek I had killed at Troy, with a plaque: *These arms, won from the victorious Greeks, were dedicated here by Aeneas.*

Reunion with old friends

"Then again we put out to sea. I gave the word, the sailors took their places, and with their oars flashing in rhythm together, the ships raced side by side past the airy citadel of Phaeacia and along the coast of Epirus to Chaonia, where we climbed up the hill to the city of Buthrotum.

"In Buthrotum we heard an extraordinary story: the local king was Helenus, another son of Priam. Apparently Pyrrhus, the man who had killed Priam, had given him his throne, along with a wife—and that wife, amazingly enough, turned out to be Hector's widow, Andromache. Pyrrhus had abducted her

and had then handed her over to Helenus, so that once again
she was married to a Trojan husband. Of course I couldn't wait
to visit Helenus and hear of his adventures. I left the ships
on the shore, and I was making my way to his palace, when
I came to a grove of trees in front of the city, on the banks
of a river that reminded me of the river at Troy. And there
was Andromache herself. She had brought gifts for the dead
and prayers to the spirits of the underworld; she had piled up
an empty barrow and covered it with grass to be a tomb for
Hector, and had dedicated a pair of altars—a place where she
could mourn for him.

"When she saw me approach-
ing, wearing my Trojan armor,
she could not believe her eyes.
At first she was frightened: she
thought I was some kind of phan-
tom. And then she recognized
me, and stood quite still, shiver-
ing and almost fainting. But at
last she spoke to me: 'Aeneas? Is
it really you? What news do you
have? Are you alive—or dead? If
you are a ghost, is Hector with
you?' Tears ran down her cheeks,
and her cries echoed through the
trees. I could scarcely make her
listen to me, and I was moved as
well. I spoke with difficulty.

"'Yes,' I said, 'I am alive—though my life is hard and sor-
rowful. But do not doubt me—I am no mirage. And you, An-
dromache—once you had lost your Hector, what happened
to you to bring you here? It can hardly be a fate that you de-
serve. You're not still Pyrrhus' mistress, are you?' Andromache
looked at the ground, and spoke to me in a low voice: 'Of all
the Trojan women, only one is happy now—Priam's unmar-
ried daughter Polyxena. She was the only one who was never

handed over to a Greek; she was never captured or hauled off to a conqueror's bed. Instead she was sacrificed at Achilles' tomb under the city walls, because Achilles had once been in love with her.

"I was not so lucky. Pyrrhus carried me off in his ship when the war was over; he treated me with arrogance and contempt, and he even forced me to have his child. But he really wanted Hermione, Helen's daughter—so he followed her to Sparta in order to marry her. He handed me over to Helenus, a slave to a slave, and then he stole Hermione from her husband Orestes, and Orestes, enraged by Pyrrhus' crimes and still madly in love with Hermione, caught Pyrrhus by surprise when he was at prayer, and murdered him. So Pyrrhus is dead. Part of his kingdom has gone to Helenus, who has called the whole place Chaonia after a Trojan warrior, and built forts on the hills above, and given them Trojan names as well.

"But you—did you come here by chance? Or did some god guide you? Did you know that I was here? Tell me about Ascanius. Did he survive the war? Is he well? I remember how in Troy... does he still miss his mother? Does he promise to be as brave and spirited as his father is, and as his uncle Hector once was?'

"She was still pouring out her questions, between fits of sobbing, when Helenus with his escort came down from the walls. He recognized us as his own people, and took us inside the palace—and he too spoke haltingly to us, through tears. I went out to admire his city: he had built a miniature copy of Troy, complete with Scaean gates and a citadel, and he had called the dry river-bed Xanthus. My companions felt at home in this friendly place. The king received them under a spacious portico; and in the middle of the courtyard, when they had made offerings to the gods, they feasted off golden plates and drank from golden cups.

"Day after day went by, and the breeze beckoned our sails, stirring them and swelling their canvas. And so I anxiously approached Helenus: 'Tell me—you can interpret the will of the gods. You know the ways of Apollo, and you understand how he prophesies from his tripod, and how the laurels smoke in his temple. You can read the stars and the cries of birds and the good omens that they bring. The gods have spoken favorably of my future voyage: all of them have persuaded me to make for Italy and lands far away—and only Celaeno the harpy foretells misfortune, speaking of revenge and famine. So tell me, what are the dangers to avoid? What advice do you have for me so that I can avoid more troubles?'

"Helenus first made the customary sacrifice of heifers, asking the gods for peace. He took the garlands from his head and led me, awed and humble, to Apollo's temple. And there he spoke words that the god had put into his mouth: 'Son of Venus—there is no doubt about the prophecy that you have already heard: your voyage is not yet over. But all is resolved: Jupiter has already drawn the lots, and events are sweeping you along. I could say a great deal, but in fact I can reveal only a little: just what you need to know in order to travel more safely across friendly seas to your landing in Italy.

Yet another prophecy and a warning of danger yet to come

"'The Fates will not allow you to know any more, and Juno forbids me to tell you. But first of all, as you get ready to go to Italy, you may think that the voyage is a short one. But you are wrong. A great distance still separates you from your destination, and you must follow an uncharted course. Before you can find a safe site for your city, you still will have to pass by Sicily, and the ocean south of Italy, and the rivers of the underworld, and Aeaea, the island where the witch Circe lives. But at least remember this: if you ever find yourself standing by a remote river, wondering what to do next— and if you see, lying alone under the oak trees on the bank, a white sow with thirty white piglets at her udders—

that will be a sure sign that you have arrived at the destined place to found your city. There for certain there will be rest from all your troubles. And do not forget Celaeno's prophecy about eating your tables.

"'You must leave my kingdom now. The fates will show you your route, and Apollo will never be far away. Avoid the coast of Italy that lies due west from here, across the Adriatic Sea. All the cities there are inhabited by Greeks who do not wish you well: the Locrians, for example, have established a colony, and Idomeneus, after his flight from Crete, has set up a garrison, and Philoctetes has founded a small walled town. But if you do cross the sea and make a landing, and if you then should build an altar and light a fire and dress in ceremonial robes in honor of the gods, be sure to keep your head covered, in case an enemy should see your face, and bring you bad luck. Make sure, too, that you and your companions—and your children after you—observe every ritual exactly.

"'But for now—when the wind takes you south toward Sicily, and you see its northern promontory of Pelorus, turn to port and take the long route around the island. Keep away from the coast of Italy, which will lie on your starboard side. And keep away from the strait that divides Sicily and Italy from each other. It has not always been there, for the island and the mainland used to be joined together. But once upon a very distant time a violent earthquake wrenched them apart and left a void between them. And the sea rushed in to form a narrow strait, dividing city from city and farm from farm.

"'On both sides of this strait is danger. On the left lurks the

implacable Charybdis. She has taken the form of three whirlpools, one after the other: she will gulp down a vast mouthful of water, swallow it deep down her steep and bottomless throat, and then spit it out again, high enough to shake the stars. And on the right, in the dark, Scylla is waiting. She peers out of her secret cave, ready to lure your ship onto the rocks. You might take her at first for a human, for above the waist she is a beautiful naked girl; but below she is all hideous monster, with the belly of a wolf and the tail of a dolphin. Though it is much farther and takes much longer, it is better to sail all the way round the southern tip of Sicily than to lay eyes on Scylla and the swells that smash onto the rocks with a noise like howling dogs.

"'And now, Aeneas, if you believe that Apollo has given me any useful ability to see into the future, and if you trust my prophecies at all, listen to this one last piece of advice, this one warning above all others, which I cannot repeat too often: never forget to pay homage to Juno. Always soothe her with prayers, and appease her with sacrifices. And then—at long last—with Sicily left behind you, you will come triumphantly to Italy. When you have landed there, you will come to Cumae, and the sacred lakes and the rustling woods of Avernus, and there you will find a woman who may seem to you quite mad. She is a priestess of Diana, one of the Sibyls, and she tells the future by writing names and words on leaves. She sets these messages in order and hides them in her cave; and there they remain unmoved and undisturbed. But if a draft swings the door open on its hinges, and any movement of the air shifts the leaves, she never bothers to pick them up as they fly about the cave, or to replace them or rearrange them. So those who come for her advice do not receive it, and they resent her.

"'Now listen: although your companions may grumble and try to make you continue your journey, and even though the wind may be favorable, you should consider that no time you spend with the Sibyl is wasted. You should go to her and ask for her oracles; you should beg her to break her silence, and speak to you. She will tell you about the peoples of Italy, and the battles that you must fight; she will tell you what troubles may be avoided and what pains must be borne. In short, if you pay her the respect that is due to her, she will show you the best course to follow. I can tell you no more then this. Now go: and by your deeds raise up a new and towering Troy.'

Final farewell to friends from Troy

"After Helenus had finished, he sent us on our way as a true friend would. He had gifts of silver and gold and ivory carried on board our ships, and copper cauldrons from Apollo's temple at Dodona, and horses and guides and extra oarsmen and weapons for all my companions. There were gifts for my father, and to me he gave Pyrrhus' own armor: a tunic woven in and out with triple-twisted threads of gold and a magnificent crested helmet.

"Meanwhile Anchises had ordered sails to be hoisted, ready to catch a breeze. Helenus approached him respectfully. 'Anchises, you are worthy to be the husband of Venus, to be well-loved by the gods, to have been twice rescued from the ruin of Troy. Italy lies ahead of you, and yet you must not make straight for the nearest point on the Italian shore. The landing-place that Apollo intends for you is much further off than that. Now go: the reverence that your son feels for the gods will bring you luck. But I have talked enough. The wind is getting up, and I must delay you no longer.'

"Andromache, too, was sad to see us go. She brought us gold-embroidered tapestries, and a Trojan cloak and other gifts for Ascanius. 'My dear boy,' she said to him, 'These are the last gifts that you will receive from one of your own people. I wove them with my own hands. As you take them, remember always how much I loved my husband Hector—and my son Astyanax. You remind me so much of him. You have his eyes, his hands, his features; and if he were still alive, he would be exactly your age.'

"Then I made my own tearful farewell: 'May you both be happy in the lot that fortune has laid out for you. The fates brought us here, and now we must move on where they send us next. For you—peace: no more travels, no more fresh fields to seek, no Italy fading ever further into the distance. You can look out on a river that is very like the Xanthus, and a

Troy that you have built yourselves—a Troy, I hope, that has a happier future in front of it, and that the Greeks will never find. But if ever I reach the river Tiber, and the land that lies by the Tiber's banks, and if ever the gods grant me to build walls there to keep my people safe, then my city and yours will be linked together—each one founded by a Trojan and each with a common history. In our hearts we will think of the two of them as one Troy risen again; and so we will bequeath them to our descendants.'

The first sight of Italy

"And so we left behind the shelter of Epirus. The crews spelled each other at the oars, and we moved down the coast to the place where Italy lies just across the water. The sun went quickly down behind the mountains, and we were glad to put in at a bay where we could stretch out on the dry sand. We were tired; we slept well. But the night was not yet half gone when Palinurus leaped eagerly from his bed, sniffing the air and listening for a wind. He observed every constellation as it slipped across the quiet sky: Arcturus, and the Hyades that bring rain, and the Bears; he checked Orion and his starry belt. Everything was still and clear. From the poopdeck, he sounded his bugle—the signal to break camp and set our course and spread our sails.

"Dawn was still driving the stars from the sky when we saw a dark smudge of hills low against the glimmer on the distant horizon. Achates was the first to recognize them. 'Italy!' he shouted, and right after him, 'Italy!' came the same excited cry from everyone else. Then Anchises took a bowl and wreathed it with flowers and filled it with wine. High up on the stern, he prayed: 'Great gods of sea and land and weather, give us an easy passage and a following wind.' And at once the breeze that we needed sprang up behind us, and in front of us appeared a place to land, a bay carved out by the east wind with a temple to Minerva set back in the hills behind it. On each side it was guarded by cliffs, jagged like battlements, and a line of rocks across the entrance sheltered it from the breaking surf. The sailors hauled in the sails and turned the bows towards the beach. But straightaway—an omen: I saw four pure white horses grazing in a meadow. 'This country

welcomes us with war,' explained Anchises. 'Horses mean cavalry, and cavalry mean a battle. And yet horses that draw a chariot can also be hitched to a plow—so there is hope for peace.' We covered our heads, and worshipped Minerva, the warrior goddess, because she was the first to receive us when we came to shore. And then, heeding Helenus' urgent warning, we made offerings to Juno, even though she favored the Greeks.

Monsters and giants around Sicily

"But we did not stay long: we couldn't trust any place inhabited by Greeks. As soon as we had finished our last prayer, we bent the sails once more to the yards. We made our way across the gulf of Tarentum, which—if the story is true—was once visited by Hercules. One town there is well-known for its temple of Juno, and another for its approaches that are dangerous for shipping. Far off across the water we could see Sicily and the peak of Mount Etna; and we could hear great waves pounding against rocks, and at the water's edge the hiss of sandbanks seething with the wash of the sea.

"'That must be Charybdis' said Anchises; 'and those are the cliffs and the dangerous reefs that Helenus told us about. We must row for our lives.' No sooner said than done: Palinurus went ahead, turning his bows to the south, away from the straits; and the rest of the fleet followed him as fast as they could. But even so the whirlpool snatched at us, lifting us and letting us fall, up to the sky and down to the deepest bottom of the sea. Three times we heard the grinding of stone on stone below us, and three times, above our heads, the stars themselves were whipped with spray. The gale did not drop until

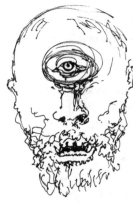

sunset, and then, too worn out to be anxious, we drifted toward Sicily, to that stretch of coast where the giant Cyclopes live.

"We came to a harbor, big and sheltered. But not far off Etna thundered threateningly: it threw a dark pall high into the sky, a roiling mass of pitch-black smoke and white-hot ash. The clouds reflected back its bursts of flame, and sometimes the mountain coughed up vast boulders, torn loose from deep in its belly. Lava rolled down its sides, boiling and bubbling from the middle of the earth. They say that one of the giants who conspired against Jupiter is buried here: his body was scorched by a thunderbolt, and then the mass of Etna was piled on top of him. But still his body shoots out fire as though the walls of his prison have split. As often as he stirs, the whole island moves, groaning and smearing the air above with soot. All that night, we cowered patiently in the woods, unable to tell exactly where the sounds were coming from, for there were no stars and no moon. Clouds veiled a dim and dreary sky.

A marooned sailor tells a bloody tale

"With the first stirring of wind from the east, dawn wiped away the shadows— and from among the trees appeared a stranger, holding out his hands to us. We stared at him. He was ragged and painfully thin, with a tangled beard and filthy clothes held together by thorns. He looked lost and bewildered. But still he was recognizable as a Greek, one of those sent to fight at Troy; and when he saw our Trojan dress and Trojan armor, he hesitated for a moment before he continued

his approach. He emerged at last onto the beach and spoke to us in fits of wild sobbing.

"'Please—by the stars and the sun and all the gods, save me! Take me away wherever you want—I don't care where. Yes, I was at Troy with the Greek fleet: and yes, I was one of those that attacked your city. If you can't forgive me for that, then take me out to sea, throw me overboard. If I've got to die, at least it'll be a comfort to have been done in by other humans.' He threw himself down, prostrate like a suppliant, and lay on the ground trembling.

"We tried to encourage him. 'Tell us first who you are. What's your family? Whatever has happened to make you speak like this?' And my father Anchises held out his hand to him, and put some spirit back into him by swearing that we would do him no harm.

"At last he stopped trembling enough to speak sensibly: 'I'm from Ithaca. My name's Achaemenides, and my dad was Adamastus. He was a poor man: so he sent me to try my fortune at Troy with Ulysses. But now I wish I'd stayed at home. We was on our way back to Ithaca after the war, but Polyphemus the Cyclops trapped us here in his cave. My mates managed to get out, but I was left behind. That cave! It's vast and dark and smeared all over with blood. And as for Polyphemus! A monster, tall as the sky, that the gods should never allow to live on the earth. He's enormous and ugly, grunts so you can't understand what he says, and lives on human blood and human flesh. With my own eyes I seen him sit there, pick up two of our lot in one giant hand, smash 'em against the wall of his cave, and their blood was collected in pools at the entrance. And I watched him, how he chewed on their arms and legs, sank his teeth into 'em while they was still quiverin' and warm and wet.

"'But he'd pay for it in the end, because he didn't know Ulysses, and he didn't realize that Ulysses would never ever let his mates down. We waits till he's finished eatin', and he's collapsed, blind drunk, in a pile on the floor; and we stands in

a circle around him as he lies there snorin' and dribblin' wine
out of the corner of his mouth and pukin' up bits of his food
mixed with blood. Then we all prays to the gods, and draws
lots as to who should do what. And we uses a sharp stick for
a drill, and we gouges out that one eye of his, the one that sits

right in the middle of his mean scowlin' forehead, an eye that
would put you in mind of a round Greek shield, or the sun.
That's how we got revenge for our poor dead mates—and hor-
rible as it sounds, we was happy.

  "'But you—you get out from here as fast as you can: you're
in trouble. Because Polyphemus isn't the only one—there's
more just like him, and just as big. They lives all along this
shore, hundreds of 'em, each one more nasty than the last,
and they wanders about in the mountains, herdin' their sheep
and milkin' 'em in their caves. I've been here for three months

now, sleepin' on leaves in the woods like the animals. I've rigged up a lookout place in the hills so I can keep an eye on 'em, scared to death if they comes near me, or even if I just hear their voices. I've been pickin' berries and nuts off the trees and pullin' up wild grasses—barely enough to keep me alive. I was scratchin' around for somethin' to eat when I seen your boats—and I says to myself, I says: I don't care what happens to me so long as I can get away from them dreadful creatures. So kill me however you want—it don't make no difference to me.'

A Cyclops pursues them

"And then we saw, up on the mountain, the monster Polyphemus himself, a huge ungainly lumpish figure. He was blind, feeling his way down to the familiar shore by using the trunk of a pine tree as a cane. His flock of sheep surrounded him—his last remaining pleasure, and a comfort for his wicked old age. Down to the beach he came, grinding his teeth in pain, and waded out beyond the breakers—though the water still did not come up to his waist—to wash the scabbed socket

where his eye once was. Taking the castaway with us in gratitude for his warning, we avoided Polyphemus as well as we could. We cut loose the bow-ropes in silence, and rowed out toward the open sea.

"But Polyphemus heard us and turned to the sound of our voices. When he realized that he couldn't grab us in his hands, or pursue us quickly enough through the waves, he lifted his voice so that the sea trembled, and even the far-off land of Italy was frightened, and the caves of Etna echoed to his howl. From the woods and hills the other Cyclopes rushed out and crowded around the harbor and the shore. We could see them all, Polyphemus' brothers, heads cocked, each vainly peering out with his single eye. They made a forbidding array, as tall as the rustling oaks or the dark cypresses that stand guard over a temple of Jupiter or Diana on a wooded mountain top. We were so frightened that we did not think where we were going: we let the sheets fly and allowed the wind to take us wherever it would, even though that meant doubling back to the north once more. We were heading straight for Scylla and Charybdis, and to certain death if we were caught anywhere between them. But at that very moment, as we remembered Helenus' warnings and realized that we must turn back, the wind changed. We turned southward with it, and as we passed down the east coast of Sicily, Achaemenides, who once had sailed with Ulysses, pointed out to us the landmarks of his wanderings.

"On an island off Syracuse, which used to be called Ortygia, is the fountain Arethusa. Its water comes, they say, from the river Alpheus, which once rose in southern Greece, and flowed to Sicily beneath the sea. There, as we had been advised, we worshipped the local gods; and then we moved on past rich fields and lakes until we rounded the promontory of Pachynus. Next we caught sight of Camerina, a city that the fates have sworn will endure forever, and the distant plains and river-mouth of Gela; then the fortress Acragas, famous for the spirited horses that are bred there; then Selinus, balmy enough for palm trees; and the tricky shoals off Lilybaeum.

A sad loss

"Finally we reached the shelter of Cape Drepanon. It was a sad landing: for here, in the port where we had arrived safe and sound at last, Anchises died. He was the best of fathers. He had consoled me in all my misfortunes and misadventures, and now, travel-weary as I was, he had left me all alone. Had he survived all those dangers for nothing? Was it for this that I had sailed so far? Helenus had not foretold my loss; nor had the awful Celaeno—but of all the trials that the fates had sent upon me, this was the bitterest of all. And yet—here I am, driven by the gods to a landfall in your country."

That was the end of Aeneas' story, the end of the voyage that the gods had planned for him. For all the time that he had been speaking, no one had moved; and now he too sat still and silent.

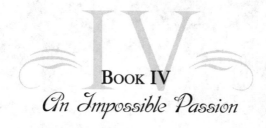

BOOK IV
An Impossible Passion

Book IV
An Impossible Passion

Dido is attracted to Aeneas. She tries to resist him...

But Dido was aware of a strange uneasiness, almost a physical pain, which she felt in every part of her body. Emotions that she did not understand consumed her. She could not stop thinking about Aeneas' courage, and the distinction of his family; his face floated always before her eyes and his voice echoed in her ears. Nothing she did could give her any peace, but when the dawn had swept away the last dewy shadows from the sky, and the sun was fully up, she went to speak to her sister Anna, who was always her sympathetic confidante.

"Anna: I have not been able to sleep at all. I cannot help wondering what kind of man he is, this stranger who has arrived in my kingdom. How can he be so eloquent, so brave, so noble? I believe—and it is no vain hope—that he comes to us from the gods. He has shown no fear; and fear would have found a weak spot in him if he were a mortal. He has been so battered about by fate and the stresses of war—what an inspiring story he has told us! And now I have a confession to make: ever since I was cheated of my first love by our brother's treachery, when poor Sychaeus was murdered and I was driven out of my home, I have been unable to bear even the thought of marrying again. I made up my mind then never to go through another wedding, but yet... this man is different. Perhaps he might be the one to wash away my grief and touch my heart. He makes me remember—faintly—what passion felt like. But still I would rather have the earth swallow me up, or Jupiter strike me down with his thunderbolt and send me down to the pale shadows and the perpetual dusk of death, before I break my promise to Sychaeus. He had my love when first we swore to stay together, and he took it with him to his grave. He has it now, and he will always keep it." Tears would let her say no more.

"You know how fond I am of you," replied Anna. "But still I must ask you—do you intend to spend the whole of your youth in mourning? Will you always deny yourself the delights of a family and the pleasures of love? Do you really believe that the ashes of the dead care about such things? Yes, you miss Sychaeus. But why have no new suitors—there were some from Tyre once, and more recently from Libya—been able to find a way into your heart? You have turned away King Iarbas and all the African chieftains who have approached you, even though they were rich and victorious in war. And have you considered how your new city is placed—on one side of it impassable sandbanks and tribes of hard-riding warriors, and on the other miles of desert, empty except for nomads and bandits? And Pygmalion may yet pursue you here, and Tyre may still attack us.

"I think that this Aeneas and his fleet have come from Troy with the blessing of Juno and the other gods. Can't you imagine what a city you could build here, and what a kingdom you could rule, if you had a husband like him? If you had the Trojans as allies, would there be any limits to the glory of Carthage? All you have to do, with the gods' approval, is to entertain him generously—and after that you can contrive all manner of reasons why he must stay here longer. You could say that it is still winter, or that there are squalls far out at sea, or that his ships have not yet been repaired, or that the sky looks threatening."

...but she cannot shake off his influence over her

Anna's words made love flare up in Dido's heart; they added hope to her hesitation, and eased her conscience. She and Anna went into the temple to pray for peace; according to tradition they selected sheep to be sacrificed to Ceres and Apollo and Bacchus and above all to Juno, the goddess of the marriage-bond. And Dido herself, from a bowl that she held in her right hand, poured an offering between the horns of a white cow and over its forehead. Sensing that the gods were watching over her, she approached the altars and throughout the day she piled on more and more gifts. Bellies of animals were torn open, and she looked deeply into the steam curling up from their entrails, looking for signs. But what do fortune-tellers know? How could she have expected that prayers, or the gods in their shrines, would help her in her perplexity? Poor Dido—she felt as if she were on fire, or that a wound was festering silently in her heart. A subtle heat ate away at the marrow of her bones, and she strayed restlessly through the city.

> Have you ever seen a wounded doe, swerving to and fro in the woods below the peak of Dicte in Crete? A shepherd has startled her and loosed off a shot; but he does not realize that he has hit her, and that she is still on her feet, with the arrowhead inside her and the shaft dangling from her flank.

So Dido, with Aeneas at her side, wandered the streets of Carthage. She explored the walls with him, she showed him her treasures and inspected the half-built monuments. But whenever she wanted to say anything, she had nothing to say.

As soon as the day came to an end, she wanted to relive the celebration of the night before. With a mad insistence she demanded to hear once again the tale of the fall of Troy; and once again she clung to every word that came out of Aeneas' mouth, until the moonlight and the torches were extinguished together, and the fading stars told her that it was time for sleep. But long after everyone else had gone to bed, she stayed up, alone and miserable in the deserted banquet-hall, lying on the tumbled covers of the couch where he had lain. Though she was apart from him, she heard his voice; though he was not beside her, she saw his face. And she put her arms around Ascanius, pretending to herself that by embracing the son she could embrace the father, and somehow deny the love that she could not put into words. And work in the city was abandoned—the harbor, the towers that had hardly been begun, the fortifications that were meant to keep them safe against a siege, the young men's military exercises. The walls stood unfinished, intimidating no one, and the lazy cranes were silhouetted against the sky.

Juno's plots to keep Aeneas in Carthage

It was as if Dido were suffering from an infection; fear for her good name did nothing to cool her fever. But Juno, the wife of Jupiter, noticed her, and she at once approached Venus. "You and your boy must be remarkable indeed, if it has taken the trickery of two gods to overcome one woman. You have brought great distinction on yourselves. I have not failed to notice your nervousness about my walls, and your resentment of my new city. But what will be the end of it all? Are we going to quarrel forever? Should we not rather arrange a lasting peace, and seal it with a wedding? You have achieved what you planned: Dido is madly in love with Aeneas, and her passion for him consumes her. Let us agree to govern their peoples jointly and to grant them equal good fortune. Let Dido marry this prince of Troy, and let her bring to him as her dowry the people of Carthage."

Venus guessed that there was a deeper purpose behind Juno's words, that she was really trying to divert Aeneas' promised kingdom from Italy to Libya. "It would be foolish," she answered, "to reject such a proposal. Who would want to quarrel with you? And perhaps fortune will indeed bring about what you suggest. But would Jupiter wish Carthaginians and Trojans to live together in a single city, side by side, allied by a treaty? Would he approve? I don't know. But you are his wife: it is for you to try to discover what his intentions are. I will follow your lead."

"Yes, I will ask him," interjected Juno. "But now listen. Let me tell you how we may carry out my plan. Tomorrow, when the rays of the rising sun sweep away the darkness from the earth, Aeneas and Dido plan to go hunting together in the country. While the huntsmen are laying out their snares along the valley, I will bring a storm down on them and lash them with hail and fill the sky with thunder. Their companions will run off in different directions, and they will all fade away into the gloom. But Dido and Aeneas will make their way into the same cave—and I will be there too. If I can be certain of your support, that is the moment when I will contrive their marriage pact and decree that she belongs to him—and that will be their wedding." Venus nodded in agreement, and laughed at the stratagem that Juno had proposed.

A hunting expedition assembles...

Meanwhile Dawn rose from the ocean and, at the first gleam of sunlight, the young men who had been invited to join the expedition assembled outside the gates of the city. They brought with them wide-meshed nets, snares, broad-bladed hunting spears, and keen-sniffing hounds; the local horsemen, who ride bareback and without bridles, came to join them. The Carthaginian nobles waited at the entrance to the queen's apartments; her horse shifted his feet noisily as he stood splendid in purple and gold, spitting and mouthing at his bit. And at last—at long last—the queen appeared. She was wearing a Tyrian cloak edged with embroidery, and her hair was held in place by a golden pin. A golden brooch gathered up her purple robe, and a golden quiver hung at her side.

The Trojans came to meet her. Ascanius was dashing enough, she thought, but Aeneas—Aeneas was the most magnificent of them all. He approached her with a kind of glory in his tread and on his face.

He had the air of Apollo when he leaves his winter home by the river Xanthus in Asia, to visit Delos where

he was born; as his attendants—Cretans, Macedonians,
tattooed Scythians—dance and sing about his altars,
the god himself floats above the mountain peaks, his
bow and jangling arrows slung across his shoulder,
green leaves and glittering gold entangled in his hair.

Together they all made their way far up into the mountains,
until there were no more paths to follow. Wild goats, flushed
out from the ridges, came leaping down the cliffs; herds of
deer abandoned the high ground and galloped across the plain
in boiling clouds of dust. In a lower valley, young Ascanius was
showing off his horsemanship. He rode in circles around one

group of hunters after another, complaining that he would
much rather be pursuing a vicious wild boar than these harm-
less deer, and wishing loudly that a mountain lion would leap
out at him from behind a rock.

*...and is
interrupted*

Meanwhile the sky had darkened. The
rumbling of thunder began, and a black
storm-cloud lashed them with hail. Flash-
floods swept down on them from above. Both the Trojans and
the Carthaginians, with Ascanius among them, were fright-
ened, and ran in all directions to find shelter wherever they

could; Dido and Aeneas found their way into the same cave. And at once Cybele and Juno gave a sign: while the whole sky stood witness, the lightning flickered like a wedding torch, and the nymphs in the mountains wailed a wedding hymn. Yet the moment marked the beginning of Dido's journey to misery and death, for this was when she began not to care what people might see or say. Her secret love affair had become in her mind a public marriage; and once she had convinced herself of this, she could ignore her guilt.

Stories spread through Libya

Rumor began her evil work immediately, slipping through the towns of Libya. Nothing moves faster than she does, for her speed is her strength, and her strength increases as she goes. She starts in a shiver of fear, skimming close to the ground; but soon she will float on the breeze and climb to the clouds. They say that the gods were angry when she was born, the last of the children of Earth: a monster of awful size, but elusive on her feet and on her wicked wings. Her body is covered in feathers: for every feather she has a secret watchful eye, and for every eye she has a whispering tongue, and her ears are alert for every sound. At night she never sleeps, but she flits between earth and sky, hissing in the shadows; by day she will settle on a roof-peak or a tower, keeping watch over an uneasy city, where truth is corrupted by the authority of her invention.

So with a smiling face she told story after story to the Carthaginians, of things done and things undone—and who should know the difference? "Your lovely queen," she said, "seems to think it right to throw herself at Aeneas, an immigrant from Troy. They are spending a whole dissolute winter together, wallowing in their lust and thinking nothing of their proper responsibilities." She slipped about among the people, putting everywhere hateful words into every mouth, and then she moved quickly on, beyond the city, to King Iarbas. What she said to him made anger simmer inside him.

Jupiter had once raped a nymph, and Iarbas was their son. He was a great chief in Libya. In a hundred temples he had dedicated a hundred altars to Jupiter, where a perpetual flame guarded the statues of the gods, and the floors were soaked with the blood of sacrifices, and the doorways were hung with garlands. When he heard the bitter gossip about Dido, he is said to have gone, in a fit of rage, to stand before his gods, and to make supplication at Jupiter's altar.

"Almighty father," he complained, "my people have arranged festivals in your honor; they have lain on embroidered couches and poured libations to you. But do you see what has happened now? Does it mean that they have trembled for nothing when you have thrown your thunderbolts at them? Have you terrified them with lightning strikes that do not burn? Should they think of your thunder as no more than a futile whimper? Look. This woman has strayed into my territory. I gave her a strip of farmland on the coast. I made a contract with her. She paid me a fee for my permission to found a city—if indeed you can call it a city. I offer her marriage. She refuses me, but then what does she do next? She welcomes Aeneas and his band of effeminates into her kingdom. He is another Paris; he wears some kind of Asian headdress and he dyes his hair. And, like Paris, he has laid his hands on stolen property. But for all my gifts to you, what do I get? Nothing but empty promises?"

Jupiter sends a stern message to Aeneas

Jupiter heard Iarbas' prayer. He turned his gaze on Carthage and on the lovers, who still seemed oblivious to what anybody thought about them. Then he spoke to Mercury: "Call the west wind, my son, and on its wings slip down to the Trojan prince. He is loitering in Carthage and paying no attention to the city that the fates have destined him to found. Speak to him; take him my instructions on the breeze. Tell him that this is not the behavior that his noble mother promised. Tell him that she did not twice rescue him from the Greeks for this dalliance. He is supposed to be a man who, after splendid feats of arms, would become a mighty king in Italy; he was to be the father of a powerful race, sprung from Trojan blood, which would govern the whole world under the rule of law. And then ask him this: if he does not wish to win glory for himself by such achievements or undertake such tasks for his own fame, does he grudge his son Ascanius the sovereignty of Rome? What does he hope for by this dawdling in a foreign country? What are his intentions? Has he no thought for his Italian inheritance or for his future foundation? He must set sail and leave at once! That is my message—and you are to be the messenger."

Mercury readied himself to obey his father's commands. First he strapped on his golden sandals; they have wings on them, which carry him as swiftly as the wind over the earth or across the sky. Then he took up his staff, with which he calls away the spirits of the dead, and opens their eyes and guides them down into the gloomy underworld; the staff with which he gives sleep or takes it away; the staff with which he rides the winds and crosses the swells of the clouds. He flew until he saw in front of him the peak and steep sides of Atlas, the mountain whose summit holds up heaven. Atlas' head is buffeted always by wind and rain, and wreathed in clouds that swirl through the pine trees. His shoulders are hunched under a cape of snow; waterfalls crash down his ancient face; his beard is glistening ice. Here Mercury rested,

with his wings spread wide. Then he swooped down like a
gull that skims low over the sea at the water's edge, looking
for fish below the cliffs. Between earth and sky he flew to the
beaches of Libya, and touched down his winged feet among
the Carthaginians' huts.

There, where the walls were still under construction,
Mercury found Aeneas. He was elegant in expensive gifts from
Dido: he wore a cloak that she had made herself, of Tyrian
purple interwoven with fine strands of gold, and a sword in a
jasper sheath.

Mercury wasted no time: "So you're a city-planner now,
are you? And like a good husband you're laying out a beautiful
capital for your queen? Have you forgotten your own kingdom,
and your own destiny? Jupiter himself, the ruler of heaven and
earth, has sent me down to you from Olympus. He asks you:
'What are your intentions? What are you doing, lazing away
your days in Libya? If you do not look to win glory for yourself,
think of the prospects of your heir, young Ascanius: he at least
has deserved a throne in Italy and an empire—the future em-
pire of Rome.'" And on that word, Mercury vanished into the
air above, the air that mortals cannot breathe.

Who can deceive a woman in love?

Aeneas was speechless, mindless,
motionless. His hair stood on end and he
could not speak or swallow. This warn-
ing, this command from the gods, was
entirely unexpected, but at the same time entirely clear: he
must leave this place, however delightful it might be. But how?
And what should he say to the queen, who was so infatuated
with him? What should be his opening words? His mind leapt
from idea to idea; but as quickly as he grabbed at a thought,
he abandoned it. But at last he came upon what seemed the
best solution: he ordered Mnestheus and Sergestus and Seres-
tus to make the fleet ready for sea, to assemble all the Trojans
at the shore—and all in secret. If questioned they should in-
vent some story to explain what they were doing; they should
be ready to fight if necessary. They obeyed him quickly and

enthusiastically, and meanwhile Aeneas himself, assuming that Dido was still happily unaware that their time of passion was shortly to be over, tried to select the most tactful moment to break the news to her, and rehearsed his best approach.

But who can deceive a woman in love? The queen, with sharp intuition, began to realize what he had in mind, to doubt all that she had been sure of earlier. Cruel Rumor murmured stories of the readying of his fleet and his preparations for departure, and her anxiety turned to anger. But there was nothing that she could do; she strode up and down the streets of the city, raging as furiously as a follower of Bacchus when she sees the ceremonial wands and wreaths brought out and hears the cry of the god echoing in the mountains. At last she summoned Aeneas to her presence.

Dido reproaches Aeneas

"Did you hope that you could fool me? Did you think that you could slip away from my country on the sly? What of the loving promises that I made to you, and the oaths that you swore to me—do they mean nothing? Don't you understand that I will die of grief if you leave me? How can you be so cruel? How can you be thinking of making your fleet ready for sea now, with winter coming on, and the wind in the north? You say that you are headed for a foreign land and an unknown destination. But even if Troy were still standing, you wouldn't dream of setting off for home in this weather. You're running away from *me,* aren't you?

"I implore you, by the tears on my cheeks and by my right hand (and in my misery what else is there that I can swear by?) to remember what I used to call our wedding and our marriage. Pity me and pity my kingdom—it is in great danger now. If ever prayers meant anything to you, and if ever I deserved well of you, and if ever you loved me, I beg you to change your mind. The people of Libya hate me; the chiefs of the desert tribes hate me; even my Carthaginians hate me— and all because of you. Because of you, I have no shame, and I have lost the good name that alone gave me favor with the gods. Now I can only die: after all, I have nothing left to live for. And whom will you leave to look after me? You are nothing more than a visitor—what else can I call you, since you are not my husband any more? Should I wait for my brother Pygmalion to destroy my city? Should I wait for King Iarbas to force me into his bed? I am left all alone, like a prisoner. And you haven't even left me with a child before you run away, some little boy like you, who would play in my palace, whose eyes would remind me of you."

Aeneas makes his excuses, but Dido will not accept them

Aeneas would not look at her. He remembered Jupiter's message, and kept his emotions to himself. But eventually he had to speak. "Dido—what you say is absolutely right, and I will never deny that you have deserved better of me. As long as I live, and have my senses about me, I will never regret my memories of you. But listen: I did not ever really expect that I would be able to slip quietly away. But you must understand that I was never actually married to you, and I made you no promises. If I had had any choice in the matter, and if I could have arranged my situation as I wanted, I would still be in Troy today. I would be attending to the graves of my friends, and Priam's palace would be standing, and with my own hands I would be restoring his citadel. But now Apollo has determined though his oracle that I should find a new love and a new land in Italy.

"You once lived in Tyre; but you had to flee to Libya, and now you are settled in Carthage. Can you then begrudge us a future in Italy? We fled from Troy, and like you we have had to look for another country. Each night, when mist and shadows cover the earth and the stars come out, as soon as I fall asleep, the awful ghost of my father Anchises appears to me.

He reminds me of my destiny, and of the injury that I would do to my son Ascanius, if I defrauded him of the kingdom that the gods have promised to him. And more than this, Mercury has been dispatched by Jupiter himself—I swear that this is true—to bring me my instructions. I have seen the messenger of the gods in broad daylight on your city walls, and I have heard his voice with my own ears. So you see, there is no sense in either of us complaining about it. I *must* go to Italy. It isn't my decision."

Dido had turned her back on him as he spoke. When he had finished she glanced back over her shoulder, and without a word, she looked him up and down. Finally she broke out bitterly: "Your mother was no goddess. You are not descended from any Trojan hero. You were born in the dry mountains of the Caucasus, and suckled by pitiless tigers. Why should I wait for even harsher treatment? Could anyone be colder than you? Did you ever feel unhappy when I was sad? Did you even glance at me? Did anything ever move you? Did you ever have any feeling for a woman who loved you? Even Jupiter and Juno cannot be indifferent to your behavior—so what is left for me to say? Promises mean nothing to you, even though I rescued you when you were wrecked, and fed you when you were starving, and recovered your ships when they were lost, and saved your companions' lives. But what is the purpose of my being angry with a man to whom Apollo and the oracles and Jupiter's own messenger bring orders that cannot be disobeyed? This, I suppose, is the sort of thing that the gods are concerned about, and these are the troubles that disturb their rest.

"So go, Aeneas—I will not keep you, and I will not argue with anything that you have said. Go—catch your wind for Italy, and seek your kingdom over the sea. But, if the gods have any power at all, I pray that they will make you suffer. If your ship is ever smashed up on some rock, I hope that you will call on me. 'Dido!' you will cry, and in the black lightning I will come to you, although you will not see me. Wherever it is that icy death comes to steal away your body from your soul, my spirit will be at your side. Yes, you will pay for what you have done. And I will hear of it, and the report of it will find me, even among the shadows of hell."

Those were her last words to him, and though he still had much to say, he was afraid to say it. She would not meet his eyes; she almost fainted as she moved away, but her maids caught her as she fell, and carried her to her marble room and laid her on her bed.

Aeneas prepares to depart, but cannot escape Dido's notice

Half in pain, and half in love, Aeneas longed to comfort her and soothe her, and talk away her grief. But first he was the servant of the gods, and he must follow the gods' commands. So he went back to the harbor, and there he found his Trojans hard at work. They were dragging the ships down to the water's edge, and setting afloat their newly-caulked hulls, in

such a hurry to embark that they had not taken time to finish the timbers that they had cut in the woods, or rub down new oar handles.

They came swarming down from every part of the city, like ants who, when they know that winter is coming on, pick apart a whole stack of grain and transfer it to their own nest. In a steady column, they follow a narrow path through the grass, plunder piled on straining shoulders. No stopping, no delays—and the whole track seething with movement.

From the roof of her palace, Dido saw it all: the feverish running to and fro on the shore, the hectic shouts coming over the water. But who knows what she thought, or what she said? The power of love will drive us to do anything, even to humiliate ourselves. By now she was determined to die, yet not quite ready to give up hope. What if more tears, more begging, might soften him after all?

"Anna," she said, "do you see all the bustle and haste down at the docks? The Trojans are as good as gone: the crews are trimming their sails to catch the wind, and they have hung good-luck wreaths on their sterns. I knew this moment was coming, and I can bear it. But do one thing for me, dear Anna. You were a friend of his. You knew his private thoughts—and you know the subtle ways into a man's heart. Go to him, arrogant and hateful though he is, and make him this one last request. Remind him that I was never at Aulis, swearing an oath along with Agamemnon to wipe the Trojans from the face of the earth; I sent no contingent to fight against Troy; I have not dug up the ashes of his father or disturbed his ghost. So why, when I speak, does he block his ears? Where is he off to in such a hurry? Ask him if he will grant this final favor to the poor woman who loves him. Ask him if he will at least wait for warm weather and light air. He has betrayed our marriage— I'm not asking for that back. And I don't expect him to give up his plans for a kingdom in Latium. I only ask for a little more time, a respite from our quarreling, until fate can teach me to live with grief and defeat. Take pity on me, Anna: I'm asking him this last kindness—and if he grants it to me, I'll repay him many times even after my death."

Anna took this sad message to Aeneas, once and then a second time. But he was not moved by her tears or convinced by her reason. The fates had made him adamant, and now he was content for the gods to make him deaf.

Perhaps you have seen an ancient oak tree standing up to northerly gales howling down from the Alps; they

batter at it with blasts from one direction after another, and the trunk creaks as its leaves are stripped and pile up in whirling heaps on the ground. But the tree holds its tenacious ground among the rocks, its top stretched up to heaven and its roots down to hell.

You will understand then how Aeneas was buffeted by Dido's requests: in his heart he suffered with her, but his sympathy did not change his mind. He wept, but his tears meant nothing.

Dido wonders if she can live without Aeneas

Then Dido became frightened. The sun in the sky gave her no more pleasure, and in her unhappiness she prayed for death. She went to offer sacrifices. As the incense wafted over the altar, the sacred water turned black and the wine was transformed disgustingly into blood, but she saw in the horror only an omen that her plan to die was right. No one else saw it, and she told no one, not even her sister. And then more omens: from the shrine that she had garlanded with skeins of wool and leaves in memory of her husband Sychaeus, she thought she heard his voice calling out to her in the night. Alone on the roof, an owl complained and complained, drawing out its cries until they sounded like the sobs of a mourner at a funeral. Distant predictions, the terrible warnings of soothsayers, floated in her head—and worst of all, confounding her confusion, were her dreams of Aeneas himself. She felt abandoned, a traveler without a companion, making a long journey through an empty landscape, searching for familiar faces. She remembered the story of

Pentheus, the king of Thebes, with the Furies on his trail, double suns and double cities dancing before his eyes. She thought of a play she had once seen about Agamemnon's son, Orestes, escaping from his mother, a fantasy of torches and black serpents and avenging spirits waiting at the gates.

So, overcome by pain and madness, she made up her mind to kill herself. She determined when and how she would do it, and approached her sister. She let nothing show in her face; she forced herself to appear calm and even hopeful. "Anna— be glad for me. I have found a way either to bring him back to me or to stop myself from loving him. In the most distant part of Africa, where the earth meets the ocean and the sun sets, where the giant Atlas turns on his shoulder the axis of the universe, studded with sparkling stars—there stands the temple of the daughters of the evening star. I have summoned the priestess who is in charge of it. She used to feed a dragon there, and protect a sacred tree by smearing its branches with honey and a drug that is made from poppies. She promises that her spells—if she so wishes—can soothe an agitated mind, or wrack it with anxiety. She can stop rivers in their courses and reverse the movements of the stars, and at night she conjures up the spirits of the dead. You can hear the earth groaning as she walks on it, and ash trees marching down from the mountains.

"And so—I swear by all the gods and by your own dear heart, Anna, that I have no choice—I have had recourse to her magic. You must secretly build a bonfire, in the inner courtyard of the palace, under the sky. On it you must heap up my shameless husband's armor, which he used to keep in our room, and his clothes and the sheets from the bed where we lay together—and where I have suffered alone. Every last wicked trace of him must be got rid of. That is what I want— and that is what the priestess has told me to do." A strange pallor spread over her face, and she said no more. But Anna did not realize that the ritual was a cover for Dido's plan for her own death; not understanding the full force of Dido's passion, she feared nothing worse than what had happened after the death of Sychaeus.

Magic cannot relieve Dido's pain

Dido knew exactly what she was doing. She spread flowers in the inner courtyard, by an altar that had been set out in the open air, and where an enormous pile of pine and split oak had been heaped up. On it was placed their bed, and on top of that Aeneas' armor, and then the sword that he had left behind and his portrait framed with a funeral wreath. At the altar, the priestess let down her hair and in a thunderous voice prayed to the three hundred gods of the underworld, to Erebus and Chaos and to the three persons of Hecate, the three forms of Diana the virgin. She flicked drops of water onto the altar to signify the rivers of hell; and she brought fresh herbs, harvested by moonlight with a bronze sickle, and dark milky poison, and, as a love-charm, the forelock of a colt cut away as it was being born. And Dido, with one foot ceremonially bare, and her robe loosened, reverently sprinkled salted grain and called on the gods and the prescient stars. "I am about to die," she said. "But if there is any spirit of justice or understanding among the gods, I ask for special protection for lovers, when one makes promises and the other breaks them."

Night. In heaven, the constellations were steady in their courses. At sea, flat calm. On the earth, not a rustle in the forests, not a sound in the fields. By broad smooth lakes and in the rough thickets of the countryside, sheep and oxen and birds were softly lost in sleep, quiet sleep, sleep under the silent stars. But not poor Dido: she could not close her eyes and her heart thudded wildly in the dark. Her pain was worse, and worse again. Once more she was maddened with love, and with love came floods of anger, and in her mind she twisted arguments to and fro: "What shall I do? Shall I approach the men who wanted to marry me before? They will laugh at me. Shall I go on my knees to the chieftains of the desert tribes? I thought them worthless enough once. Or shall I follow the Trojan fleet, and do what the Trojans tell me? Will they help me because I helped them? Will they be grateful if they remember what I did for them? If I decide to go to them, will they welcome me? Their ships intimidate me, and they despise me. I don't know, lost soul that I am—and I certainly cannot guess at the limits of Trojan treachery. And what after that? Could I survive, a refugee, all by myself among taunting Trojan sailors? Or should I take my own Carthaginians with me? I have uprooted them once, from their homes in Tyre. Is it fair to force them to move again, to put to sea a second time? Death is all that I deserve. Only a sword can end my misery."

And then she reproached her sister: "I fell foolishly in love, and my tears persuaded you to help me. It was you who brought on this trouble. He should have been my enemy and you pushed me into his arms. Why did you not let me live out my life without a mate, like an innocent creature of the woods? But you made me forget my honor—and break the promise that I made at Sychaeus' grave."

Aeneas' departure is hastened by the gods

High on the poop of his ship, Aeneas was dozing. The hour for sailing was fixed, and all the proper rituals had been carried out. In a dream he saw the image of the same god who had visited him before—the same voice and coloring, the same blond hair and slender build: it was Mercury. And again a warning: "Son of a goddess, is this a time to sleep? You are mad not to see the danger that surrounds you. Don't you hear the wind in the rigging? Dido has made up her mind to die; but the tide of her anger is rising, and she is planning some ruse or crime or horror. Why don't you go as fast as you can, while the going is good? If you are still lingering here at daybreak, you will see the sea churned up by the oars of Dido's navy, and torches flaring. The whole waterfront will be in flames. You must act—at once." And, as he faded away into the dark: "You are dealing with a woman—and a woman's mind and moods can never be trusted."

Aeneas started up, frightened by this sudden visitation. He barked orders: "All hands on deck! Oarsmen—stand by your thwarts! Make ready the sails! I have had a message from Olympus; we are told to be on our way once more, to cut away our mooring lines for yet another voyage." Then he prayed to the god: "Whoever you are, we will follow you, and once more we will obey your commands without question. Stay with us, and bring us a calm journey, and have the stars look down favorably upon us." He drew his glittering sword from its scabbard, and sliced through the lines; and a simultaneous excitement seized all the crews. No one hesitated, no one held back. Behind the fleet the shore fell away; the open sea lay before it. Oars dipped and swung. Spray flew. The ships' stems cut smoothly through the blue water.

Dido curses the Trojans... Dawn left her golden bed and touched the earth with sunlight; from her tower, the queen saw the first pale gleams, and then looked out to see the Trojan fleet under full sail. The waterfront was deserted; no sign of movement in the docks. Again and again she pounded her breast and slashed at her beautiful hair.

"Will you let him go, Jupiter?" she cried. "How can this stranger be allowed to insult my kingdom? Why aren't my sailors arming themselves and pursuing him? Why don't they launch their ships? Where are their weapons, their torches, their oars? What am I saying? Where am I? Is my mind playing tricks on me? Should I only now be regretting what I have done? The time for regret was when I handed over my authority to him. To *him?* What did oaths and promises mean to *him?* And yet this was a man, they say, who brought his gods with him, who carried his old father on his shoulders. I could have torn his body to pieces and scattered them at sea; I could have massacred his companions and cut up his son Ascanius and served him up for his father to eat. So why didn't I?

"War is always risky—but I should have risked it. What did I have to fear? I was going to die in any case. I should have set fire to his camp and his ships and burned up his entire family—father and son together. And then I should have thrown myself on top of the pile. But now I can only pray. Listen to me, Sun—your searching light lights every act of man. Listen to me, Juno—in your wisdom you understand the pain of love. Listen to me, Hecate, as you howl through the cities and lurk at crossroads in the dark, and you avenging Furies and any of the gods who may attend my death. Listen, and punish where punishment is deserved. If the fates require that this wicked man come safely into port and step ashore once more, then let that be the end of it. But I want him embroiled in war, hard-pressed by a brave opponent. I want him exiled, separated from Ascanius. I want him to beg for help and see his men die miserably. I want him to have to surrender under the most humiliating conditions, and never to enjoy his kingdom or the happy life he wishes for. I want him to be cut down before his time and lie unburied, out on some empty beach.

"And now—as I die—this is my last request. This, my people, is the promise that you must make over my grave. Between you and Aeneas, between your children and his children, there must be no glimmer of friendship, no whisper of peace—but only everlasting hatred. Warriors will spring from my bones. They will take vengeance on the Trojans long after they have settled in Italy. They will hunt them down with fire and sword, now and always, for as long as Carthage shall stand. I call for generation after generation of war: fleet against fleet, army against army, iron against iron forever."

...and makes a terrible decision.

Then she thought of her own end, and looked for a way to escape from a life that she had come to loathe. She spoke briefly to Barce, Sychaeus' old nurse—her own was buried back in Tyre—and asked her to take a message to Anna. "Tell her to sprinkle herself with river-water, and bring sheep for sacrifice. Then she should come to me herself. And wind a wreath about your own temples: I am going to finish the offering to Jupiter that I have begun, and put an end to my sorrow, and set fire to Aeneas' pyre."

Barce hurried off with the quick step of an old woman anxious to please, but Dido remained behind, trembling and restless, frightened by her own terrible determination. Her eyes were red and there were patches of color high on her cheeks, but her face was pale, already bloodless. With her mind in a maze, she made her way to the inner courtyard and climbed the steps to the top of the pyre. She drew Aeneas' sword; it had been her gift to him, and she had never considered what its final purpose might be. She looked at the clothes that he had brought from Troy, and for a moment she wept, remembering. Then she lay down on their familiar bed and spoke her final words.

"These are reminders of a happier time that the fates allowed me once. Now, gods, receive my spirit and release me from my cares. My life is over, and my ghost is about to pass below the earth. I have faithfully followed the road that fortune laid out for me: I have founded a great city, whose walls went up before my eyes. I have avenged my husband and seen his murderer punished. History would have thought me lucky—too lucky, perhaps—if only those ships had never arrived from Troy."

A pause. She buried her face in the coverlet.

"I will die unavenged—but at least I am going to die."

Another pause.

"I am happy to go now. I hope that from far out at sea

Aeneas will see these flames, and will never be free from the guilt that my death portends."

Silence. Then in full view of her attendants, she fell upon the sword, and blood welled up around the blade and spattered over her hands. A cry went up in the palace, and Rumor raced through the bewildered city. Everywhere weeping and groaning and women's lamentation echoed across the sky, exactly as if Carthage—or old Tyre—had been sacked by invaders, and set on fire, and the houses of the citizens and the temples of the gods were all ablaze together.

Anna heard the noise, and, half-dead herself with fear, tore at her face with her fingernails and beat her breast with her fists. She ran to her dying sister, and spoke to her: "Dido, what have you done? You deliberately deceived me, didn't you? You didn't tell me that this was what the pyre was for, or the fire, or the altar. Whom should I weep for first, now that I am left alone? As you die, have you forgotten me? You should have summoned me to meet the same end as you. We have shared the same sorrows, and I would have shared your sword. I built this pyre and called on our father's gods. Should I not have been with you when you lay upon it? You have made an end of yourself and me together, and of your people and your ancestors and your city. Let me wash your wound, and, if you have one last breath, let me catch it on my lips."

As she spoke, Anna had climbed the steps of the pyre. She took her sister in her arms, and between sobs she wiped away the blood with her robe, but still it seeped from the wound beneath Dido's breast. Dido tried to look up at her, but she could not. Three times she almost lifted herself up onto her elbow, but three times she fell back. Her eyes shifted. She was looking for the sunlight—but when at last she found it, she sighed.

It should then have been the duty of Proserpina, the queen of the dead, to take a lock of hair from her head and escort her to the underworld. But she had not yet arrived, because Dido was dying before the time that had been planned for her by fate: her end was undeserved, brought on by unexpected passion. And so Juno took pity on Dido's painful struggle, and from Olympus she sent down Iris to set her spirit free and relax her stiffening limbs. And Iris, leaving behind her a trail of a thousand different colors, the colors of the sun shining through the drops of dew that sparkled on her wings, flew down to stand by Dido's head and cut off a lock of her hair.

"It is the gods' command," she whispered. "I make this offering to Hades, and release you from your body."

At that very moment, a chill slipped through the room: it was Dido's spirit, fluttering off upon a breeze.

Book V
Funeral Games and Burning Ships

Bad weather compels the Trojans to take shelter in Sicily, where Anchises is buried

By this time the Trojan fleet was far out at sea, holding a confident course to the north across the darkening sea. Aeneas took a last look back at the walls of Carthage, and behind them he saw the flickering of flames. The Trojans did not know that they were the flames of Dido's funeral pyre; but they understood the pain of a love killed by the gods, and a premonition of what a maddened woman might do sent a shiver through their hearts. But soon the land was out of sight, and there was nothing to see but water and sky.

A squall brought with it cold and a steep chop. Ominous blue-black shadows streaked the waves, and up on the poop-deck of Aeneas' ship, Palinurus the helmsman talked to himself. "What does this sudden overcast mean? What do you have waiting for us, Neptune?" And he ordered the sailors to check their lines, bend to their oars, and trim the sheets. "Aeneas," he called. "If I read these signs correctly, we're not going to make Italy in this weather. There's a westerly gale coming up on our beam; I don't like the look of those clouds. We're not going to make any headway now, however hard we try. We should follow Fortune's lead—she is more powerful than we are—and head wherever she suggests. If memory and my reading of the stars serve me rightly, I think we are not far from the coast of Sicily—your brother Eryx' land."

Always mindful of the gods' intentions, Aeneas agreed with him: "I read the weather exactly as you do. You can't make any more progress north. Change course, then, at your discretion. What could please me more than to bring my tired crews to that part of Sicily where Acestes, my old friend from Troy, is king, and where the bones of my father Anchises are laid to rest?" So their bows were turned, and the westerly wind filled their sails. On a following sea they came happily to the beach by Drepanon that they remembered so well.

From far off, on the top of a high mountain, Acestes was at first surprised to see the Trojan ships approaching, but then he realized that they were friendly and came down to meet them, wearing the hide of a Libyan bear and surrounded by a bodyguard bristling with javelins. As he welcomed them, he thought of his parents—Crinisus the river-god was his father, but his mother was from Troy—and brought out whatever he could to make the Trojans feel at home.

Aeneas announces funeral games in honor of Anchises

When the next day's dawn had put the eastern stars to flight, Aeneas called together his men from their camp along the shore. He climbed up onto a mound to speak to them: "My Trojans, members of a great race born from the gods: it is a year ago that we laid the bones of my father in the earth here and sadly made sacrifices at his grave. And now, unless I am mistaken, the day has come again that I shall always keep as a bitter memory—though, as the gods would wish, an honored one. Even if I had been cast up among the sand-dunes on the coast of Libya, or if I had been forced ashore in Argos or Mycenae, I would celebrate this day each year and with due ritual raise an altar and bring offerings to it. But now I have arrived of my own free will in a friendly harbor—though I think that the gods had a hand in it too—and I am standing at the very spot where my father is buried. This is a good time to honor him, and then to pray for fair winds. And later, with the king's permission, I will found a city here and make annual sacrifices in temples that I will dedicate to my father's memory. But for now, Acestes, who was born in Troy, will give to each of you two bulls. Bring your own household gods, and let us not forget the gods whom Acestes worships. For eight days we will remember Anchises, and after that, if the dawn of the ninth day brings us warm sunshine, I will organize funeral games for him. First, we shall have a boat-race; next we shall see who is the fastest runner; then we will find out who is the best shot with a spear or arrows—a test of strength and nerve—and finally who can show the most guts in a boxing match. All of you should compete—and there will be prizes of palm-wreaths for the winners. Now: silence—and crown your heads with branches."

A good omen

Aeneas took a garland of myrtle, the tree sacred to his mother Venus, and put it on his head. Old Acestes and his companion Helymus did the same; so did the boy Ascanius, and the rest of the Trojan young men. And with a great crowd following him, and his escort pressing close around him, Aeneas walked from the meeting of his council to his father's tomb. Onto the ground he poured two cups of wine as an offering to Bacchus, and two cups of new milk and two of consecrated blood. He scattered red flowers and addressed his father's ashes, and his spirit and shade: "I have come, dear father, to greet you, even though I seem to have rescued you from Troy in vain, because the gods did not allow you to accompany me all the way to Italy and the river Tiber. Wherever it is I am destined to go, I must now make my search alone." As he was speaking, a snake slithered out from the innermost part of the shrine, and Aeneas stood still and hushed at the sight of it. Seven times, in seven silent circles, it coiled about the tomb and about the altar, and on every scale

of its blue-bespeckled back, a glint of gold caught the light, just as the thousand different colors of a rainbow are splashed across the clouds by sudden sunshine. Between the dishes and bowls laid out for sacrifice the snake twined its long length, flicking its tongue at the offerings on the altar, just tasting them, and then it slid harmlessly away back into the depths of the tomb. Aeneas did not know whether the snake was a guardian spirit of the place or his father's own attendant, but it was a sign for him to bring yet more honors to his father. He killed two sheep and two pigs and two black bullocks, and he poured out more wine and spoke to Anchises' spirit, and to his ghost that had been sent back from the underworld. The rest of the Trojans cheerfully brought whatever gifts they could. They piled up slaughtered bullocks on the altar; or they laid out a line of bronze cooking-pots on the grass, and set them over hot coals, and roasted the animals' entrails on spits.

The horses of the sun drew in the ninth dawn bright and clear: it was the day appointed for the games. Report of them—linked with Acestes' famous name—had gone out to the neighboring tribes, and they had come crowding happily along the shore to see Aeneas' men—and some of them were ready to compete themselves. The prizes for the winners were spread out in full view: sacred tripods, green wreaths and palm leaves, weapons, purple-dyed robes, and a great weight of silver and gold. Then a trumpet blast from the high ground announced that the games could begin.

The boat race   First, four ships, equally matched, were selected from the fleet for the boat-race:

• *Pristis*, with Mnestheus in command: he would one day be known as Italian Mnestheus, and from him the Roman Memmius family is descended.

• *Chimaera*, as big as a town, with Gyas in command: his young crew sat in groups of three, and by threes their oar-blades rose and fell.

• *Centaur*, with Sergestus in command: from him the house of Sergius gets its name.

• *Scylla*, painted bright blue, with Cloanthus in command: he was the founding father of the Roman clan Cluentius.

Far out at sea, and visible over the surf that roars onto the beach, there is a rock. Sometimes it is submerged, covered by the waves whipped up by the northwest winds of winter that sweep clouds across the stars; but sometimes it sits quiet, rising out of the calm sea as a level platform for the gulls, who like to warm their feathers there. Here Aeneas set up a green branch from an oak-tree to serve as a mark for the oarsmen, so that they would know where to turn and begin the race's long homeward leg.

The coxswains drew lots for their lanes and went to stand on their poop-decks, resplendent in gold and purple. The crews had garlanded their heads with poplar leaves, and rubbed oil over their bare shoulders. They sat ready on their thwarts, hands on the oars, waiting, waiting, intent on the starter's signal, excitement and desire for glory thumping and pounding in their hearts.

The trumpet blared. They were off. A burst of orders from the coxswains—shoulders swinging into the first stroke—an explosion of spray—oars in a single rhythm, and knife-edge prows, cutting and slicing—the whole sea torn up, convulsed. You never saw the start of a chariot race like this: however quickly the drivers give the horses their heads, and lean forward lashing with their whips, chariots never burst out of the gate with so much energy so violently released. The woods shook with applause and enthusiastic shouting, as some supported one ship and some another; the cheering rolled along the shores of the bay and echoed back and forth between the hills.

Impelled by the roaring of the crowd, Gyas' *Chimaera* went out in front first. After Gyas came Cloanthus in *Scylla*; his crew rowed better, but his ship was slower because of her weight. Then came *Pristis* and *Centaur*, neck and neck, each straining to get in front. *Pristis* had the lead, and then *Centaur* passed her, and then they were side by side again, as if they were joined together, cutting through the water on a single keel.

They approached the rock, and had the turning point in sight, when Gyas, in the lead and with the open sea heaving under him, called to his coxswain Menoetes: "Why so far to starboard? Straighten up. Stay close to the edge of the rock: cut it as fine as you can with your port-side oars. The others can take it wide if they like." But Menoetes, nervous that part of the rock was invisible under the surface, still held his course out to sea. Gyas shouted at him again: "Why are you sheering away?" and again: "Make for the rock, Menoetes!" He glanced back at Cloanthus, who was coming up from astern. Cloanthus took the corner closer, and slipped by him on the inside, between Gyas' port side and the rock, taking the lead and leaving the mark safely behind him. Then frustration and shame burned through young Gyas' bones, and tears ran down his cheeks. He forgot his own reputation and the safety of his crew, and he grabbed the cautious Menoetes and pitched him over the side. And he took over the steering oar himself, shouting the orders and turning his ship back to the shore. And the Trojans laughed when they saw Menoetes falling in, and laughed again when they saw him swimming; and when they saw him coughing up salt water, they laughed some more. But Menoetes, who was stout and elderly, bobbed up from the bottom and hauled himself out onto the rock, where at last he sat high and dry—except for his dripping robe.

At this point the two lagging captains, Sergestus in *Centaur* and Mnestheus in *Pristis*, began to hope that they could overtake Gyas, who was moving more slowly now. Sergestus was ahead as they came up to the turning point, but he did not have clear water and *Pristis* was coming up fast, only half a length back. Mnestheus paced up and down in the well, encouraging his crew. "Come on now, put your backs into it, you heroes, you second Hectors. You were the ones I specially chose in the last days of Troy. Remember the Libyan sandbanks? Remember the Ionian sea, and the riptide of Malea?

You showed me then what you had. So show me again. I'm not asking to win—let Neptune decide that—but it would be a disgrace to come in last. Give me one last effort to avoid the worst." And his oarsmen drove in their blades harder than ever: the bows lifted and the bronze sternpost vibrated in its socket. Muscles and lungs and dry throats quivered, sweat ran down their backs. And then, in return for their hard work, chance gave them the success that they wanted.

Sergestus, still moving fast on the inside, for a second let his excitement overcome his concentration: he let the *Centaur* slip sideways onto a rock that lay just below the surface. She hit it hard, her port oars were snapped off, and her prow caught on a jagged edge. She went fast aground. "Way enough!" shouted someone, and the sailors leaped up from the benches to push her off with iron-tipped boat-hooks and spars, and to reach for their broken oars in the swirling water.

But Mnestheus in *Pristis* was elated, and seizing his opportunity, called on his men to pick up their cadence and the gods of the winds to flatten the seas. And so he ran down into clear water.

> Perhaps you have seen a dove driven out of a cave where she has her comfortable nest in a dark shadowy niche? Something has scared her, and she flaps wildly out into the open; but soon she becomes calm again and she is gliding in the quiet air, without even moving her wings.

That was how *Pristis,* running on smoothly between the oarstrokes, began the last leg of her journey. Sergestus was left far behind, struggling between the steep rock and the shallow water, and shouting for help in vain: he would have to find out for himself the best way to row a ship with broken oars. But Mnestheus overtook Gyas and the enormous bulk of the *Chimaera*, which without a coxswain was steadily losing way.

The finish was just ahead, and Mnestheus had only Clo-
anthus in *Scylla* ahead of him. He chased him hard, not for a
moment letting his crew relax. The crowd yelled louder than
ever, cheering for *Pristis* as she moved into second place, and
the whole world seemed filled with their noise. But, to the
crew of *Scylla*, any praise and honor they had already gained
meant nothing, unless they could hold on to it by winning the
race. They would have been happy to trade even their lives for
glory, but their own success inspired them: "We can do it, as
long as we think we can."

Pristis and *Scylla* might have finished in a dead heat, if
Cloanthus, stretching out both his hands to the sky, had not
called on the gods. "Help us, you who rule the sea, and in
whose waters we sail, and I will happily sacrifice that white
bull that is standing there on the shore, and I will bring you its
entrails along with bright wine. That is my promise." And the
whole company of sea-nymphs and sea-gods who live beneath
the waves heard him, and they lifted their hands and, quicker
than the south wind itself, or a winged arrow, they nudged
him just ahead. So *Scylla* flew in towards the land, and in the
deep anchorage her sailors rested on their oars.

Then Aeneas called everyone together according to cus-
tom. He had a herald announce Cloanthus' victory, and placed
a garland of laurel on his head. He allowed the crews of the
ships to choose three bullocks as gifts, and wine and a great
weight of silver, and there were special prizes for the captains.
To the winner went a gold-embroidered cloak, with a double
border of Syrian purple and a designs portraying young Gany-
mede In one scene he was chasing stags on the green slopes
of mount Ida, and throwing his spear at them; and in anoth-
er, just as he was catching his breath, and while sheepdogs
barked madly and the old shepherds lifted up their hands in
vain, Jupiter's eagle snatched him away in its talons to Olym-
pus. For Mnestheus, who had come second, there was a tunic
triple-stitched in gold, a wonderful thing for him just to pos-
sess, let alone to protect him in battle. It had once belonged to

a Greek called Demoleos, but Aeneas had taken it from him on the banks of the river Simois, under the walls of Troy. It was so heavy that it took two slaves to carry it on their shoulders, but Demoleos had worn it to hunt down Trojan stragglers. The third prize was a pair of bronze cauldrons and polished silver cups chased with elaborate patterns.

But when they had all been given their prizes, and were still swaggering about in their wreaths, Sergestus came ashore from his dangerous adventure on the rock. Although he had been very ingenious in bringing in his crippled ship with his starboard oars alone—the rest had been lost—he still had to suffer laughter instead of receiving praise.

> It is not uncommon to see a snake half-dead at the side of the road, run over by the wheel of a cart or crushed by a stone that a traveler has thrown at it. It tries in vain to get away, and part of it still has some fight in it: its long body coils and recoils, its eyes burn and it lifts its head to hiss. But part of it is so badly injured that it can only bend itself into knots and twist itself uselessly back upon itself.

In such awkward fashion, with only half of her oars, the *Centaur* limped home, but her mast was up and she came into port under sail. And to show how pleased he was that Sergestus had saved his ship and brought back his crew, Aeneas gave him the gift that he had promised: a slave-girl from Crete, skilled in arts and crafts, and her twin babies.

The foot race   With the first event completed, Aeneas moved on to a grassy plain, surrounded by woods and gentle hills, where a race-course was laid out in a valley, in a natural amphitheater. There he stood on a mound among the thousands of spectators, and here he laid out prizes to encourage the ambition of those who wanted to compete in the footrace. Sicilians and Trojans crowded round together, but the first to step forward were Nisus and Euryalus—Euryalus famous for his good looks and raw youth, and Nisus for his reverent love of Euryalus. After them came Diores, from Priam's family, then Salius the Acarnanian and Patron from Tegea in Arcadia; then two young Sicilians, Helymus and Panopes, friends of old Acestes; and many more whose names are now forgotten.

Aeneas spoke to them all: "I have good news for everyone: everyone will win a prize. To each competitor I am offering two javelins from Knossos with brightly shined points and a double axe inlaid with silver. The first three to finish will be garlanded with fresh olive leaves. In addition, the winner will receive a horse with a breastplate; the prize for second place will be an Amazon quiver filled with Thracian arrows, complete with a gold belt and a jeweled pin; and the third prize will be this helmet from Greece."

The runners took their marks. At the signal they were off, eyes fixed ahead, springing from the starting line in a blur like a puff of cloud. Nisus glided into an early lead, far in front of the others, quicker than the wind or lightning. Salius was a distant second. A little behind him was Euryalus, and Helymus after him. Then Diores, coming up very fast, tapped his foot against Helymus' foot, and jostled him, and if he had not been boxed in he would have slipped past him and beaten him without any question.

They were coming up to the finish now, all of them tired and nearly at the end of their strength. But then Nisus, already celebrating his win, had the bad luck to slip on a patch of blood that had been poured onto the ground during the sacrifice of the bullocks and left the grass still wet. Nisus' feet skidded from under him and he went flat on his face in the mud and blood. But he did not forget Euryalus and how much he loved him: as he got to his feet, he managed to obstruct Salius and trip him, and Salius rolled over and over in the sand beside the track. Euryalus, as handsome as ever, flashed past him and won the race, inspired by the noisy support of the crowd and taking advantage of his friend's generosity. Helymus came in next and Diores was third.

But Salius complained bitterly, to the elders in the front row and to the assembly that filled the whole amphitheater, that he had been robbed: "I lost the prize by a foul, and it should be given back to me." But the spectators were on Euryalus' side: he was in tears, which seemed appropriately modest, and in any case his beautiful body was as impressive as his athletic skill. And he was further supported, loudly and passionately, by Diores, who realized that he would lose his third prize if Salius were reinstated.

Aeneas made the final decision: "The result will stand. You will have your prizes as arranged. But allow me to sympathize with the accident of my unfortunate friend." And he presented to Salius the hide of an enormous shaggy African lion, with gold claws. But then Nisus said, "If losers get such wonderful prizes, and if that's how you pity people who fall over, what do you have for me? I would have won the first prize, if I hadn't been overcome by the same bad luck as Salius." And he pointed to his face and arms and legs all covered in mud. Aeneas laughed, and gave orders that this excellent young man should be given an excellent gift—a shield made by the famous artist Didymaeon that had originally hung from a doorpost of the temple of Neptune in Troy, but had been torn down by the Greeks.

The boxing match

The racing and the distribution of awards were over. But then Aeneas made a new announcement: "If anyone has strength and spirit in him, let him come forward and bind on the gloves and put up his fists." He proposed a double honor for the boxing match: for the winner, a bull-calf wreathed in gold and garlands, and a magnificent sword and helmet as a consolation prize for the runner-up. He did not have to wait.

At once the Trojan Dares volunteered, a man of such immense size that the crowd murmured in admiration. He was the only one who had been able to spar with Paris, and at Hector's funeral games he had knocked down the enormous Butes (a fighter from Bebrycia, home of fighters, and a kinsman of its king Amycus) and left him half-dead on the sand. Now, at the suggestion of a match, Dares lifted up his head and bared his mighty shoulders and threw imaginary punches, first with his right and then with his left. Who would challenge him? But from all that great gathering, no one dared to approach him or bind on gloves to fight him.

So Dares, thinking that every other contestant had withdrawn, walked quickly up to Aeneas and without hesitation he grabbed the bull by its left horn and said: "Son of a goddess, if no one dares to put himself forward to fight me, why am I still standing here? It's not right to keep me waiting any longer. Have the prizes brought out." And the Trojans called for all the promised gifts to be given to him.

King Acestes then turned gravely to his friend Entellus, who sat next to him on his turf bench, and reproached him. "Entellus, you were once the strongest of my warriors. Does that mean nothing to you? Have you no compunction? Will you allow such splendid gifts to be carried off without a contest? What would you say to Eryx, the son of Venus, who was your instructor? Have you forgotten what he taught you? Where is that reputation that you earned through all of Sicily? What about all the trophies that hang in your house?"

Entellus replied: "My love of honor hasn't left me; my desire for glory hasn't been driven out by fear. But I'm getting older and my blood has become chilled. I'm short of energy, and not as fit as I used to be. If I were what I once was, if I still had the self-confidence of that brash fellow, if I were just not so *old*, I wouldn't need any beautiful calf to bring me out, or any other prize for that matter. It's not the *gifts* that I care about." When he had finished, he tossed onto the ground a pair of huge boxing gloves, which the champion Eryx had bound onto his hands with lengths of sinew. Everyone was astonished by the gloves: they were made from the hides of seven bulls, with pieces of lead and iron sewn into them to stiffen them. Even Dares was intimidated and would not go near them, but Aeneas was bold enough to pick them up and heft their weight and touch the immense bindings that were used to hold them in place.

Entellus turned to Aeneas and said: "So you're impressed, are you? Your brother Eryx once wore these gloves, Aeneas. You can still see the bloodstains on them and the remains of spattered brains. He last wore them to stand up to the mighty Hercules—and you should have seen what Hercules had on *his* hands!—and on this very beach they fought till your brother was dead. After Eryx, I used to wear these gloves myself—in the days when my blood flowed thicker than it does now, and my chief opponent, old age, hadn't yet salted my temples with gray. But if Dares doesn't like the look of these weapons of mine, and as long as Aeneas and Acestes approve, we'll fight on equal terms. He needn't worry—I'll put away Eryx' gloves, as long as Dares takes off those overweight Trojan mitts."

With that Entellus stripped off his double-layered tunic, and bared his shoulders, arms and legs—all enormous—and went to stand in the middle of the sandy arena. To both of them Aeneas offered gloves of exactly equal size and weight, and bound them on. Each of them went up on his toes, and saluted the gods without any sign of fear. Then they began to fight, ducking and weaving with their heads, pounding each other with their fists, Dares quicker on his feet because he was younger, Entellus superior in weight and power—even though his knees were shaking, and his whole body trembled from his deep-heaving breath. Neither of them could hurt the other seriously, but they hammered— thud thud, thud thud—at each other's

ribs, and each of them, though he missed with a flurry of blows to the side of the other's head, managed to deliver a damaging punch to the jaw. Entellus never shifted his feet, and simply swayed from the waist up to avoid Dares' attacks, never taking his eyes off him. But Dares, as if he were storming a city with battering rams, or besieging a fort on a hill, moved with great skill from opening to opening, from one side to the other, sticking to no pattern and always varying his approach.

Finally Entellus bored in, threatening with a swinging sledgehammer right; but Dares saw the blow coming, ducked, stepped back—and the punch met nothing but air. Down went Entellus, thrown by his own massive weight and his own momentum. He fell full-length, like a hollow pine-tree uprooted from a mountainside. All the young men rushed forward, shouting wildly; but the first to reach Entellus was King Acestes, who anxiously helped his old friend to his feet. Entellus was not slowed by his fall, however, and his nerve was unaffected. With his strength regained in anger, and his courage reborn in shame, he threw himself back into the fight. He went right after Dares, and chased him round the ring. With rights and lefts one after the other, piling on his punches like bursts of hail clattering on a roof, he pounded Dares with a two-handed assault that dizzied him and wore him down.

By this time both boxers had lost their tempers, and Entellus was quite out of control. So Aeneas stepped between them and drew the exhausted Dares aside. "My poor fellow, you must see what is happening," he said gently. "Aren't you aware that you are up against supernatural strength? Entellus is possessed. Your opponent is a god—yield to him." And so he stopped the fight.

Dares' seconds led him away to the ships: his knees had no more spring in them, his head was flopping from side to side and he was spitting out thick blood and teeth. They took the sword and the helmet for him, and they left the garland and the bull for Entellus. And Entellus, glorying in his victory and his prize, gloated to Aeneas and the Trojans: "That was nothing—you should have seen me in my prime. But at least you can imagine what kind of death you would have had to rescue Dares from." And then he stood in front of the bull that had been given him as a prize; he lifted his gloved hand into the air above its horns, and smashed it down viciously into its skull so that its brains squirted out. The animal fell to the ground, quivered and lay dead. And Entellus stood over it and called out: "To you, Eryx, I dedicate this creature's spirit; it is a better one than Dares'. So now I end my career—a champion to the end."

The archery competition

Aeneas next invited entries, and announced the prizes, for the archery competition. With his own hands he un-stepped the mast from Serestus' ship and looped a line around the top of it, from which he hung a dove to serve as a target for their arrows. The competitors gathered and determined their order of shooting by drawing lots from a bronze helmet. The first name out, amid much excitement, was Hippocoön, the son of Hyrtacus. Next was the runner-up in the boat-race, Mnestheus; he was still wearing his olive-wreath. Then came Eurytion, the brother of the sharpshooter Pandarus, who during the war had been persuaded to break a truce between the Greeks and Trojans by sniping at the Greek generals. The last name from the helmet was that of the king, Acestes—an old man daring to try a young man's sport. Each of the archers strung his own bow—a demonstration of strength in itself—and pulled out the arrows from their quivers. Hippocoön was the first to send an arrow singing through the air from his bowstring: it stuck in the wood at the top of the mast. The mast quivered and the bird flapped its wings in panic, and everyone broke out into applause. After him, it was Mnestheus' turn, and he took careful aim along the line of his angled shaft. He was not quite good enough—or, perhaps, not lucky enough—to hit the bird itself; but his point cut through the knot of the line that tethered it by the foot to the mast. Up on the breeze it flew, but Eurytion, who had already fitted his arrow to the string, kept his eye on it as it fluttered happily away, silhouetted against a dark cloud. He loosed off his shot, in dedication to his brother—and hit it. With Eurytion's arrow still in its side, the dove fell to earth, but it left its spirit among the stars.

Now only Acestes was left. He had lost his chance at the prize, but nevertheless he shot his arrow straight up into the air, just to show that he had not lost his skill. And then, right before their eyes, there appeared a remarkable sign, an omen for their future history: the soothsayers made their usual gloomy prognostications, but events themselves would teach them what it had really meant. Acestes' arrow, as it flew into the clouds, burst into flames. You could follow its path in a line of light until it burned out in the upper air, like those shooting stars that escape their fixed positions and flash across the sky, leaving a trail of sparks behind them.

The Trojans and the Sicilians stood without moving, in reverent amazement; but Aeneas recognized the importance of the omen by embracing the happy Acestes and loading him with gifts. "This is a sign," he said, "that Jupiter wanted *you*—not simply someone who was drawn by lot—to win the prize. In honor of old Anchises you must accept this embossed bowl, which Cisseus the king of Thrace gave my father many years ago, as something to remember him by, and as a sign of his affection." He put a wreath of green laurel around Acestes' temples, and before everyone named him as the winner. And, although Eurytion alone had actually hit the dove, he was sportsman enough not to envy him the title. Another gift went to Mnestheus, who had cut the bird's tether, and another to Hippocoön, who had put his arrow into the mast.

An exhibition of horsemanship

But Aeneas was not yet done with the games. He sent for Epytides, the bodyguard and companion of Ascanius, and whispered into his faithful ear: "Go to Ascanius and tell him to put on his armor. Make sure that he has his group of boys lined up and their horses ready. It's time for the parade of cavalry squadrons in honor of his grandfather." He told all the gathered crowds to fall back in a big circle and to clear a level space. Both Trojans and Sicilians murmured in admiration as the boys rode in under their fathers' eyes, glittering in their armor, with their horses held on a tight rein. They wore neat wreaths on their hair, and round their necks, lying along the line of their collarbones, were torques of plaited gold. Each carried a pair of dogwood lances tipped with iron, and some had lightweight quivers slung across their shoulders.

The whole formation was stiff and smart: three squadrons, each one headed by its own captain and twelve lieutenants. Priam the younger, the son of Polites but named after his grandfather, whose family line he would continue in Italy, led the first, riding a big dappled horse from Thrace, with white fetlocks and a white blaze on its forehead. Atys, Ascanius' friend since childhood, led the second—the Roman Atii would be descended from him. And the handsome Ascanius led the third, on a Carthaginian horse that Dido had given him as something to remember her by, and as a sign of her affection. The rest of them rode Sicilian horses belonging to Acestes.

The boys were nervous, but the Trojans received them warmly, especially delighted when they recognized the sons of distinguished parents. After they had finished showing themselves off to the admiring crowd, Epytides saw that they were ready and in the distance cracked his whip as a signal: the three squadrons galloped forward in line abreast, then split apart to wheel on each other with lances leveled. Each intertwined with the other, circling in mock advance and mock retreat, one moment leaving their backs exposed and the next whirling round to counter-attack, then smoothly reforming the line to finish side by side.

A spectator might have been reminded of the legend of king Minos' maze: its tangle of forks and blind alleys would send you off in a thousand false directions, and if you made a mistake you never knew it, and then it was too late.

So the Trojan boys played their complicated game of alternating retreat and advance, twisting and turning like the dolphins in the sea off Libya or Crete.

Later, when he had finished building the walls round Alba Longa, Ascanius taught the inhabitants of Latium those same cavalry maneuvers that he had learned when he was a boy; the people of Alba Longa passed the tradition on to the Romans; and the Romans preserved it in deference to their ancestors. To this day, when celebrations are held in honor of the city's founders, the boys who take part in such exhibitions of horsemanship are said to be "from Troy" and to ride in a "Trojan" formation.

Juno is still angry with the Trojans

And now, for the first time since they had left Carthage, their luck changed: Juno was still angry with them, and revenge was as ever on her mind. So while they were absorbed in the ceremonies and games before Anchises' tomb, she sent Iris on a waft of air down to the Trojan fleet. Iris flew off quickly, seen by no one, following the path scored by her rainbow's arc. She observed the great crowds below her, and then she moved further along the shore, where the harbor was deserted and the fleet unguarded. Far off, separated from the rest on a lonely beach, all the women from Troy were weeping together for the dead Anchises, and, as they looked out to the blank horizon, they wept again that so much sea was still left for them to cross. They were already exhausted from their long voyage, and they longed for a city where they could make themselves new homes.

Iris in disguise approaches the Trojan women

Iris knew well how to stir dissension. She took off her goddess clothes and her goddess face; and so that she might slip unnoticed in among them, she disguised herself as Beroe, an old woman, the wife of Doryclus, who came from an old family and once had had distinguished children and a famous name. And as Beroe, she said to the Trojan women:

"I feel sorry for you all because after the war at Troy the Greeks did not drag you off and kill you. And because you were spared then, what kind of death, do you think, does Fortune have in mind for you now? Seven years have gone by since our city fell. And all that time we have either been at sea, or living in strange countries, or cast up on unfriendly rocks under unfriendly stars—and still we haven't arrived in Italy, which always seems to lie further off the more we're tossed about on the waves.

"Now here we are in the land of Eryx, Aeneas' own brother. King Acestes has certainly made us welcome. So what is to prevent us from tracing out new walls here, and founding a city for ourselves in Sicily? What was the purpose in abandoning our own country and rescuing our household gods from the enemy? Will there ever again be a city that we can call Troy? Will I ever again see rivers such as the ones that Hector loved, the Simois and the Xanthus? Help me: we must set fire to the ships, before they carry us away into yet more trouble. In a dream I have seen the ghost of the prophet Cassandra. She put a blazing torch into my hands, and she said to me: 'Sicily is where you should look for your new Troy. The site of your new home is here.' Isn't it clear what this omen means? We should act **now**. There are four altars here, dedicated to Neptune. The god himself will give us torches—and the will to use them." And with a great show of indignation, she lit a firebrand and waved it about in her right hand, ready to throw it.

The women listened closely, but without emotion, until the oldest of them, Pyrgo, the nurse of many of Priam's children, cried out: "This isn't Beroe. This isn't Doryclus' wife. Look at her shining eyes—this is a goddess. All the signs are there: her breath, the expression on her face, the sound of her voice, the way she walks—it's unmistakable. In any case, I've just been sitting with Beroe—she's ill, and upset because she's the only one who hasn't been able to pay her respects to Anchises or bring him the honors that are due to him."

The Trojan women are persuaded to set their own ships on fire

The women hesitated. They looked uneasily at the ships, but they were still torn between their eagerness to stay where they were and a desire to move on to the land where the fates were summoning them. But at that moment, Iris spread her wings to lift herself into the sky; and her curving rainbow cut a path for her through the clouds. Her transformation astounded the women. Driven by a sudden impulse, they grabbed fire from the hearths inside their houses, and a few of them even stole it from the altars. They threw blazing leaves and twigs and torches into the ships, and the flames raced without a check along the thwarts and the oars to the painted pinewood sterns.

Word that the ships had been set on fire was brought and to the spectators in the amphitheater and to Anchises' tomb. Everyone could see the cloud of black smoke curling up into the sky. Ascanius, who had been happily engaged in the maneuvers, was the first to break away. He ignored the sentries who tried feebly to stop him; and with Aeneas and the rest of the Trojan army right behind him, he galloped to the camp, which was in complete confusion.

"Have you gone mad?" shouted Ascanius. "What are you trying to do, you poor women? You are not attacking an enemy or destroying a Greek camp. You are setting fire to your own best hopes for safety." He took off the helmet that he had worn for the mock battle, and threw it on the ground in front of them. "You must know me—I'm Ascanius."

But the women were frightened. They scattered all along the beach, and hid wherever they could in caves or in the woods. But they had come to their senses now, and they recognized their friends. No longer under Juno's influence, they were ashamed of what they had done—but the fire still burned relentlessly.

For all the men's efforts, for all the water that they threw on it, the caulking smoldered even where the wood was damp, and poured out rolling clouds of smoke. A slow heat ate at the ships' planks, like an infection that creeps through every limb of the body. Aeneas tore off his tunic and called on the gods for help. "Almighty Jupiter, you used to have some sympathy for human sufferings. If any of your feelings remain, and if you don't despise every last one of us, allow our fleet escape these flames and save the Trojans, frail as they are, from death. Or, if I have done you wrong, strike what is left of us with your thunderbolt, and destroy us with a single gesture."

He had hardly finished speaking, when a black squall with sheets of rain struck them, a whirling blinding downpour from all across the sky. Mountains and plains trembled at the thunder and the wild gusts of wind. The ships were filled to the gunwales, their half-burned timbers completely soaked. The flames were extinguished, and all except four of them were saved.

Aeneas is discouraged, but Anchises' ghost cheers him up and tells him what to do next

Aeneas was bewildered by these events, and anxiety consumed him. In his heart he considered and reconsidered first one plan and then another: should he settle in Sicily after all, ignoring what the fates had told him, or should he continue on to Italy? Then an old man called Nautes—he had been Minerva's student, and she had made him famous for his skill in interpreting the anger of the gods and explaining the mysteries of the future—comforted him. "Son of a goddess," he said, "we must go on, following in whatever direction it is that the fates may lead us. Whatever fortune brings, bear it—and you will see that it can be survived. Why don't you take Acestes into your confidence—he is of Trojan blood—and make him your friend and ally? Hand over to his care those who have lost their ships and those who have no more patience for your adventure. Leave with him the men who are too old, and the women who are weary of the sea, and whoever else is sick, or afraid, or exhausted. Allow them to build their own town here. Perhaps they can call it Acesta."

But even though he was encouraged by the words of his old friend, Aeneas remained in doubt. But when the earth was already shadowed by the dark night's chariot, he thought he saw his father Anchises slipping across the sky and calling to him.

"My son—you were dearer to me than my life while life remained, and now the fate of Troy rests on your shoulders. I have come here at the command of Jupiter. He has put out the fire in your ships and now, looking down from heaven, he pities you. Take the excellent advice that Nautes has given you. Only the young men, the bravest men, should go with you to Italy. The enemy that you will have to fight in Latium will be hard, tough and without experience of civilized life. But before that, my son, you must go below the earth to the house of Hades, and deep in the underworld you must seek out a meeting with me. You will not find me among the gloomy ghosts of hell; I am in the Elysian fields, in the pleasant company of the spirits who are dear to the gods. The Sibyl of Cumae—through blood, through the black blood of sacrifice—will bring you to me, and then I will tell you of the future of your race, and what cities you are to found. But now night's gentle journey is half done, and in the east I hear the snorting horses of the sun. Farewell." And, like a puff of smoke, he was gone.

"Where are you going? And why so fast?" Aeneas called after him. "Why won't you stay? Why can I not hold you in my arms?" He stirred up a sleepy flame from the embers on the altar, and dutifully made an offering of sacred grain and incense to the gods of Troy and of his own house.

Immediately then he summoned Acestes and his companions, and told them what Jupiter had commanded, what his father had advised and what he intended to do himself. He and Acestes at once began to plan a new town, and the women were put ashore, along with any volunteers who had no more interest in making a splendid reputation for themselves. The rest of the Trojans—there were not many of them, but they were filled with fighting spirit—went to work on the ships. They put in new benches and replaced the timbers that had been burned; they refitted the oars and rigging. Meanwhile Aeneas traced a boundary with a plough, and allotted houses: the divisions of the town, he said, were to be named after the various parts of Troy. Acestes was delighted with this addition to his kingdom: he laid out its forum and brought together all the old men to establish its constitution. A temple to Venus was raised on the starry summit of the mountain where Eryx was buried, and a priest was appointed to tend Anchises' tomb and the grove in which it stood.

The Trojans set sail once more; Neptune promises safe passage to Italy

For nine days, days without a stir of breeze, they celebrated, with ceremonies at every altar. But then the south wind beckoned them to sea again. All along the shore, for a whole night and a whole day, the Trojans wept and embraced each other. The women, and the men who had so recently complained of the intolerable misery of life at sea, were now suddenly willing to set sail again after all, and put up with all the discomfort that another voyage might bring. But Aeneas cheered them up with his kindness and gentle words and, himself in tears, commended them to Acestes' care. Three heifers were sacrificed to Eryx, and a lamb to the god of storms, and then he gave orders to cast off. Standing by himself in the bow, with his head wreathed with sprigs of olive, he held up a bowl from which he made his own libation to the sea. A following wind sprang up. Oars rose and fell together. Their wake foamed behind them.

Venus is anxious that Juno may try to prevent their progress...

Venus, however, was not easy in her mind, and she poured out her anxiety to Neptune: "Juno is still angry with the Trojans, and her intransigence forces me to approach you. Nothing makes her change her mind: not prayers, not the passing of time. Jupiter's orders do not move her, and the fates do not forestall her. Is it not enough for her insatiable hatred that she has destroyed Troy and its people, and dragged the survivors through every possible humiliation? The city is in ruins, but she will not even let alone its ashes or the Trojans' bones. Does even she know why she is so furious? You yourself saw how she raised up that storm against the Trojans off the Libyan coast. You saw the frenzy of waves and winds, you saw the gale that she had Aeolus whip up—in vain, as it turned out, but only because she had had the gall to interfere with your own intentions. You saw how she tricked the women into setting the ships on fire—so that now the Trojans are compelled to continue their voyage with half their fleet lost, and to leave many of their own people behind in a foreign country. What can happen to them next? At least, I beg you, let them have a safe passage to Italy and the Tiber—if that is where it is ordained that they should settle at last."

...but Neptune reassures her

"You have done well to come to me," Neptune replied. "I am the god of the deep sea where you were born, and you can trust me. On many occasions, to help your Aeneas, I have calmed furious storms, and soothed a mad confusion of sea and sky. And—the gods of Troy's rivers will tell you that this is true—I have protected him on land as well. In the middle of the battle before Troy—when Achilles was driving the Trojans back towards the walls, pressing them hard and killing so many hundreds of them that the rivers were clogged with corpses and Xanthus could not find his way down to the sea—there came a moment when he and Achilles stood face-to-face. But because Achilles was much stronger and the gods were on his side, I hid Aeneas away inside a cloud. What I really wanted to do was to knock down the walls of Troy—walls that I built myself, and then I was cheated of my pay. But I supported Aeneas and I still do. Do not fear for him. As you wish, he will come safely into port near the gateway to the underworld. Only one life will be lost in the swirling sea; one man must give his life for all the rest."

So Neptune smoothed away the cares from Venus' heart. He put gold bridles on his horses, and set bits in their foam-

flecked mouths and let the reins run slack through his hands, so that he flew lightly over the whitecaps in his sky-blue chariot. Under his thundering wheels the swells were flattened, and the clouds dispersed into the desert of the sky. After him crowded the sea-monsters that attend the old gods of the sea; and on his left flew Thetis, the mother of Achilles, and her company of nymphs.

A night passage, and a man overboard

Aeneas felt less troubled now, and peace sifted into his heart. The wind was fair, and he ordered all masts to be stepped, and canvas spread on all the yards. The crews sheeted in their sails on the port side, and let them loose to starboard, taking turns round the horned cleats or shaking them out. Aeneas' ship, with Palinurus at the helm, moved out at the head of the fleet.

As it came to the middle of the night, the sailors shipped their oars, and stretched themselves out on their hard benches. The god of sleep came softly down to them from the starlit heaven, slipping through the darkness and the shadows in the shape of one of Priam's sons. He was particularly looking for Palinurus, and sat on the stern-rail next to him, dropping subtle temptation into his guileless ears: "The sea is smooth... the breeze is light... all's well... you've earned your rest. Why don't you lay down your head and close your eyes... just for a moment? And I'll stand your watch for you."

Palinurus barely looked at him. He kept a firm hand on the steering-oar, and his eyes on the stars. "Are you telling me that I don't understand the ways of the cruel sea?" he asked. "And are you suggesting that I betray Aeneas' trust, just because the weather's good? I've been around long enough to know that any wind can tell a lie, and that even a flat calm can be misleading." But the god leaned over him, and took a twig that he had dipped into the river Styx, and shook drops of the water of Forgetfulness over Palinurus' temples; and after that Palinurus could stay awake no longer. He swayed on his feet, and the god unbalanced him, and tossed him through the rail. Over the side he went, down, straight down into the sea, with the steering-oar still in his hand. If he called for help, there was no one to hear him; for the god had already spread his wings and flown up into the empty air.

The fleet sailed on. Unharried and unharmed, as Neptune had promised, it passed by the Sirens' rocky coast, harsh and white with the bones of mariners shipwrecked long ago. The surf crashed against the distant cliffs, and the cliffs sent the sound back out to sea. When Aeneas woke, he found his ship adrift and his helmsman missing. He took over the steering himself, and through the night he wept for the loss of his friend.

"Palinurus? How could you think there was no danger in a peaceful sea and a cloudless sky? Now you lie far away on some deserted strip of sand, naked and alone."

Book VI
The Golden Bough:
Aeneas in the Underworld

Apollo's temple at Cumae

Even while he mourned for Palinurus, Aeneas kept his ships at sea, moving up the west coast of Italy as far as Cumae. Here they turned at last toward shore, and here they dropped their anchors and drew up their sterns all along the curve of the beach. The young men went ashore, full of excitement: some looked for flints that they could use for starting cooking-fires, and others explored the woods in search of places in the underbrush where small game might lurk, and streams to provide fresh water. But Aeneas' first thought was for the gods. He made his way high up into the mountains sacred to Apollo, to find the secret cave where the Sibyl lived—Apollo had breathed into her his own prophetic spirit and revealed the future to her—and they came upon a grove sacred to Diana, and a gilded temple.

The story goes that Daedalus had fled here from Crete; he had dared to entrust himself to wings—an unnatural feat—for a freezing journey to the north. He had alighted on this mountain top near Cumae, and here he had dedicated to Apollo the wooden feathers that he had made for himself, and had built a vast temple. On its doors he had engraved his story. In the first panel, the king of Athens had murdered Androgeus, Minos' son, and in retaliation Minos was demanding that each year seven unfortunate Athenians should be chosen by lot and delivered to him for punishment. The next scene was set in

Knossos: Minos' wife had seduced a bull, and their appalling lust had produced the Minotaur—half bull, half man. He was kept inside a maze—and no one who entered it had ever found his way out. Daedalus felt sorry for the princess Ariadne (who had fallen in love with one of the Athenian victims), and revealed to her the maze's secret: "However complicated are the twists and turns," he said, "a way out can be found by paying out a length of thread behind you." No doubt his son Icarus, who flew away with him, might also have had a place in the design, but Icarus had fallen into the sea, and his father could not bring himself to depict his death. Twice he had tried, and twice his hands had dropped down.

They would all have spent much time examining the doors, if Achates, whom Aeneas had sent ahead, had not returned with the Sibyl, the priestess of Diana and Apollo. "This is not the moment," she said to Aeneas, "to be looking at pictures. You must make a sacrifice: from herds that have never been touched before, choose seven heifers and seven lambs." Aeneas at once obeyed her, and then she summoned the Trojans into the temple.

The Sibyl's cave: her divine frenzy

Inside, the face of the cliff had been hollowed out into a gigantic cave. A hundred paths led up to it, and it had a hundred mouths from which the utterances of the oracle could emerge. As they approached the threshold, the Sibyl announced: "This is your time! Ask for your future! The god! Ask the god!" And all at once the color faded from her face, her hair unraveled, her breath came short and shallow, her heart beat in a disordered rhythm. She grew taller, and her voice changed too: no longer like a mortal's, but with the soaring inspiration of a god's. "You are too slow to pray, Aeneas," she said. "You are too slow to make your vows. But until Apollo hears them, there will not be a single word of comfort from his oracle." Then—silence.

The Trojans felt a cold fear creeping in their bones, and Aeneas thought for a long time before he made his answer.

"You have always pitied the Trojans in their troubles, Apollo. When Paris killed Achilles, you guided his hand and his aim. During my long journey you looked out for me, whether I was wandering inland among barbarians or was caught on some treacherous coast. And now I have come at last to the shore of Italy, which has always seemed to withdraw from me the nearer I approached it. Can this be the end of the bad luck that has haunted Troy forever? Surely even the gods who hated us before will spare us now. Most sacred Sibyl—you can look into the future, and I ask nothing that is not fated for me—grant to the Trojans a place to settle in Latium, along with their gods who have been wandering homeless for so long. I will build a marble temple for Apollo and Diana, and I will establish a festival in Apollo's name. And there will also be a shrine for you, great Sibyl, in my new kingdom: here I will publish for my people your prophecies and the future that only you can foresee, and I will pick attendants to serve you." And then he made his last request: "Do not give me your words written on leaves, which will only be whirled away on the frivolous winds. Speak to me yourself."

But Apollo still possessed the Sibyl. The more she tried to shake him from her heart, the more he put wild words into her mouth and madness into her spirit and made her the agent of his will. The hundred mouths of the cave opened of their own accord and carried her reply out into the open air.

The Sibyl's prophecy

"You have survived great dangers at sea, but worse await you on land. The Trojans will indeed arrive in Latium—you can be sure of that—and yet they will wish that they had never come. I see war, vicious war; I see the banks of the Tiber awash with blood. At Troy you fought beside a river; you will fight beside a river again. At Troy there was a city and a siege; there will be a city and a siege again. Another Achilles has already been born; and like Achilles, he is the son of a goddess. Once more the cause of war will be a woman; there will be another Helen in another Paris' bed. And Juno, of course, will never cease to harass you. In the difficult times that await you, there will not be a single tribe of Italy, not a single city, to which you will not appeal for help. But you must never let disaster diminish you; on the contrary, you must be more determined than ever. Wherever your fortune leads you, you must push on. Salvation will come from where you least expect it, from a town that was founded by a Greek."

Inside the cave, Apollo drove his spurs into the Sibyl's side and whipped on her dance. She gasped out her terrifying words—but what did they mean? They might be true—and yet they were unintelligible. As soon as she became calmer, and her mad mouth was stopped, Aeneas said to her: "Nothing can happen that I have not expected or experienced already. No horror can surprise me, and in my heart I have lived through every possible twist of fate. But I ask one thing of you. They say that this is the entrance to the kingdom of Hades, and this dank marsh is the place where the river of hell has overflowed its banks. I am instructed to go down to meet my dear dead father face to face once more. Will you show me the way and open the gates? I carried my father on my shoulders through cascading arrows and the flames of Troy, and however hard the enemy pressed us, I kept him safe. He stayed with me through all my travels; together we went through storms and a shipwreck that he should never have had to suffer in the frailty of his old age. Now he has spoken to me and told me to approach you. I beg you, then, have pity on a father and his son. It is not beyond your power: it was not for nothing that Diana has made you the guardian of the country of the dead. With the music of his lyre, Orpheus was able to charm Hades into releasing his dead wife Eurydice. When Pollux died, he was allowed to go to the underworld and return again and again, sharing immortality with his twin brother Castor. Did not Theseus contrive to come back from the dead—and the hero Hercules? But *I* am born from the stock of Jupiter." He placed hands on the altar and waited for the Sibyl's reply.

The Sibyl explains the way to the underworld, and tells Aeneas how to pick the Golden Bough

"To go down to hell is easy," she said. "The gates are open all day and all night. But it is another thing entirely—difficult and daunting—to come up once more into the upper air. Only a few have ever managed it. Perhaps they were the children of the gods, or Jupiter particularly loved them, or their own bright virtue lit their way. Between this world and the next there is nothing but forest, and a river winding drearily around it. And after that there is a lake, and a black wall: you will have to cross them on your way in, and then again on your way out. But you are the son of Anchises of Troy, sprung from immortal blood: if your heart is set on it, and if you are rash enough to want to make this journey, listen to what you must do first.

"Lost in the deepest shadows of a valley, hidden in the woods, there is a tree; and on that tree is a golden bough, with golden leaves and twigs. It is sacred to Proserpina, the queen of the underworld; anyone wishing to go there must pick it and bring it to her as a gift. As soon as it is picked, another will grow in its place, and will sprout golden leaves as before. So look carefully for its hiding place and take hold of it. If the fates are with you, it will come away easily in your hand; if not, however hard you pull, or even if you take a knife to it, you will not be able to tear it off. And one more condition: though you do not know it yet, one of your friends is lying dead and unburied near your ships. The fleet has become polluted while you spend your time at the mouth of my cave, seeking my advice. You must bring him to his last resting place and build him a tomb, and make a sacrifice to expiate your neglect. And then at last you will see the valley of the river Styx, and Hades' kingdom, which no mortal has ever entered."

The death and burial of a Trojan trumpeter

She closed her lips tightly, and Aeneas left the cave, going over in his mind all that she had said. His eyes were on the ground. His expression was grim. Achates, loyal as ever, came up to walk with him and worry with him: who had died and who was it that must be buried? But when they returned to the beach, they found the body of Misenus, suddenly and painfully dead. Misenus was famous for his courage, and also for his skill with a bugle: he had no equal in stirring up soldiers' spirits for battle. He had fought side by side with Hector in the war; then, after Hector had been killed, and believing Aeneas' cause to be equally worthy, he had joined the expedition to Italy. But he had done a foolish thing: he had picked up a hollow sea-shell on the beach and, while he was blowing flourishes to the waves, he had challenged the sea-gods to a musical competition. His arrogance, not surprisingly, infuriated Triton, the son of Neptune, who had plucked him up and drowned him in the surf among the rocks.

Aeneas—always wary of the anger of the gods—and the rest of the Trojans gathered round his body with cries of horror. Then in tears they went to find wood for an altar and a tomb, which they intended to raise fast and high, according to the Sibyl's instructions. In the forest and in the hills, the wild animals heard the sound of their axes felling the ancient trees—pine and oak and ash—and their mallets driving in wedges to split the timber, and the crashing of the trunks as they were rolled down the mountain.

Aeneas was especially moved by Misenus' death; he worked side by side with his companions, and encouraged them by his example. With a sad heart he looked back into the tangled woods and whispered: "The Sibyl certainly told us the truth about you, Misenus. I wish that she would show us the golden branch she spoke of." The words were hardly out of his mouth when two doves swooped steeply down from the sky and settled on the grass in front of him. Aeneas recognized them as his mother's particular birds and called out to them with relief.

"You are my guides: you fly and I will follow. Take me to the magic branch; it is hidden somewhere among the shadows. And Venus will be at my side if I should lose my way."

**Aeneas finds
the Golden
Bough**

He observed closely whatever signs they showed him, and went wherever they did through the wood. They fluttered ahead of him, stopping to feed and keeping just in sight; but when they reached the opening to the underworld they shot up towards the sunlight and settled side by side at the top of an oak tree. And in the gloom below them he saw something glittering, a sharp spark of light; it reminded him of the mistletoe, the uninvited guest that winds itself around the trunk of its unwilling host, and sprouts new green leaves and pale berries even in the coldest days of winter. There it was—the golden bough: bright leaves against dark bark, and a rustle of golden foliage in the breeze. He seized it eagerly and tore it off—it was only a little stiff—and took it back to the Sibyl.

Meanwhile on the beach the Trojans mourned Misenus and brought him their last sad gifts of oil and incense and consecrated food. For his funeral they built an enormous pyre of pinewood, sticky with resin; round the base they wove a circle from the dark branches of wild cypresses and laid his armor on the top. Then they brought water to the boil in metal cauldrons; they washed and oiled his cold body, and with great lamentation they laid it, wrapped in his familiar crimson robe, on a high couch. They brought torches to the bier—reluctantly, but it was the custom of their ancestors—and with their faces turned away they lit the fire.

After the pyre had collapsed into ashes and the flames were out, wine was poured over Misenus' remains and left to soak into the dust. Corynaeus gathered up the bones and put them away in an amphora of brass; and Corynaeus blessed his close-crowding friends with fresh water and touched them with an olive branch to purify them, and bade Misenus a formal farewell. But it was Aeneas who saw to it that a great mound was constructed as Misenus' tomb, with his armor on it, and his oar, and his trumpet. His name was given to the promontory that overlooks the mound, and today Cape Misenum keeps his memory alive forever.

The cave of Avernus

Between jagged rocks a deep cleft gaped wide open, leading down to a cave. Black standing water protected it, black shadows arched over it, black breath seeped from it in swirls of poisonous air. As a result, the place is called in Greek **Aornos** (and in Latin **Avernus**, which means "place without birds"). The Sibyl selected four black heifers and splashed wine over their foreheads, and cut off the tufts of hair between their horns and threw them into the flames on the altar; then she prayed to Hecate—Diana's name when she rules below the earth. As his Trojans cut the heifers' throats and held bowls to collect their blood, Aeneas himself slaughtered a black lamb for the mother of the Furies and her sister, and for Proserpina a cow that could never bear a calf. He dedicated an altar to Hades, the king of the underworld, and through the night he made him burnt offerings of bulls' flesh and dripped rendered fat over the entrails. And then, at the first light of dawn, to show him that Proserpina was near, the ground creaked beneath his feet and the trees on the mountain swayed and dogs howled. Possessed again, the Sibyl cried out: "Keep out and keep away! If you do not revere the gods, this is no place for you. Draw your sword, Aeneas, and begin your journey. It will demand all your courage and determination."

Into the opening of the cave she went, and without hesitation he followed close behind her. The world that they entered was sunk in the darkness under the deep earth; if mortals have ever heard of it, is only by leave of the gods who rule it. It is a formless country of smoldering water and ghosts and shadows and silence stretching endlessly through the night. Can you imagine trying to find your way through an unfamiliar wood after sunset? Can you imagine no

light, no shade, no color—just the moon flickering vaguely in a cloud-smudged sky? They traveled across the dreary, empty land, and came to the gates of hell, and the chamber where Mourning and Anxiety have made their beds. Pale Sickness lies there too, and Age and Fear; and Famine that strips men of their consciences, and Poverty that undermines their affections; and—ghastly in the different forms they take—Pain and Death; and Death's brother, Sleep; and that Delight that comes from wicked thoughts. On the other side of the doorway stands War the assassin, and the shackled Furies, and empty-minded Violence, who binds her bloodstained hair with a garland of vipers.

An enormous elm tree spread over them. There is a story that dreams drift among its branches, and cling to the underside of its leaves, but the dreams mean nothing. All kinds of monsters lurked there: the Centaurs in their stable just inside the gate; a giant with a hundred arms; a fire-breathing dragon; a serpent with nine cruelly hissing mouths; dog-women, and women with snakes for hair; birds of prey with human faces; and a shifting three-bodied phantom. They loomed above Aeneas, and in a fit of panic he threatened them with his sword. But the Sibyl restrained him; she knew that they were not real. "They are all creatures of air and imagination," she said. "It is foolish to attack them; you cannot kill a shadow."

The river Styx

From here a path led down to a river, seething furiously among deep marshy pools. Mud-bubbles swelled and burst and spat up ooze scoured from the bottom. Looking out over the water, unkempt and scowling, stood the master of the rust-gray ferry that carried the dead across the river; he steered it and tended its sails himself. A filthy cloak was twisted over his shoulders, an untidy white beard rambled down his chin, and above it his eyes glowed in their sockets. He was very old, though for an immortal god still young and green. A great crowd pressed down to the edge of the river, as many as the leaves that fall from the trees at the first snap of frost, as many as the birds that, warned by cold weather that it is time to depart for the sunshine of the south, flock together for their stormy migration across the sea. There were mothers and husbands, warriors who had sacrificed their lives in battle, little boys, unmarried girls, young men who had died before their parents—and each one of them begged to be taken across the river first, reaching out their hands to the boatman in their passionate desire to reach the farther side. Some of them he took on board, but others he held off and pushed back roughly.

Aeneas was puzzled by the confusion, and asked the Sibyl: "What does it mean, this dreadful river and this crowd of spirits? What do they want? How does the boatman know which ones to turn away, and which ones to ferry across?"

The priestess answered him briefly: "I will tell you, but only because you are the son of Anchises and a goddess. This river is the Styx. If a god swears an oath on it, he dares not break his word. The boatman's name is Charon, and round him crowd the spirits of the dead. But he may only carry across the spirits whose bodies have been buried. The others do not even have a pauper's grave, and as long as their bones have not been laid to rest, he cannot take them over the churning water, away from this dismal shore. For as long as a hundred years their ghosts will flit up and down the bank, and then at last they are allowed to come back here to ask again."

Aeneas meets his lost companions

Aeneas stood still, pitying those who were separated out by this merciless distinction. He saw familiar faces—Orontes from Lycia, and Leucaspis, drowned with all their crew on the voyage from Troy to Africa, and both unhonored with a funeral; and then Palinurus, his own helmsman, lost overboard as he was navigating by the stars during their northward passage. Aeneas barely recognized him in the sad shadow where he stood, but he called out to him: "Palinurus—tell me. Which of the gods was it who grabbed you and threw you into the sea? Surely not Apollo? He foretold that you would come safely to port to Italy. I have never known him not to tell the truth before, but now he seems to have deceived me."

"No," Palinurus replied. "Apollo has not lied to you. I was not thrown into the sea by any god. I was holding to my course, as you ordered, when I was jerked off my feet. My hand was firm on the steering-oar, and I went straight over the side still holding it in my hand. The swells were high, but I swear that they did not frighten me so much as the thought of your ship with her gear lost in a rising sea, and her helmsman missing. For three cold nights, I was tossed about by a gale, far from land. But on the fourth day, swept up high on the crest of a wave, I caught sight of the coast of Italy. Slowly I made my way to shore—and I almost made it. I was all weighed down by my wet clothes, and I was hanging on by my fingertips to the rocks that were just showing in the surf, when some fishermen mistook me for their prey and attacked me with their spears. Now my body lies among the breakers and the wind tumbles me along the beach. And so—by the stars and the sky, and by the memory of your father, and by the great hopes that you have for Ascanius—I beg you to release me from my suffering. I'm sure that you could make your way to Velia, where I am, and bury me there; but, since it is obvious that you have the gods on your side—you certainly could not cross the Styx without their help—perhaps the mother of the gods can show you another way to let me rest in peace. Give me your hand and take me with you across the river."

The Sibyl interrupted him. "How dare you, Palinurus? How can you think that you can even set eyes on the Styx when you have not been buried? How will you reach the bank without the permission of the gods? And how can you believe that prayer can alter the destiny that has been laid down for you? But listen to me carefully: your troubles will soon be ended. Signs from heaven will guide the local people to the beach where your body lies. From their towns, however distant, they will come to honor your remains. They will raise a tomb for you, and at the tomb they will perform the rites that are due to you, and the place will forever be called Palinurus after you." And at her words his anxiety faded away and the pain in his heart was lifted; he was happy that his name would not be forgotten.

He takes the ferry across the river

Now they continued on their journey, and approached the river. Charon had been watching them from his boat as they came through the silent wood and made their way to the bank, and now he challenged them brusquely. "What do you mean by coming down to my river with a sword in your hand? Stop, whoever you are—and tell me what you want. This place is for ghosts; it's always nighttime here, and time for the dead to sleep. If you're alive, I've got no room for you on my boat. I made a mistake when Hercules came down here and I let him on board, and the same with Theseus and his friend Pirithous—they were the children of gods and much stronger than any mortals. Hercules stole the watchdog Cerberus from right under Hades' nose; he put a leash on him and dragged him away with his tail between his legs. And the other two wanted to kidnap Proserpina out of her own palace."

"We have not come to trick you," answered the Sibyl quickly. "Hold on to your temper. This sword is not intended to threaten you; we have no plan to prevent Cerberus from frightening away the ghosts with his barking, or to distract the chaste Proserpina from her watch at Hades' door. This man is Aeneas. He comes from Troy, and he is as famous for his duty to the gods as he is for his courage in battle. He has come down to the underworld to visit his father. If you do not know how much he respects the gods, then you will certainly recognize *this.*" From under her robe she drew out the golden bough. Charon was shocked. He had not seen it for many years, but he knew what it meant; his irritation subsided and he did not protest any more. He turned his pitch-stained stern into the bank, and cleared a space for Aeneas and the Sibyl among the spirits who were sitting on the thwarts. The boat creaked under their weight, and water spurted through the cracks in its planking, but at last it brought them safely to the slippery mud and gray swamp-grass of the far bank.

They came next to another cave; the dog Cerberus blocked the entrance, and snarled at them from all his three throats. The Sibyl waited until she saw snakes begin to sprout from his necks, and then she threw him a piece of bread soaked in honey and soporific herbs. He opened his three mouths wide, and gulped it down hungrily; then he staggered and flopped down on the floor. Aeneas stepped across his sleeping body and went inside, leaving the river of no return behind him.

Judgment of the dead

At once he heard voices raised, complaining and lamenting, and the crying of children who had died before their time, on a black and bitter day that had found them still at their mothers' breasts. And beside them were those who had been falsely accused and condemned to death; but now they had a new judge, whose name was Minos. He summoned them to stand in silent assembly before him, and interrogated each one of them. "What were the charges against you? And what did you actually do?" And he shook lots from an urn to decide their fate. After them came the suicides: innocent of any crime, they had hated the light of the sun and thrown away their lives. Perhaps poverty or unremitting misfortune did not seem so intolerable to them now, and they wished that they were back up in the upper air. But it was too late: they were trapped by the gloomy marshes of the Styx, which flowed in nine enclosing circles round them.

Aeneas meets the ghost of Dido...

Not far off the ground leveled out into what was called the Mourners' Field. Here, moping beneath myrtle trees, or hiding on secluded paths, were those who had wasted away from love. They were dead, but death had still not eased their misery. Passion or lust or fatal obsession had consumed them, or their lovers had betrayed them; one woman had been changed into a man when Neptune tried to rape her, then back to a woman again. And among them, in a thick wood, with the blood from her wound not yet quite dry, was Dido. In the shadows Aeneas did not recognize her until he was standing quite close to her; and he felt like a man who sees, or thinks he sees, a new moon rising through the clouds. His eyes filled with tears and he spoke to her affectionately.

"My poor Dido: is it true that you killed yourself? Did you die because of me? I swear to you—by the stars and the gods in heaven and whatever divine powers there are down here—I did not leave your kingdom of my own free will. It was the gods who forced me to leave, the same gods that now compel me to travel through these sad shadows, to make this journey in a darkness like the darkness of night. How could I have known that if I left you it would bring you so much pain? Wait. Do not turn away from me. Where are you going? This is the very last time that I shall be allowed to speak to you."

As he tried to soothe her, he was weeping. But she was implacable and there was no softening of her eyes; she kept them fixed on the ground, refusing to look up at him. However much he pleaded with her, her face remained expressionless, as hard as flint or Parian marble. At last she turned away and moved off among the formless trees, back to her long-lost husband Sychaeus, who was waiting to comfort her and to return her love. Aeneas was overcome with regret for what had happened to her, and his pity made him follow her until she disappeared.

...and those of the Trojan heroes killed in action...

Their journey continued. They came now to the farthest part of the plain, where the ghosts of the Trojan war-heroes were gathered: Tydeus, and the courageous Parthenopaeus, and Adrastus, so much paler than he used to be, and all the others who had been killed in action, but were still missed by those who had stayed alive. Through his tears he saw the endless line of them: Glaucus and Medon and Thersilochus, and the three sons of

Antenor, and Polyboetes the priest of Ceres, and Idaeus, sword in one hand, chariot-reins in the other. The spirits clustered all around him. It was not enough for them simply to see him; they had to stop him and walk with him and find out why he had come. And there were Greeks there too, officers from Agamemnon's army; but when they saw Aeneas and his armor glimmering in the dark, they became frightened. Some of them fled, just as long ago they had looked for safety by their ships, and some of them raised a feeble attempt at a battle-cry—but no sound came out of their mouths.

...including a son of Priam who had been betrayed by Helen

Beyond them lay Deiphobus; he was one of Priam's sons, and he had married Helen after Paris died. He had been horribly mutilated: there were deep cuts all over his face and both his hands; his head was crushed, his ears ripped away from his temples, his nostrils sliced open. But he tried to cover up his wounds, and trembled so much that Aeneas scarcely recognized him—but he spoke to him anyway, hoping that he would know his voice.

"Deiphobus, how could this happen to you? You were of royal blood, a great warrior. Who has desecrated your body so viciously? I heard that you had collapsed, exhausted from the fighting of that last night, on a confused pile of corpses. So I built a tomb for you, my friend, and three times I called upon your spirit. Your name and your armor are preserved there on the shore—but I could find no trace of your body, and I could not lay you to rest before I left the city. Your tomb is empty."

"You have done all that you could," Deiphobus replied. "You owe me nothing. My sufferings come from the gods and the treachery of Helen: she left me these wounds to remember her by. You know—of course you do—how we spent that last night in stupid pointless celebration? After the wooden horse, with its belly full of soldiers, had passed so easily over the walls that were supposed to protect us, it was Helen who led the other women in a wild procession through the city, pretending to be dancers in a Bacchic orgy. It was Helen who went up to the roof of the citadel with a torch and flashed the signal to the Greeks. I was worn out with worry, and so I came home and lay down on our bed, I drifted into a sleep as heavy and peaceful as death. But Helen—my dear wife Helen—had removed all the weapons from our house and even stole the sword that I kept under my pillow. And then she sent word to Menelaus—he was waiting outside—and opened the door to him. That, she thought, was how she could make amends to her first husband, and put an end to all the old gossip about her. So Menelaus came bursting in and attacked me—the details are not important—in our own bedroom. And Ulysses, who of course was behind the whole scheme, was with him. I pray that the gods will repay them for what they did. But tell me, how do you come to be here, if you are not yet dead? Did you lose your way on your travels, or did the gods tell you to come here? What can have happened to make you enter this sad and sunless country, this place of misery?"

At this moment in their conversation, the chariot of the morning reached the mid-point of its journey across the sky. Aeneas would have used up all the time that had been granted to him, if the Sibyl had not given him a sharp warning. "Night is coming on, and we are spending every hour in weeping. Here there is a fork in the road: if we go right, the way leads beneath the ramparts of Hades, and we will come to the Elysian fields, where virtue is rewarded. But on the left is Tartarus, where sins are punished."

"Great Sibyl," said Deiphobus, "do not be angry with me. I must depart to complete what I have to do, and return to my proper place among the shadows. Gallant Aeneas—you deserve a better fate than…" But, before he had finished his sentence, he was gone.

Past crime and present punishment

Aeneas looked behind him. He saw, under the cliff to his left, a fortress surrounded by a triple wall, and the river Phlegethon, which whirled and boiled and tumbled, rocks below and flames above. In front of him was a gate with posts of granite, too strong to be moved by men or even by the gods when they are at war; and there was a tower made of iron. On the tower sat Tisiphone the Fury, sleepless, wrapped in a bloodstained cloak. From behind the gates that she guarded by day and night came groans and the hiss of

whips and the clanging of chains dragged across flagstone floors. Aeneas stood and listened in terror; then he asked the Sibyl, "What are these sounds? Who is being tortured? Who is being punished?"

"You are a good man," she replied, "and this is no place for you. When Hecate put me in charge of Avernus, she explained to me exactly how the gods inflict their penalties. The sinners appear before their judge Rhadamanthus; he listens to them with pitiless impartiality as they plead their cases. He forces confessions from those who, while they were alive, expected smugly that their crimes would go unsolved—but after death they discover that it is never too late to be found out. Tisiphone takes immediate revenge upon the guilty. She assaults them with her sneering tongue and with the slashing whip of hard-eyed snakes that she holds in her left hand; and she calls her fierce sisters to help her. Then, and only then, do the gates of Tartarus whine open on their hinges.

"Do you see the guard sitting in the courtyard and watching the doors? Do you see his face, and his fifty snarling black mouths? He is fiercer than the many-headed Hydra. Behind him is the opening to Tartarus itself: it drops sharply and steeply down into a pit that lies twice as far beneath where we are now as Olympus rises above us. Hecate showed me, writhing at the very bottom, the firstborn children of Earth, the

Titans, banished there by Jupiter's thunderbolt. And there were the twin offspring of Aloeus: they too are giants, who tried to split heaven apart with their bare hands and expel Jupiter from Mount Olympus. And Salmoneus was there, still suffering the punishment given to him for pretending to be the king of the gods. He used to prance all over Greece in a four-horse chariot, brandishing a torch above his head; he rode in triumph through the cities of Elis, demanding that divine honors be paid to him. He was mad, of course: with a brass gong and the dust kicked up by his horses' hooves, he thought he could imitate Jupiter's clouds and his inimitable thunderbolt. But from Olympus Jupiter threw the genuine article at him—not just a torch or a sooty firebrand—and sent him spinning down to his doom. And I saw Tityos, another giant, another child of Earth: his body lies stretched out over nine acres of land, and a vulture picks constantly at his liver and the entrails hidden beneath his ribs. But as fast as the hooked beak nibbles at them, they grow back—a perpetual delicacy for the vulture, and perpetual agony for Tityos.

"Do you want to hear more—about Ixion and Pirithous, or about the sons of Lapithes? Some of them must roll a huge stone perpetually up a hill or hang bound to the spokes of a turning wheel. The unhappy Theseus sits waiting for his punishment… and must sit… and sit… and sit. And the insistent voice of Phlegyas, the most miserable of them all, gives a warning to the other ghosts: 'Be reverent—respect justice—do not despise the gods.' Above him a black boulder seems always on the point of falling, and he must cower under its threat

forever. Before some of them, a lavish feast is laid out; the gleam of golden furnishings invites them to a festival; but the chief of the Furies sits on a couch nearby and prevents them from approaching. She towers above them, screaming, and the flames from her torch scorch their hands if they reach out to the food.

"If anyone ever sold his country for gold and set a tyrant on the throne; if anyone ever took a bribe to make laws or to repeal them; if anyone ever broke into his daughter's bedroom and raped her—he will be there. With him will be all those who, while they were alive, hated their brothers or beat their parents or cheated their clients or kept their money to themselves and did not share it with their relations—there are a lot of them. And there are adulterers, and rebels, and traitors. They are all imprisoned down there, waiting for their sentences. Do not ask me to tell you what will become of them, or to what depths they have already sunk. I can only tell you that they have dared to do what the gods have forbidden, and they will pay for their rashness. But even if I had a hundred mouths and a hundred tongues and a throat of iron, I could not rehearse their crimes or name their punishments.

"And now come along. We must hurry," said the Sibyl, when she had finished her explanation. "It is time to complete the task you came to do. Over there is another gate, in the walls that the giant Cyclopes built in their workshops. Do you see the arch that curves over it? This is where the gods have ordered us to lay down the offering that they have prescribed." Through the darkness they went side by side until they stood in the open space before the doors. Under the arch Aeneas sprinkled himself with fresh water, and to the lintel he attached the golden bough.

Rewards for virtue in the happy fields

When the ritual was over, and Proserpina's dues were paid, they came at last into a green and pleasant country—the gardens of good fortune and the resting-place of the blessed. Here a softer light spread over the plain and bathed it with glowing warmth; for these spirits had their own sun and their own stars. They played games and wrestled on the turf, or raced each other on the sand. There was dancing and singing and poetry. Orpheus, dressed in a priest's robes, accompanied it on his lyre, plucking a progression of seven chords with his fingers or with his ivory plectrum.

An entire generation from ancient Troy was here, handsome and brave, and born in happier times: Ilus and Assaracus and Dardanus the founder of the city. It was wonderful to see from far away their arms and their empty chariots; they had stuck their spears into the ground and their horses, unharnessed, grazed at will over the plain. Now that they were beneath the earth, they still took the same pride in their weapons as they had while they were alive, and the coats of their horses were kept as glossy. On every side Aeneas saw them: some feasting outdoors, some singing cheerfully under the laurel trees, where a wide river meandered through the forest. He saw warriors who had been wounded fighting for their country, or priests and prophets and poets, who had lived blameless lives in fear of the gods and felt Apollo's inspiration. And he saw artists who by their imagination had made the upper world a better place, and would deservedly be remembered. Every one of them was garlanded with bright white flowers.

They gathered close around the Sibyl, and she spoke to them all, but especially to Orpheus' pupil Musaeus, who stood in the middle of the crowd, taller than all the rest. "Tell me, happy spirits—and tell me, best of prophets—where can we find Anchises? It is because of him that we have come here and crossed the rivers of hell."

"No one here lives in any particular spot," Musaeus answered. "We spend the days under the trees, and we sleep where we will on the banks of rivers and in the water-meadows. But, if you really want to find him, climb up here, and I will put you on an easy path." He led the way to the top of a ridge and showed them the sparkling landscape that stretched out far below them on the other side.

Aeneas meets the shade of his father Anchises

They went down from the high ground into a deep green valley—and there was Anchises. He had been pondering the fate of those souls who were about to go up into the light; and by chance he was at that very moment thinking of his own family—of his beloved grandchildren and what would become of them, whether they would be rich or poor, bad or good. When he saw Aeneas approaching him over the grass, he stretched out both his hands and spoke to him with tears streaming down his cheeks.

"You are here at last! You loved your father enough to make this terrible journey—and the gods have allowed me to see your dear face and to hear your voice and answer your questions. I thought that perhaps—just perhaps—you might come. I was wondering how long it might be—and here you are. What countries have you visited? What seas have you crossed? What dangers have you had to face? How worried I was that you would somehow come to grief in Carthage!"

"No," replied Aeneas. "Our fleet has reached Italy. But your anxious face has been always before my eyes, father, and it was you that brought me here. Give me your hand. Do not pull away from my embrace." His cheeks, too, were wet. Three times he tried to put his arms around Anchises' neck, and three times his father's ghost slipped out of his grasp, like a whisper of a breeze or a forgotten dream.

The river of Forgetfulness

Then Aeneas saw within the valley a secluded stand of trees and rustling bushes, and flowing through it Lethe, the quiet river of Forgetfulness. People of every race—so many he could not count them—were milling about like bees that settle on the blossoms of midsummer grasses, or hover around white lilies, so that the whole meadow hums and murmurs. Aeneas was puzzled; he did not understand what was happening. "What is this river, and who are the men who are crowded together on its banks?"

"These are the souls to whom fate must give another body," answered Anchises, "and they have come to drink the water of Lethe to free themselves from their past cares, to forget forever all that they once knew. I have long wished to show you, to let you see for yourself, the generations of our family that are yet to come, so that when you have made your mark in Italy you may share my pride in them."

The secrets of life, death and rebirth

"Is it possible, then," asked Aeneas, "that some souls can be transported from this happy state to the upper air, and again inhabit mortal bodies? What makes them desire so fiercely the light of the painful world?"

"I will answer you at once, my son," said Anchises. "I will explain it to you, point by point. From the beginning some interior spirit has informed the heaven and the earth and the sea and the glowing moon and the stars that the giants placed in the sky. And an intelligence, implicit throughout the entire universe, brought to life what was once a lifeless mass. It moved to action men and animals and birds and whatever creatures lurk beneath the mottled surface of the sea. They all have their origin in fire: their energy derives from heaven, but their limbs are tied to the dull earth. Disease slows their step and they know that there is no escape from death. Fear and desire, sorrow and joy—all come from their sense of their mortality; and from their dark prison they cannot see the sky. So, in the end, they die. But even then they are not entirely free from grief and pain; in some strange sense they still cannot shake off their material past, however distant. Old crimes, still unexpiated, must still be punished. And so some souls are left to be scoured clean by the wind; others must have their sin, like an infection, washed away under a jet of whirling water or burned out by fire. Each of us is purified according to the way that we have lived. Then we are sent on our long journey to Elysium, and a few of us will reach the happy fields. The passage of circling time purges every mortal wrong until there is nothing left but disembodied sensibility itself, an airy flame. And when the wheel of a thousand years has come to rest at last, the god calls the souls together to drink the river Lethe. When they remember nothing, they are given permission to revisit the world above. They begin to wish to be restored to a human form."

Anchises shows Aeneas the heroes of future Roman history: first, his own children...

When he had finished, Anchises guided Aeneas and the Sibyl through the murmuring crowd onto a mound. From here he could look closely into the faces of the spirits as they passed by him in a long line, and recognize them.

"Now: I will describe to you the glory that will come upon the future generations of Trojans. I will tell you who our Italian descendants will be, and what distinction they will bring to our name. Do you see that young man leaning on a simple spear? He has, by lot, drawn the spot closest to the light of the upper earth, and he will be the first to have in his veins a mixture of Trojan and Italian blood. He will be your son Silvius. His mother will be called Lavinia: she will conceive him in her old age, and he will be born after your death. She will bring him up in the woods to be a king and the father of kings—the kings who, named after him, will rule over the city of Alba Longa. And there are his glorious successors, next to him. Look especially at Silvius Aeneas, who will share your name: if ever he comes to the throne, he will be remembered equally for his devotion to the gods and for his courage in war. What excellent young men they are—don't you think?—decked out so proudly in their wreaths of ceremonial oak. They will found cities on hilltops near Alba Longa—some, like Gabii or Fidenae, to be well-known, and some to be forgotten.

...then Romulus, the founder of Rome...

"Next comes Romulus: he will be the son of Mars and Rhea Silvia, herself descended from my grandfather. Do you see the double plume on the crest of his helmet? And how he is marked out by his father to be a god himself? He will be the founder of Rome—a wall will enclose her seven hills, but her empire will reach to the farthest edges of the world, her fame to the heights of Olympus. She will be fortunate in the race that she will nurture. She will be like Cybele, who rides through the cities of Asia in her turreted chariot, happy to be the mother of the immortals, embracing a hundred children who live and reign in heaven.

...and Romulus' descendants, including the current emperor Augustus

"Look now at the race of the Romans themselves, your Romans. Here are all the members of the Julian clan; they are descended from Ascanius, whose other name is Julus. And here is the man, the son of a god, whose coming you have so often heard of: the emperor Augustus Caesar. He will again establish a golden age in the land of Latium, which once was ruled by Saturn. He will extend his reign to the African desert and as far as India, a land that lies beyond the stars, beyond the path of the seasons and the sun, where sky-supporting Atlas turns on his shoulder the axis of all the constellations. As the gods announce his approach, the shores of the Caspian Sea and the Crimea are already trembling, and the estuaries of the seven-mouthed Nile run rough with fear. Even Hercules, in pursuit of the famous bronze-footed stag or the wild boar of Erymanthus or the seven-headed Hydra, did not travel as far as Augustus' rule will stretch; nor did Bacchus, whenever he came triumphantly down from Mount Parnassus, holding back his tigers on a tight rein made of vine-tendrils. You see how you must not hesitate to match your courage with deeds, or let fear prevent you from setting foot in Italy.

Early kings and consuls, statesmen and generals

"And who is that, standing over there, carrying bowls for sacrifice, stately in his olive wreath? I know his hair and his white beard: it is Numa Pompilius. He will be brought from poverty in a little Sabine town to be a mighty king of Rome, to settle the city under the rule of law. Tullus will succeed him: he will disturb his country's peace and call its complacent citizens to arms, and lead them to victories that they had not known before. And after him will come Ancus, too pleased with himself and too easily led by the pleasure he will take in his popularity. And do you want to see the Tarquins' line, and Brutus, the founder of the republic? He will have the spirit and the courage to avenge the Tarquins' cruelty and take away from them their insignia of office. He will be the first to hold that awesome symbol, the consul's axe; and, for the sake of the liberty he loves, he will have his own rebellious sons put to death. Poor man! whatever else historians may say of him, they cannot deny his love of country—nor his greed for praise.

"Next come all the heroes of Rome's early wars: look at Torquatus, who too will execute a disobedient son, and at Camillus, who will restore to Rome the trophies lost to her enemies. And look at those two in their polished armor: one of them is Julius Caesar, and the other Pompey. They are friends now, and friends for as long as they stay down here. But, when they reach the light of day, they will take up arms against each other. You cannot imagine the forces that they will collect, or the ferocity of their conflict, or the number of the dead. Even though Pompey's wife is Caesar's daughter, Caesar will attack him from his province beyond the Alps, and Pompey will stand ready to oppose him in the East. But listen to what I am going to say to them: 'My sons, have you come to put your faith only in war? Will you stab your country in the heart? You, Caesar, you should be the first to hold back, to lay your weapons down—for you are born from the gods, and your blood is mine!'

"And who are these? They are the Roman generals destined to conquer the Greeks. One of them will celebrate the sack of Corinth, in a triumphal procession to the Capitol; the other will overrun Agamemnon's fortress at Mycenae, and will defeat an opponent descended from Achilles himself—and so at last avenge his Trojan ancestors and the desecration of Minerva's temple. Next after them, don't miss the great statesman Cato, and the family of the Gracchi, protectors of the people, and Cossus, who is to be victorious over the Etruscans. Then come the scourges of Carthage—Publius Cornelius Scipio and his grandson, two thunderbolts of war. And Fabricius, incorruptible even in poverty; and Cincinnatus, farmer and statesman. And the Fabius family—can I forget them? Especially Quintus Fabius Maximus: by his judicious inaction he will save his country.

The manifest destiny of Rome

"To sum up: there are some places where smiths and sculptors will shape bronze more subtly or carve more lifelike portraits out of marble; in others, orators will argue more persuasively, and astronomers will observe more accurately the motion of the heavenly bodies and predict the rising of the stars. But *you*, remember, are to be a Roman, and the Romans' art is to be of a different kind: the art of government, of ruling nations. Your task is to impose peace by law and order: to protect the downtrodden, and to crush the arrogant in war."

Marcellus, the war hero; and Marcellus, Augustus' heir

Aeneas and the Sibyl listened in astonishment, and Anchises continued: "Look carefully at who is coming now. It is Marcellus, the most distinguished warrior of them all. At the moment of Rome's greatest danger he will stand firm against the Carthaginians, and ride out against the Gauls. And then—the highest possible honor—he will dedicate, for the third time in history, the captured armor of an enemy general to his city's gods."

But Aeneas' attention was held by a young man walking beside the hero, remarkably handsome and radiant in full armor, but with a dejected expression and downcast eyes. "Who is that, father?" he asked. "And why are his companions so excited? Is he Marcellus' son? Or some other relation? He certainly has the family looks—but a black and dreary shadow hangs over his head, like night."

"In him there is nothing but sorrow for your descendants," answered Anchises, with tears shining in his eyes. "Do not ask me to talk about him. The fates will allow him to appear only briefly on the earth; they will not let him linger. Perhaps, if such gifts as his were to appear among the Romans for long, the gods would be afraid that they would become too powerful. The city will never have heard such cries of grief as will come from the soldiers out on the field of Mars; the river Tiber, as it curves past the site of his tomb, will never have known such a funeral. No other child of Trojan blood will stir such hopes among the Latin people, nor will the land of Romulus be so proud of any of its sons. We can only mourn his reverence for the gods and our ancient traditions; we can only weep for his invincible prowess on the battlefield. No one, mounted or on foot, would have been be able to stand up against him."

And then, directly to the boy, he said: "Yes, my poor child: you too are called Marcellus—and Augustus' heir, if only you could escape your sad fate. Though funeral gifts mean nothing, at least I can offer them to your spirit. Give me armloads of lilies—I will scatter their purple petals on your bier."

The way out of the underworld

And so they wandered on, staring about at the broad bright plains of Elysium, and attending closely to Anchises' words. And Anchises fired his son with a desire for future glory, as he told him of the battles he had yet to fight, and of the people of Latium and Italy, and of his future trials—when he should turn away and when he should take a stand.

As we sleep, visions come to us from the underworld: they come through two gates—one made of horn, the other of burnished ivory. The one provides an easy passage for the ghosts who may be trusted; through the other the spirits of the dead send deceitful dreams. Anchises accompanied Aeneas and the Sibyl as far as the ivory gate. Without hesitation Aeneas passed through it, and returned to his ships and his companions.

From Cumae they set their course directly for Caieta, and there they dropped anchors from their bows, and drew up their sterns on the beach.

BOOK VII
The Gates of War

Book VII
The Gates of War

The Trojans land in Latium, and their task begins in earnest

Aeneas' nurse had died at Caieta. If we are to remember her anywhere, it must be here in Italy, where her name has been given to the place where her bones were laid to rest and her honor is preserved. Dutifully Aeneas carried out her funeral rites and raised a mound for her tomb; then he left the harbor in pleasant weather and again set his course to the north.

Even at nightfall the breeze did not drop. They sailed on under the light of the moon, palely reflected in a glimmering sea, and made their way past Circe's island. From deep in the woods, where no mortal has ever set foot, they could hear the witch's endless humming, and the quick sound of her loom, whirring to and fro in the night; and they caught the scent of the cedar-wood which smolders in the lanterns hanging from her roof. They could hear too the sound of the men whom Circe, by her herbs and spells, had transformed into animals: lions strained against their chains, whimpering or roaring in the dark; bristling boars and short-tempered bears paced anxiously in their cages; wolves howled. But Neptune kept the Trojans safe: if they had come to shore there they might have been trapped themselves, but he filled their sails with wind and swept them past those dangerous waters.

And now, as the chariot of the dawn touched the sea and the sky with the colors of morning—red and pink and saffron yellow—the wind dropped to a flat calm, and they rowed through a sea like polished stone. Aeneas sighted a stand of trees on shore, and between the trees the river Tiber, colored by the sand that its eddies had picked up, moved steadily towards the sea. The place was full of songbirds of every kind, fluttering among the leaves or swooping over the water. He gave the order to his men to change course toward the coast and they cheerfully approached the shaded estuary.

Now the story takes on a more serious tone, and below it lies a yet more universal theme. And certainly, without guidance from the gods, it could not be told at all. A terrible conflict must be described: armies on the march, reinforcements levied, the passion and death of kings—all Italy at war. But first must come a digression on the rulers and history of Latium, and the state of affairs when the Trojan strangers first arrived on the shores of Italy; and then an explanation of the original causes of the fighting.

The early history of Latium; the Trojans' arrival foretold

In the beginning, the god Saturn had a son called Picus. Picus was the father of Faunus, and Faunus and the nymph Marica were the parents of Latinus. Latinus was king of Latium—he had ruled it in peace for many years—and now he was getting old. It was the will of the gods that he should have no male heir—his only son had died young—but he did have a daughter Lavinia, still at home and waiting to choose a husband. She had many suitors from Latium and from all over Italy; but the most handsome of them, and the most pressing, was Turnus, who was from an old and powerful family and the leader of the Rutulian tribe. Latinus' wife, Amata, approved of him and supported his cause; but various disturbing omens, sent by the gods, stood in his way.

In an inner shrine in Latinus' castle was a laurel tree; its leaves were held sacred and it had been preserved carefully for many years. The story went that Latinus himself, when he was first laying the foundations of his town, had discovered it and dedicated it to Apollo—and so the Latins were also known as Laurentians, after Apollo's sacred laurel. It may be hard to believe, but one day a swarm of bees flew in and settled at the top of the tree—each bee packed tight against its neighbor, buzzing and humming among the foliage. Latinus had consulted a soothsayer, who had said, "The bees foretell the arrival of a foreigner—and an army, moving with a common purpose to be masters of your citadel." And this was not the only sign: while Lavinia was standing beside her father and holding a torch to light the fire at the altar, her long hair caught fire. Her headdress crackled with heat, her jeweled crown glowed red; and then she was hidden in smoke and yellow light. Flames flickered all through Latinus' castle. It was an amazing sight, and horrifying as well: it meant that she herself would be famous, but that a great war would come upon her people.

The king was anxious at these portents, and went to consult the oracle of his father Faunus. High up in the mountains there was a dark copse, and in the middle of it a spring spewed out foul-smelling vapors. It was a place where all the tribes of Italy sought advice when they did not know what to do. A priest would bring gifts, and lie down on sheepskins in the silence of the night, and try to sleep: in his dreams he would see strange fleeting shapes and hear voices, and he would converse with the god and speak to the spirit of Acheron, one of the rivers of hell. Here too Latinus came; after sacrificing a hundred sheep, he stripped off their shaggy skins and spread them on the ground and lay down. Suddenly a voice came out from among the trees. "Do not plan to marry your daughter to any of the Latins, my son. Do not put your trust in any marriage that you have already arranged. A son-in-law, with his companions, is coming to you from a foreign land. Because of the children that he will father, our name will be famous among the stars. From the eastern sea where the sun rises to the western sea where it sets, his descendants will rule the whole world as it turns beneath their feet." That was his father Faunus' prediction, and those were the warnings given to him in the silence of the night; but unfortunately Latinus did not keep them to himself. And so, at the very moment when the young men of Troy were making fast their ships to the grassy river-bank, Rumor on her busy wings had already spread the word through the Italian towns.

A prophecy fulfilled

Meanwhile, Aeneas, with Ascanius and his captains, gathered under the wide shade of a tree for a celebratory feast. On the grass beneath their food—on the advice of Jupiter—the Trojans laid out flat pancakes, and piled up apples on top of them. When they had eaten everything else, they were still hungry and started on the pancakes; without hesitation they picked up the square-shaped crusts and sank their teeth into them, without realizing that their action had any particular significance. "Look: we are eating our tables," said Ascanius. He meant it as a joke, but his remark in fact meant that the first stage of their troubles was over. As soon as he heard it, Aeneas was astonished; he recognized it as a sign from the gods, and he would not let his son say any more. "At last," he said, "we have brought the household gods of Troy to the land that fate intended for them. This is our new country; our new home is to be here. Now I recall my father's words: this was the secret that he left with me. He said: 'When you have landed on an unknown shore, and, when all else fails, hunger compels you to eat your tables—remember then, tired as you are, to look for a place to settle; that is where you must build your first houses and fortify them with a wall.' Now I see clearly what he meant. At last the moment has come which will mark an end of our sufferings. At first light tomorrow we must move out from this harbor to explore. We must find out what people live here and where their capital is. But first refill your cups: let us make an offering to Jupiter and send grateful prayers to my father Anchises."

He wound a wreath around his temples and prayed to the local spirits and to the earth-mother, the first of the gods, and to the nymphs of the river that he did not yet know. Then he called on Night and the stars of Night, and on the gods who had protected Troy, and on his mother in the heavens and his father in the underworld. And three times almighty Jupiter sent thunder from the clear sky, and with his own hand he showed them a cloud radiant with light and gold. And at once the word spread amongst the Trojans that the time had come to found their fated city. Happily they set out a feast and filled their bowls with wine and hung wreaths around their cups.

An embassy is dispatched to king Latinus

As the first lamp of daybreak shone upon the world, they explored the shore and the countryside inland. They found the pool where the river Numicus springs, and the river Tiber; they encountered the tough people of Latium and brought back reports of the imposing walls of their town. Aeneas picked out a hundred delegates, had them put olive wreaths on their heads and instructed them: "Take gifts to the king, and tell him that the Trojans wish for peace. Waste no time, leave at once." He himself dug out a shallow ditch around their landing-place to mark a line for its defenses; then he circled it with earthworks as though it were a military camp. Meanwhile his envoys made their journey to the Latin king. First, from a distance, they observed his towers and houses; then they approached his walls. In front of the town, boys and young men of remarkable fitness were exercising on horseback or racing chariots round a dusty track; they were practicing archery or spear-throwing, and challenging each other to foot-races and boxing matches. A mounted messenger reported to the king the arrival of a group of strange warriors in exotic dress; and Latinus, after ordering that they should be brought inside his castle, waited for them on his ancestral throne.

The throne-room was impressive. It had been built on a hill by Latinus' grandfather: a hundred columns supported its roof, and the presence of ancient gods could be felt in all the surrounding woods. These gods had ordained that here each king should first take up his scepter and hold the symbols of his power. It served both as a temple and as a meeting-place for the king's council; it was also a banquet hall, where the elders would sit together at long tables after they had sacrificed a ram. Trophies of war were hung over the doors: captured chariots and battle-axes and enormous deadbolts and javelins and shields and the figureheads of ships. There were statues of the Latins' ancestors, carved long ago out of cedar wood: Italus, the founder of the Italian race; Sabinus, who introduced the vine, shown with a pruning knife in his hand; the venerable Saturn; Janus, with one head looking to the future and the other to the past; and many other kings from distant history, who had been wounded fighting for their country. Most prominent was Latinus' grandfather Picus, famous for his skill with horses. Circe had once fallen in love with him; she had touched him with her wand, and with her potions had turned him into a gaily-colored bird. But here he was represented bare to the waist, his official staff in one hand and his shield in the other.

Here, in this hallowed hall, Latinus sat in state, and called the Trojans into his presence. When they came in, before they could say anything, he addressed them in a gentle voice. "We know where you have come from, and who you are; we have heard all about your voyage. Now, Trojans, tell us what it is that you want? Why have you come so far over the sea to the shores of Italy? What has brought you here? Was it an error in your navigation? Were you driven off-course by storms, or by some other of the misadventures that sailors suffer so often on the high seas? Well, whatever it was, here you are. You have sailed up our river and you have come to anchor in our harbor. Do not suppose we will not welcome you.

"You should be aware that the Latins are not a slave people. We are not subject to any despotic law; but we live of our own free will under a tradition of justice given to us by Saturn, from whom we are descended. I remember well—though it was a very long time ago—a story that was told to me by some old men I used to know: that Dardanus, the founder of your city, was born not far from here. From Corythus' seat in Etruria he set out on his travels to the island of Samothrace, and from there to mount Ida in Asia. Now he sits in a golden palace, another of the gods, on a throne among the stars."

The Trojans' spokesman was Ilioneus, who answered him without hesitation: "Latinus, we have not arrived in your country driven by any winter storm; we have made no mistake in our landing place; and we have not misread the stars. We have come on purpose, under no compulsion. We have been driven from our homeland, which was once the greatest kingdom that the sun ever looked down on. We are sprung from Jupiter: our young men are proud to have him as our forebear. From his line comes our king—Aeneas of Troy—and he has sent us to speak with you. There is no one, however far he may live from the sea, however cut off from civilization he may be by heat and desert, who has not heard of the storm that blew across the plains of Ida from cruel Mycenae and the collision of Europe and Asia. We were swept away by the flood of war, and since then we have traveled countless miles over the sea in search of a simple resting-place for our country's gods. We ask only for water to drink and air to breathe, and a place to settle safely. It will be no disgrace for you if you shelter us, and you will achieve no passing attention from us, but rather our undying gratitude. Italy will not regret that she welcomed Troy. You should not think less of us because we come to you with gentle words and carrying branches of supplication. By Aeneas' life, and by the right hand with which he has sworn loyalty to his friends and fought his enemies, I promise you this: there are many tribes and many peoples who have wished for an alliance with *us*—but the fates, in all their power, have ordered us to search for an alliance with *you*. Yes, Dardanus was born here, and now he returns; and Apollo, whom we cannot disobey, has directed us to the Tiber and to Numicus' sacred spring. Aeneas sends you these small gifts from our happier days, which we rescued from the flames of Troy. This is the gold cup from which his father Anchises used to pour offerings onto the altars; this is the scepter that Priam held, whenever he assembled the people and gave them laws; this is his crown, and this is a robe that the women of Troy made for him."

Latinus listened without expression to Ilioneus' speech, sitting motionless on his throne and staring straight ahead. The gifts of the royal robe and Priam's scepter did not stir him as much as his own thoughts of his daughter's marriage and old Faunus' prophecy. Aeneas must be the man, he decided, that the oracle had spoken of, the man who would come from a foreign country to be his son-in-law. The gods would unite their kingdoms, and Aeneas' children, by their extraordinary courage and power, would rule the world.

Latinus welcomes the Trojan ambassadors

At last he answered, and his voice was full of happiness. "May the gods continue what we have begun, and may their prophecies be fulfilled! What you have asked for, we will give you. We accept your gifts; and, as long as I am king, you will have land as fertile and riches as abundant as you ever had in Troy. And as for Aeneas himself—let him approach us as our friend, our guest, our ally. He will find nothing but the friendliest of welcomes, and I myself will take his hand in peace. Now take back to him this message: I have a daughter; but our own oracle and many other omens have foretold that she is not to marry any of her countrymen. Our soothsayers have said that the future of Latium lies in new blood from abroad; and in new blood will our name be raised to heaven. I am convinced that the fates have chosen your king to be my daughter's husband—and I desire it to be so."

When he had finished, Latinus took the Trojans to his stables. There he kept three hundred gleaming horses, and he picked out one for each of them, and ordered them to be paraded in front of them—all in embroidered purple blankets, with golden trappings and golden medallions on their chests, and golden bits between their champing teeth. But his gift for the absent Aeneas was a chariot with a pair of fire-breathing horses; the ingenious Circe had bred them by mating her own mare with a stallion stolen from her father the sun. The Trojans, delighted both with what Latinus had said and what he had given them, rode back on their new horses and reported that their embassy had been entirely successful.

Juno resolves to hinder Aeneas' progress

But Juno was not so happy. She was making her way back from Argos, flying on the wind, when she had caught sight of Aeneas and the Trojan fleet from as far up in the sky as they were from Sicily. She saw that they had disembarked and, feeling that they were safe, had begun to lay out a settlement. She was filled with bitterness.

"I loathe them still, and this is not at all what I had devised for them," she muttered, with an irritable toss of her head. "Were they not supposed to die on the beach at Troy? or at least to be taken prisoner and held in chains? Did the flames consume the city but not the citizens? Not these at any rate: they found their way out through the fire and the enemy lines. My powers must have been exhausted, or perhaps I was over-wrought by the intensity of my hatred. Even when they were forced to leave their country, I did not cease to harry them. Wherever they sailed, I stood in their way however I could. But all the powers of the sea and sky have been used up, and still these Trojans survive. What good did the shoals of Libya do, or the monster Scylla, or Charybdis the whirlpool? Safe from me and safe from the sea, they have finally found shelter between the Tiber's banks. Mars was quick enough to punish the hubris of the Lapiths; Jupiter himself let Diana deal with the ancient city of Calydon—and what were the misdeeds of the Lapiths or Calydon in comparison with these people's? I am Jupiter's wife, and I have left nothing undone which I could; I have tried everything, and yet I am outmaneuvered by Aeneas. But if my own strength is insufficient, I will not hesitate to ask for help wherever I can—and if I cannot move heaven, then I will try beneath the earth. Apparently I cannot prevent Aeneas from becoming king of Latium, or from marrying Lavinia—that is fixed by fate. But I can at least delay the progress of events, and throw up obstacles before him. I will annihilate the Latins and Trojans together; this will be the price that they will pay—both the new husband and the father of the bride. And so, Lavinia, your wedding gift from Trojans and Italians will be blood, and the goddess of war will be your bridesmaid. Before Paris was born, his mother dreamed that she was would give birth to a firebrand that would destroy Troy. Now Venus' child will be a second Paris—another torch of death in another Troy."

Terrible in her anger, Juno swooped down to the underworld, and from among the Furies she summoned up Allecto, the contriver of all evil, who always nurses in her heart rage and ill-will and cruelty and treachery and war. Allecto's father is Hades, but even he despises her; and so do her sisters. She is a monster of shifting faces and hateful forms, wreathed in writhing snakes.

"Daughter of Night, I have a task well-suited to you," said Juno. "I will be left without honor or reputation if the Trojans are allowed to settle in Italy or ally themselves with Latinus by a marriage pact. You can make the most loving brothers turn against each other; you can split up the happiest of families. Your whips bring them agony and your torches death. You have a thousand names and a thousand ways of doing harm—you must contrive a way to make these young men, now contentedly at peace, first to wish for hostile action, then to demand it, and then to take it. I want you to cause a war."

Queen Amata is driven mad

So straightaway Allecto, with poisonous intent, made her way to Latium and Latinus' castle, and sat silently in the doorway of queen Amata's room. Since the first arrival of the Trojans, the queen—as any woman would—had been anxious about the marriage she had planned between Lavinia and Turnus;

but now she was becoming angry. So Allecto planned to throw the whole house into confusion by driving Amata mad. She took one of the snakes from her own hair and placed it by magic

next to Amata's heart, beneath her robe. It slipped over the smooth skin of her breasts, yet it did not touch her; Amata did not know where it was, though she thought she could feel its breath. The snake became a long golden collar around her neck; then a band across her forehead, then jewels in her hair and sliding slithering ornaments on her wrists and ankles. And a fever crept through her bones and her senses became dull, though the venom had not yet involved her mind. She did not yet feel the blaze that would soon consume her. For now she only wept a mother's tears for her daughter and her approaching marriage to the man from Troy, and she spoke gently to her husband.

"Latinus, have you decided to give Lavinia away to the Trojan refugees? Do you have no pity for her? Have you not thought about yourself—or me? This man, at the first puff of wind, will be off to sea again with my daughter, leaving us behind without a thought. You haven't forgotten how Paris wormed his way into Sparta and abducted Helen, have you? And what of the oaths that you have sworn? What of the love that you have always had for your family, and the promises that you made to Turnus? If you are determined to obey your father Faunus, if it is settled that you must look for a son-in-law who is not from Latium, I would suggest that that any land not actually ruled by you is, in some sense, foreign—and this is surely what the gods mean too. And, for that matter, if you look back far enough, you will find kings from Greece in Turnus' ancestry."

But Latinus would not listen to her arguments; and by this time the snake's venom had worked its way through her whole body. The poor woman: strange shapes and visions taunted her and, all dignity lost, she rushed out into the street.

You must have seen little boys whipping a wooden top, making it swerve in great loops and circles round an empty room; the children crowd round it, fascinated—and the harder they hit it, the faster it spins.

And that was how Amata was impelled into the town and out of it, through the rough country villages, convinced that she was a follower of Bacchus, with ever greater horror mounting in her mind and ever wilder passion. She fled into the woods, and there she hid her daughter: at least now she could hold her out of a Trojan wedding and a Trojan wedding-bed. In her frenzy she called on the god Bacchus, screaming that he alone was worthy of Lavinia, and that she would follow him and join his holy dances, with an ivy-bound staff in her hand and her hair grown long. In the town the women talked urgently among themselves, and magically they became aware that they were discontented with their lives at home. On impulse they deserted their families, bared their breasts and let their hair fly free. Some of them filled the air with high-pitched wailing, or carried vine-wood spears and dressed in animal-skins. And among them Amata set a pine-branch on fire and brandished it, singing a wedding song for Lavinia and Turnus. Her eyes were bloodshot and her voice was shrill. "Listen, you mothers of Latium, wherever you are: if you owe any favors to poor Amata, if

you understand anything of a mother's secret rights, let down your hair and dance with me."

Turnus is provoked into action

So the first stage of Allecto's scheme was complete: under the lash of Bacchic frenzy she had driven Amata deep into the woods and the corners where only wild animals lived; and the madness she had caused had thrown Latinus' plans and all his household into confusion. Now she flew on her dark wings to the walls of Turnus' town, the home of his Rutulians. It is said to have been founded by Acrisius' daughter Danae, when she came to Italy from Argos on the sharp south wind. The place was named Ardea by its first inhabitants, and Ardea it still is, though less splendid than it used to be. It was the middle of the night, and in his fortress Turnus was fast asleep. Allecto shed her grim Fury's face and form, and appeared in his dreams as an old woman; she gave herself a forehead furrowed with wrinkles and white hair bound up with olive-leaves, so that she could have been taken for one of the priestesses from the temple of Juno.

"Turnus," she said, addressing him as he lay before her. "Are you going to allow all your hard work to be wasted, and the kingdom that might have been yours handed over to Trojan colonists? King Latinus is denying you the wife and dowry and kinship that you had expected, and he has picked out a foreigner to be his heir. You have been made to look a fool; all your courage in the face of danger is meaningless. These enemies from abroad must be destroyed, and Latium left in peace. And so great Juno herself has ordered me to bring you this message, while you sleep calmly through the crisis. This is the command of the Olympian gods. Call your young men to arms; let them be ready to move out from behind their gates to destroy these barbarian interlopers who have made camp by your lovely river, and burn their painted ships. And finally, if king Latinus will not keep his word to you, if he still refuses you your rightful wife, let him see what it is to have Turnus as his enemy."

Smiling in his sleep, Turnus laughed at her. "I am not as ignorant as you think; I am well aware that a fleet has sailed up the Tiber. Don't try to frighten me—Juno is looking out for us. But your age has worn you out, and gives you no understanding of the truth. It makes you too concerned with what does not concern you. When kings take up arms, a prophet is filled with pointless fear. It is your job to guard the statues and temples of the gods; but it is men's job to fight. War—and peace—is made by men."

When Allecto heard Turnus' sneer, she could not contain her temper. She sent a sudden fit of trembling over Turnus even before he had finished speaking; he stared straight ahead, unable to comprehend the monstrous hissing form that she now took. Her flaming eyes glared at him when he hesitated and wanted to say more; and every strand of her hair became… a snake? a whip? She lashed at him, a double stinging stroke, and quickly spoke again: "So my age has worn me out, has it? And it gives me no understanding of the truth? And when kings take up arms, a prophet is filled with pointless fear? I come from the house of the Furies, and my hand brings war and death." And with that she threw a torch at him, sooty, black and smoky. It struck him just below the heart—and woke him up. Sleep was replaced by panic. Sweat broke out all over his body, and even trickled into his bones. Mindlessly he called for a sword; he looked beneath his bed, then through every room. His search for weapons became desperate, his desire for war beyond reason—but above all he was angry.

Imagine a wood fire crackling under a brass cauldron,
and flames licking up around its sides: the water leaps
and foams, a swirl of bubbles explodes upwards in
scalding steam.

So did Turnus' energy boil as he charged his young men to abandon all treaties and march on king Latinus: "To arms—Italy must be protected! Expel the intruders! Latins or Trojans—

I will go against them both!" Then he called on the gods to support his cause, while his Rutulians urged each other on—some anxious to show off their youth and good looks, others moved by the memory of their ancestors, or by their reputations as warriors.

Ascanius is tricked into starting a war

Allecto left Turnus engaging his people with dreams of glory, and on her wicked wings flew off next to the Trojan camp. By her magic she was able to spot the handsome Ascanius as he went hunting: he was setting traps for small game, and tracking other animals on foot. At once she filled his hounds' nostrils with the familiar scent of deer, and made them give furious chase—and that was how she first stirred up the country people and contrived an occasion for war.

It happened that King Latinus' estate and flocks were managed by a man called Tyrrhus. He and his children had once taken a fawn from its mother and had brought it up: it had grown into a beautiful stag with enormous antlers. His daughter Silvia had lovingly tamed it to do whatever it was told. She would twine flowers around its horns, and comb its coat and fetch water from the spring to wash it. Wherever it wandered

off into the woods, it knew its way home, and however late it was it would always return to eat from her hand.

It was this creature that Ascanius' hounds had scented—it was not far off, standing in the river to cool itself, close under the grassy bank—and Ascanius himself, always eager for praise and honor, raised his bow and took aim. The gods were with him, and he made no mistake: the arrow tore straight through the

stag's flank and into its belly. The wounded animal ran home
and stood outside its stall, covered in blood and whimpering.
The whole household heard it; it was almost like a baby cry-
ing. Silvia clapped her hands and called out to the shepherds
for help. They came at once, armed with sharpened sticks or
knotted branches or whatever their first impulse made them
pick up: they still did not know what danger they might have
to face in the silent forest. Tyrrhus was at their head, encour-
aging them hoarsely; he had been splitting oak with wedges,
and he still held a gigantic axe in his hand.

A call to arms Allecto, watching carefully, seized the
moment to do her damage. She perched
on the roof-peak of the stable, and from there she sent a signal
out over the fields, a trumpet-blast straight from the country of
the dead. Every tree shuddered and the echoes rustled through
the deepest forest, as far away as Diana's lake, or the sulfurous
white water of the river Nar, or Velinus' spring. Mothers heard
the sound, and held their children closer. But the farmers of
Latium were not afraid: they grabbed their weapons and did
not hesitate to answer Allecto's awful call—at exactly the same
time as the young Trojans poured through the gates of their
camp to help Ascanius. Lines of battle formed. But by now
the farmers had exchanged their wooden clubs and stakes for
sharpened iron; by now the drab colors of the fields were shot
with splinters of light, reflected back from shields and sword-
blades naked to the sun. They approached like a wave as it
begins to break: first a line of white foam, then a slow lifting to
a sharper crest, and finally a tower of water rising from seabed
to sky. Almo, Tyrrhus' oldest son, was the first to die, struck in
the throat by an arrow; blood muffled his voice and blocked
his last feeble breath. But after him there were many others,
including Galaesus, an old man who died trying to arrange a
truce. He was respected more than any man in Latium for his
sense of fairness and for his wealth; he had owned five flocks
of sheep, and five flocks of cattle, and it took a hundred plows
to till his fields.

The skirmish proceeded, and neither side gave ground. Allecto had delivered what she had promised—conflict and blood and death in battle. With satisfaction, she left Italy behind and flew across the sky to Juno.

"Well, I have brought about the quarrel that you asked for," she said triumphantly. "Who will persuade them now to settle their differences and come to an agreement? The Trojans now are splashed with Latin blood. But, if you will, I can spread rumors in the neighboring towns and draw them in as well. I can make them fall in love with war, and they will come from all directions to join in. I can turn the whole of Italy into a killing field."

"No," answered Juno. "Enough now of fear and trickery. A cause for war is well established, and they are already at each other's throats. Fate has sharpened their swords; fresh blood already stains them. What kind of wedding can King Latinus and Aeneas celebrate now? But Jupiter, who rules heaven and earth, would not wish you to spend further time up here; go back to where you came from. If there are any further twists of fortune to arrange, I will deal with them myself."

And so Allecto—her snakes still hissing on her wings—left the upper world and departed for her home in hell. Everyone has heard of the valley of Amsanctus; it is right in the center of Italy, high up in the mountains. On every side it is deeply shaded by thick foliage. A waterfall crashes down from the cliff-top and drops into a cleft between the rocks, where the air is foul with poisonous fumes that float upward from the river Acheron far below. It is a passage into Hades' kingdom—and into it Allecto vanished. She is a vicious spirit: earth and heaven were better for her going.

King Latinus cannot prevent the outbreak of hostilities

But now Juno gave her close attention to the brawl. The shepherds had hastily retreated into the town, bringing back their dead—young Almo and Galaesus, scarcely recognizable because of his wounds—with prayers to the gods, and protests to Latinus.

But Turnus was waiting for them, and he made them more nervous still with his warnings of fire and slaughter. "The Trojans have invaded our kingdom. They want to mix their Asian blood with ours. I have been driven out of my own inheritance!" And the men whose wives were still out dancing in the woods under the spell of Bacchus (to say nothing of Amata's influence) came together in front of Latinus' castle, pressing him to action. Regardless of omens, prophecies, or premonitions, all that they wanted was war. But Latinus was adamant, like a rock in the sea with a storm raging against it. Waves pound it and lash it; stones and pebbles rattle down its sides; the seaweed is ripped from it and washed away—and still it is unmoved. But he could not dissuade his subjects from their foolish intentions; Juno, not he, was in control of them. He called on the gods, but it might as well have been on the empty air. Then he turned to the crowd and said: "Fate has broken us. We are wafted off on the wind. You will all pay for what you have done with your blasphemous blood. And as for you, Turnus: you are to be dreadfully punished, but when you turn to the gods again, it will be too late. My own conscience is at peace; I have come to the end of my voyage, and the only thing that I regret is the chance of a happy death." After that, he had no more to say, and he locked himself up in his castle. Whatever happened now, the responsibility would not be his.

When the people of Latium decided to go to war, there was a particular ritual which had to be carried out. The ritual was later passed on to Alba Longa, and then to Rome. To this day, whether they intend to bring blood and tears to the tribes of Asia, or to recapture battle-standards lost long ago, or to march beyond India to the dawn, the Romans follow it exactly. It involves two gates—the Gates of War—that are sacred to Mars and therefore held in great awe. They are held closed by a hundred bronze bolts and bars of everlasting iron, and the spirit of old king Janus stands eternal guard over them. But when it is clear that the Senate has chosen war, the consul himself, in a robe of scarlet stripes and a ceremonial sash, must push them until they swing back, grating against their stone threshold. He shouts a war cry, and young men echo him with fanfares on bronze bugles.

It was this tradition that the Latins, eager for a formal declaration of war against Aeneas' forces, now tried to persuade their king to follow. "Open the gates," they shouted.

But he refused to touch them. "This is a duty that I cannot perform," he said, and turned away into the darkness. But Juno flew down from Olympus and with her own hand pushed against the hinges. The hinges gave way—and the Gates of War stood open.

Passions in Latium now ran unchecked: there were no more questions to be asked. Infantry drilled in the fields, cavalry pirouetted in clouds of dust. Everywhere the Latins brought out their armor, smeared shields and javelins with grease, sharpened axes, hoisted standards and obeyed the bugle-calls. In five towns—Atina, Tibur, Ardea, Crustumeri and turreted Antemnae—anvils were set up for new weapons. Everyone fitted on headgear, beat out breastplates from bronze and greaves from silver, wove new wicker shield-bosses. Work in the fields with plows and sickles seemed tedious now, and as for the smithies—who would not rather re-temper his father's sword? The farmers sounded bugles, passed watchwords. They snatched down helmets from their places on the wall. They hitched snorting horses to chariots. They tried on armor and elaborate tunics, and buckled on faithful old swords.

A roster of Turnus' allies
Now is the moment to make a formal list of the kings who came down into the plain with their armies to fight. Now is the time to show how all Italy burst into flower with young men in armor. Yet only the gods of history remember for certain who they were; and if it were not for the gods, this famous tale would float to us only as a memory on the wind.

• Mezentius first, a cruel man who despised the gods: he brought reinforcements from Etruria, and with him came his son Lausus. They said that only Turnus was better looking than

Lausus, who was also famous for his skill in breaking horses and his persistence in hunting down wild game. In the end, though, it was to no purpose that he led out his thousand men from their city of Agylla. He would have been happier in his father's kingdom if Mezentius had not been his father.

• Aventinus, driving his prize-winning chariot and pair, a handsome son of handsome Hercules. On his shield were engraved a hundred serpents and the hundred heads of the monster Hydra, which made up his father's emblem. Hercules, on his way home to Greece from Spain, where he had killed Geryon and stolen his cattle, had stopped in Latium to wash them in a stream. There he had seduced the priestess Rhea— he was a god and she was a mortal—and she gave birth to Aventinus in secret on the wooded slopes of the hill which is now called after him. Aventinus' men carried spears and pikes into battle, and they fought with both stabbing-swords and javelins. He himself marched into Turnus' stronghold dressed like his father, with the hide of an enormous shaggy lion slung across his shoulders and its teeth gleaming over his forehead.

• Catillus and Coras, brothers from a fort at Tibur: Tibur is called after their brother Tiburtinus, but they came originally from Argos. They would always be found in the front line wherever the fighting was fiercest, brash as a pair of cloud-born centaurs who come charging down from the peak of some snow-covered mountain in Thessaly. The trees part to let them through and the undergrowth lies flat under their trampling feet.

• Caeculus, the founder of Praeneste: he had been abandoned as a child, but was thought to be a son of Vulcan the fire-god. He was king over a country of shepherds, and they followed him from the heights above the town or the grazing-land or the spray-splashed banks of icy mountain streams. They were a ragged army: only a few had conventional armor or shields or chariots. Most of them were armed with slings from which they shot lead pellets, and some carried a pair of javelins. They wore caps of fawn wolf-skin, and their custom was to walk with their left feet bare and their right feet laced into boots.

• Messapus, son of Neptune: a famous horseman and invulnerable to fire or sword. His people were unadventurous and inexperienced in war—some lived high up on the peak of mount Soracte, some lower down in the fields or forests, or in woods beside a lake—but he had brought out his weapons again and lined them up for battle. They marched to the steady beat of a song in honor of their king, but their singing might have reminded you of the cries of long-necked swans, which you can hear all over the marshes and rivers of Asia as they return from their feeding grounds. And you would never have thought that they were a formation of troops in full armor: they looked more like a gaggle of raucous birds clapping in to shore from far out at sea.

• Clausus, born from the ancient blood of the Sabines: he led a mighty force—and indeed he was a mighty force in himself. Ever since the Romans allied themselves with the Sabines, his descendants, the Claudian family, have been widespread through Latium. His soldiers came from every town and valley, every rocky hillside or olive grove, along the whole length of the Tiber and the Tiber's tributaries. They came from both banks of the Allia—a bad omen, because later a Roman army would be defeated there. They were as countless as the breakers driven onto the Libyan coast by the gales which spring up when Orion sets into the winter sea; or as the ears of wheat rippling gold under the spring sun on the plain south of Troy, or in the wheat-fields of Lycia. They beat out a rhythm on their shields and the ground cowered under the tramping of their feet.

• Halaesus, a son of Troy's greatest enemy Agamemnon: he rode in a chariot at the head of thousands of ferocious tribesmen eager to fight for Turnus. Their fathers had sent them to the war from the hills of Aurunca or the flatlands of Sidicinum, or from the valley of the shallow Volturnus river, where they scratched up the rich soil with mattocks in order to plant vines. Their traditional weapons were javelins which they threw by means of leather thongs. In their left hands they carried small round shields, and for close work they used swords curved like sickles.

• Oebalus, rumored to be the son of the nymph Sebethis and Telon, king of Capreae: Telon was old now, and Oebalus, not content with the territory that his father ruled, had added to it much of the surrounding land, including the water meadows by the river Sarnus, and the apple-orchards which lay below the walls of Abella. His soldiers, like the Germans, fought with long javelins. Their headgear was made of bark stripped off the cork-tree, but their lightweight shields and swords were made of gleaming bronze.

• Ufens, from the mountain town of Nersae: he was always fortunate in battle and of admirable reputation, and his people were the Aequi, tough above all others whether they were hunting or plowing their hard lumpy soil. They wore their armor even when they were working in the fields. They loved to rob their neighbors, and they lived off what they stole.

• The courageous Umbro: he was a priest, sent by king Archippus from Marruvia, and he wore on his helmet a sprig of lucky olive. He could put vipers and poisonous water-snakes to sleep by the touch of his hand and the sound of his voice; he could soothe their anger and cure their bites. But his magic was not proof against a Trojan spear, and neither his lullabies nor the herbs which he picked in the mountains could heal a battle-wound. The trees and pools of his home country, and the glassy water of Lake Fucinus, would mourn for him.

• Virbius, sent by his mother: in answer to Turnus' summons, he brought his eager chariot-team across the plain at a full gallop. He had been brought up near the fountain of the nymph Egeria, where there is a pleasant and peaceful altar dedicated to Diana. He was beautiful and brave, the son of Hippolytus, whose stepmother was Phaedra. According to the legend, Phaedra told slanderous lies about him to his father, and his father banished him. As he fled from his father's vengeance,

Hippolytus' horses were spooked by sea-monsters; his chariot overturned and he was killed. But because Diana loved him, he was brought back again to the upper air by the medicine of the god Aesculapius. Jupiter, angry that any mortal should return from the underworld to light and life, struck Aesculapius with a thunderbolt (even though he was the son of Apollo) and threw him down into the river Styx. But Diana hid Hippolytus in a secret place and then sent him off to Egeria's grove, where he survived, unrecognized and with a changed name. And to this day horses are not allowed into Diana's temple or her sacred precincts.

• Camilla, at the head of a column of cavalry, drawn up by squadrons and bright in their bronze breastplates: she was from the Volscian people—a warrior-woman who knew nothing about looms or wool-baskets or Minerva's arts, but could fight all day without tiring, and outrun the wind. You might almost think that she could fly over the tops of the standing crops without disturbing a single green blade or delicate ear; or make  her way over the surface of the sea, skimming the waves and not touching their crests with the soles of her feet. Young men left their huts or the fields to watch her go by, and women came out in crowds to admire her. In silence they wondered at the royal purple swinging across her smooth shoulders, at her hair gathered up with a golden pin, at her quiver of arrows and her rough-cut myrtle spear.

• And finally, Turnus himself: he was outstanding for his physique and stood a head taller than all the others. His helmet had a triple crest, and on it was engraved Chimaera, a monster who breathed fire like the volcano Etna: the more she raged and spat her flaming poison, the more the battlefield ran with blood. His shield was inlaid with golden images of Inachus and his daughter Io: he had become a river, flowing from a decorated waterspout, and she had been miraculously transformed into a heifer, sprouting first bristles and then horns, with the hundred-eyed Argus always on watch over her. Behind Turnus a cloud of footsoldiers spread across the plain, shields at the ready: his own Rutulians, reinforced by young recruits from Argos, veterans from Sicily, and contingents from many of the Latin towns. They came from the Tiber valley or Numicus' spring, from the Rutulian hills and a ridge named after Circe. They came from the farms of Anxur which Jupiter especially protects, and from the woods loved by Feronia, the goddess of all green things. And they came from the dreary marsh of Satura, where a freezing river winds along the valley bottom and tips into the sea.

Book VIII

New Allies and New Armor

Book VIII
New Allies and New Armor

The Latins look for reinforcements from southern Italy, while Aeneas receives a promise from the god of the river

The war began.

Turnus cracked his whip, and from his citadel he gave a signal, which the hoarse bugles passed on. Anticipation of action stirred every heart in Latium, and set every young spirit on fire. Messapus arrived with the first reinforcements, then Ufens and Mezentius who despised the gods. All able-bodied men had enrolled, and the fields were empty. A messenger was sent to the city of the Greek hero Diomedes in the south; he was instructed to explain that a band of Trojans had landed in Latium, and then to ask for help. "Aeneas has brought ashore the gods of his conquered city and he claims that it is his destiny to be our next king. Many local tribes support him and all over Latium we hear more and more talk about him. What will be the end of this beginning? What will be the outcome of the struggle, if fortune is on his side? You would perhaps know this better than either Turnus or Latinus."

This, then, was the situation in Latium. Aeneas observed it all, and his mind was flooded with anxiety, with courses of action chosen and then rejected. What should he do for the best? His thoughts moved off in one direction, then swiftly in another; they were like the shattered reflections of the sun or the moon in a bowl of water, which flicker across the walls and in the air, and dance at random on a coffered ceiling.

Night: when birds and animals were everywhere at rest, he lay on the riverbank under the cold stars, restless with plans for the impending war. At last he fell asleep. In a dream he saw the god of the place rising from among the poplar trees, the god of the pleasant river, wrapped in a cloak of floating gray linen, with reeds entwined in his hair. It was old Tiber himself.

"Son of Venus," he said in a soothing voice. "You have brought Troy here, safe from her enemies; and here you will rebuild her to stand for ever. On the soil of Italy, in the land of Latium, we have been waiting for you. This is to be your home; and here your household gods will find protection. Look at me: you must not be frightened by any threats of violence. The gods are no longer angry with you. And to prove to you that this is no false dream, I promise you that soon, among the oak trees on the bank, you will find a great white sow; she will be lying on the ground, suckling her new-born piglets—thirty of them, and they will be white as well. This will be the site of Alba Longa, the famous city which Ascanius, thirty years from now, will found. There can be no doubt of it.

"Now listen—I will tell you briefly how you may emerge successfully from your present difficulty. Not far from here there is a community of Greeks: they are descended from an early king of Athens. They came to this place with their king Evander, and they have built a town in the hills, which they call Pallanteum after their founding father. They are perpetually at war with the Latins; you should therefore make them your allies, and strike a treaty with them. I will take you to them. Follow the river upstream, and I will make sure that your oarsmen make good progress against the current. As soon as the stars set, you must make your prayers to Juno and appease her with sacrifices. And then, when you have won the war, you may honor me. I am the river: it is I who glide between these banks and curve through these fertile fields—blue Tiber, the river that the gods love most. This is my home; and from here great cities will one day spring." He turned away and disappeared, down to the bottom of his deep pool.

It was already morning, and Aeneas could sleep no longer. He stood and looked toward the rising sun, and then he scooped up water in his hands, and poured it on the ground as a libation. "My prayer is to all the water-nymphs of Latium," he said, "and especially to you, father Tiber. Take me under your protection and keep me safe. Whatever form you may have when you take pity on my misfortunes, lake or waterfall or spring, I will always honor you and offer the sacrifices that are due to you. Horned river-ruler of the waters of Italy, stand by me and let me feel your presence."

Aeneas follows the river-god's advice and travels up the river

After his prayer was finished, Aeneas made ready two ships to be rowed up the river, and saw to it that their crews were well armed. And there in front of them, lying on the green grass under a tree, was a white sow, with her white piglets beside her. It was a miracle, an omen not to be ignored—and Aeneas immediately cut their throats, and laid them on an altar as a sacrifice to Juno. All that night, as long as it was dark, Tiber smoothed out his wrinkled surface for the Trojans, and the current lost its force; it was as if he had turned it into a lake or a reed-sheltered pool, a shiny floor of water. The crews hardly needed to pull on their oars, and they talked gratefully to each other as their ships slipped on with increasing speed. The river and the trees on the banks had never seen such wonderfully shining shields, such cheerfully painted timbers. They rowed on through that day and the next night, round long shady bends on water green with reflections of overhanging leaves. At noon on the second day, they caught sight of walls and battlements in the distance, and occasional rooftops. It was Evander's capital—in those days a town of little distinction, but today the place where the towers of Rome go up to scrape the sky. They turned their prows toward the bank.

Aeneas addresses King Evander

On that day, in a grove in front of his gates, Evander happened to be presiding over a banquet in honor of Hercules and the other gods. Pallas, his son, attended him, with his chief warriors and an unassuming group of advisors. They looked up from the swirling incense and the blood still hot on the altars, to watch the warships sliding silently in to shore beneath the trees. They were alarmed and jumped up from the table; only Pallas had the presence of mind to warn them not to interrupt their ceremony. He seized a spear and went to face the strangers. "Why have you come here, so far inland?" he called, standing above them on the bank. "Where are you going? Where are you from? Who are you? Do you bring war or peace?"

Then Aeneas stood up in the stern of his ship and held up an olive branch as a symbol of peace. "We are from Troy. We are armed because the Latins have insolently declared war on us, even though we tried to avoid it. We are looking for king Evander. Tell him, if you will, that envoys from the Trojans have come to seek alliance with him."

The mention of the great name of Troy astonished Pallas. "Come ashore, whoever you are," he said. "You are welcome. You must come to speak to my father." They clasped hands, and together they went from the riverbank into the grove.

Aeneas addressed the king courteously: "My lord, I count myself fortunate that I can approach you and hold out these signs of friendship. You were distinguished among the Greeks; but though you are of the same family as Agamemnon and

Menelaus, I see no reason to fear you now. I am known for my courage, and I am obedient both to the prophecies of the gods and the commands of the fates; and you are famous throughout the world. Since, moreover, we are related by blood, it is only right that we should be linked together. According to Greek legend, Dardanus, the first founder of Troy, was the son of Electra, and Electra was the daughter of Atlas, who holds heaven and earth on his shoulders. Your father was Mercury, and his mother was Maia, who gave birth to him on the cold summit of mount Cyllene. But Maia—if the story is to be believed—was also a daughter of Atlas. So you and Dardanus are of the same blood.

"Relying on these family connections, I have not sent ambassadors to represent me, nor have I made my approaches to you by any complicated diplomacy; I have come myself, in person, as a suppliant to your door. The Latins are at war with you—and now with us as well. If they drive us out, nothing will satisfy them till they bring all of Italy under their control, as well as the sea to east and west. You have my word; now give me yours. Our hearts are ready for war, our spirits are high, our young men are hardened in battle."

Evander's answer

As Aeneas was speaking, Evander never took his eyes off his face. When his speech was finished, he continued to examine him carefully before he answered. "It gives me great pleasure, sir, to receive you in friendship, as my guest. You were indeed distinguished among the Trojans, and I remember your father well—both his face and his voice. Priam of Troy once went to visit his sister in Salamis, and later he came to Arcadia, my country. I was young then—my beard was just beginning to show—but I still recall how much I admired the Trojan princes, including, of course, Priam himself. But it was Anchises who really stood out. I longed to speak to him—I was only a boy—and take him by the hand. And I did actually go up to him and show him round the walls of the famous town of Pheneum; and when he left he gave me a wonderful quiver and arrows, a cloak interwoven with gold, and two gold bridles which I have passed on to my son Pallas. So, as you wish, I will join my hand with yours to seal a pact. At the first sign of light tomorrow morning, I will give you reinforcements and supplies, and send you on your way.

"And now you are our allies. Sit down with us. And in the future, to celebrate our friendship, you must come to us each year to join us at this banquet—an appointment which you must not miss, or it will bring you bad luck."

Evander ordered the food and wine to be put back on the table, and showed the Trojans where they should sit on the grass; but for Aeneas, who was the guest of honor, he threw a lion-skin over a wooden throne. A priest and selected young men took turns to serve Aeneas and his companions. They offered wine and bread in baskets and the rump of a roasted ox, whose entrails were put aside for sacrifice.

The story of Hercules and Cacus

When everyone had finished eating, and everyone's hunger was satisfied, Evander stood up. "My honored guest," he said," I should explain to you that we have not met here for this feast and these rituals because of any vague superstition, or a misunderstanding of the gods' intentions. We honor the gods in this way because they once saved us from a terrible disaster. Do you see that rocky cliff-face? No one lives up there now, and landslides have left nothing except a jumble of scattered boulders. But there used to be a cave there, set back in a valley in permanent shadow, the lair of a half-man, half-animal called Cacus. He was very dangerous. The ground was always warm with the blood of passersby that he had caught. He murdered them, and then he would hang up their heads to rot at the opening of his cave. Cacus' father was Vulcan the blacksmith god; and as he lumbered about he would pant Vulcan's fiery black breath. We prayed to be rid of him, and in time a god arrived to bring us help.

"It was Hercules, on his way back home in triumph after slaughtering the three-headed monster Geryon, and he was driving the cattle he had taken as plunder—there were so many of them that, when he brought them down to the river, they seemed to fill the whole valley. To Cacus' criminal mind they offered a challenge: he would always try to steal anything that did not belong to him. He removed four fine bulls from their enclosure, and four fine heifers. And he dragged them back to his lair by their tails, so that their tracks pointed in the opposite direction to the one in which they were actually going, and he hid them among the rocks. No one who came looking for them would see hoof-prints leading to the cave.

"The next day, Hercules prepared for his departure. But as he let his cattle out of the enclosure, they began to bellow. They were reluctant to move, and their protests echoed to and fro across the valley and up into the hills. But from deep inside Cacus' cave, one of the stolen heifers bellowed in answer, and Cacus' hopes of tricking Hercules were undone. Hercules lost his temper: he snatched up his knotted oak club and went bounding up the mountain. For the first time, we saw Cacus confused and frightened. Fear put wings on his feet, and quicker than the wind he fled back into his cave. Over the entrance he had suspended a huge boulder by iron chains—he had made them using skills learned from his father. He released the chains, the boulder came down to block the doorway, and he shut himself up inside.

"But Hercules was close behind, looking over the entrance from every possible angle and grinding his teeth with rage. Three times he explored all round the mountain; three times he tried to break down the stone door, and three times he returned exhausted to the valley. Behind the cave, as high

as the eye could see, rose a sheer smooth cliff, a safe place
for birds of prey to build their nests. At the highest point of
the cliff a peak leaned leftward over the river. Hercules put
his weight against it: he forced it back to the right, struck
it sharply to loosen its roots—and ripped off the top of the
mountain. There was a crack, like thunder. Riverbanks leapt

apart. Terrified streams reversed their flow. The cave of Cacus
was opened up to human eyes, and its darkest corners held
no more secrets. It was as if the earth had split open to reveal
the underworld, as if the pale palace of Hades, so detested by
the other gods, had been suddenly unveiled so that the spirits
of the dead, cowering in the flood of light, could look upward
into the abyss of heaven.

"Trapped inside his cave, Cacus was unexpectedly caught
in the glare. He howled with frustration, but Hercules stood
above him and pelted him with spears, then called for us to

come and attack him too with heavy timbers and millstones. There was no way for Cacus to escape. But—can you believe this?—he belched out such a gust of soot and smoke that the cave was filled with a toxic blackness, except for flames flickering in the furthest corners—and we could no longer see him. But there was no holding Hercules: he leapt straight down where the smoke was thickest, and grabbed hold of Cacus, still futilely spitting fire. First he twisted his limbs into knots, and choked him till his eyes popped out and the blood stopped flowing in his throat. Then he broke down the door of the cave and let in the light: his cattle were revealed and the gods could see exactly how Cacus had tried to hide his crime. Finally he dragged out Cacus' corpse by the feet.

"No one could have enough of gazing at the hairy half-human body, the fearsome eyes and the mouth still blackened by the traces of extinguished flames. Ever since that day, we have celebrated our deliverance, and the younger generation is happy to continue the tradition. That's why Hercules has a temple here: the priest in charge of it has built an altar that we hold most sacred—and we always will." Evander wound a spray of blossoming poplar—Hercules' own tree—in his hair, so that the leaves shaded his face. He lifted up an enormous goblet. "So, my young friends," he charged, "remember those great deeds: put garlands on your heads, worship the god that we all share, and with a cheerful grace make libations to him." And round the table they all made toasts and praised the gods.

By now evening was creeping down the slopes of Olympus. The high priest and his colleagues came forward, as was their custom, dressed in animal skins and bearing torches. They brought fresh food so that the feasting could begin again, and more dishes filled with offerings for the gods. Then priests, garlanded with poplar, danced and sang hymns at the altars, and choruses of old and young men took turns in praising Hercules and telling stories of his feats. They recounted how he had with his bare hands strangled the two snakes sent by Juno to his cradle; how he had destroyed mighty cities;

how he had carried out a thousand tasks set him by king Erys-theus and arranged by the angry Juno. "Unconquered Hercu-les," they sang. "The cloud-born centaurs could not escape you, the monstrous bull from Crete could not defeat you, the lion of Nemea could not overcome you. You smoothed the wa-ters of the river Styx, you entered the blood-splashed cave of Cerberus and tamed him as he snarled among his half-chewed bones. You feared no monster, whatever its shape—not even the giant Typhoeus in his armor. You outwitted Hydra, the many-headed serpent. Come to us, true son of Jupiter. You have increased the glory of the glorious gods. Look with favor on us and on the feast that we hold in your honor." In songs and dances that echoed through the hills and forests they re-membered every one of the hero's achievements—and above all they celebrated the destruction of Cacus' cave and the end of the fire-breathing Cacus himself.

Evander shows Aeneas around the future site of Rome

When the rituals were complete they returned to the town. The elderly king Evander walked with his son on one side of him and Aeneas on the other; in their eager conversation, he forgot how tired his long day had made him. Aeneas was fascinated by every-thing that he saw along the way, and with great curiosity he asked to hear all the old legends. And Evander, who had him-self established the fortress which was one day to be the cen-ter of Rome, told him the story of his town. "Woodland spirits were once the only inhabitants of this spot. Then a race of men was born from the trees; they took their strength from the trunks of oaks. They had no traditions, no common way of life. They did not know how to yoke oxen for plowing, nor how to bring in a harvest or keep seed for another year. They survived by hunting, and by gathering fruit and leaves. When the old god Saturn, banished from Olympus by Jupiter, came to them as an exile, he found them disorganized and scattered up and down the mountain slopes. He brought them togeth-er and gave them laws. And he called their country Latium, which in their language meant "safe hiding place." The time of peace and quiet that they knew under his protection we now call the Golden Age. But as the years went by the gold became gradually tarnished by greed and a mad desire for war. Tribes from Greece and Sicily mingled with them, and the people of Saturn lost their old identity. They were ruled now by kings, including the fierce Thybris, from whom the river Tiber got its present name (it used to be called Albula). I come from Greece myself. I was exiled from Arcadia, and, after a long and adventurous voyage—there is no arguing with Fortune or the fates—I settled here, in a place that was ordained for me by Apollo and my mother, the nymph Carmentis.

As they continued, Evander pointed out the altar and the gate which the Romans still call Carmentalis in honor of his mother; she could foretell the future and was the first to prophesy the greatness of Aeneas' family and of Pallanteum. He showed him too the wood where later Romulus would shelter the outcasts who made up the first population of Rome, and the spot under the cool shade of a rock which the Arcadian people say belongs to the god Pan—later to be called the Lupercal: "the place of the wolf." He showed him the Argiletum—a stand of trees whose name means "death of a man from Argos." He showed him the Tarpeian rock—now Rome's splendid Capitol, but then covered with creeper and briars. In those days, the country people thought it was haunted, and they were afraid of it and the forest around it.

"And in the next wood," Evander went on, "at the top of the hill, is the home of a god. We don't know which god it is, but the Arcadians claim that they've often seen Jupiter himself up there, beating on his shield and summoning the thunderclouds. And you see those two ruined hamlets? They date from very long ago, and the walls they once had have fallen down. They both used to have castles in them, one built by Janus, and the other by Saturn—so they are called Janiculum and Saturnia."

At last they arrived at Evander's house: it was not much of a place, and there were herds of cattle wandering about and lowing in what is now the Roman forum and the elegant Street of the Carinae. "Don't forget that Hercules once passed through these doors," Evander said, "and slept under this very roof. It's hard to understand that riches are not everything; but if you conduct yourself as he once did, and don't think any less of me because I am poor, you are welcome." He led Aeneas to a room beneath the gable, and gave him a bed of leaves with the skin of a Libyan bear as a coverlet. Night came on fast, and wrapped the earth in her soft dark wings.

Venus visits Vulcan and asks him to make new armor for Aeneas

But Venus was perturbed—and, as Aeneas' mother, rightly perturbed—by the hostility of the Latins. She was afraid that much trouble was approaching. And so she invited Vulcan the smith into her golden chamber and spoke softly and lovingly to him.

"My dear husband, did I ever ask you to help the poor Trojans, even when their city seemed certain to fall to the Greeks and go up in flames? Did I ever ask you to work for them, or use your skill to protect them? No—because I did not wish you to use your power to no purpose, however much I owed in those days to the children of Priam, and however hard it was to see Aeneas in such trouble. Aurora once came to you in tears, and so did Achilles' mother, Thetis: they were able to soften your heart, and you granted their requests. But now the time has come when I must implore a favor of you—because I love you, and because I love my son. Aeneas is standing today on the shore of Italy because Jupiter has commanded him; and now he needs new armor. The Latins have massed together behind their walls—look at them! Their gates are closed against Aeneas; their weapons are sharpened for war. They are determined to destroy my people—and me."

Vulcan hesitated. But when Venus put her arms round him, and gently pressed herself against him, he felt a sudden surge of warmth, a familiar heat. Like a flash of light that glitters along a rift between two thunderclouds, it entered his heart and weakened his limbs;. And Venus was glad when she felt him stirring at her beauty, and his resolve undone by love. "You are casting about too far for reasons to persuade me," he said. "Have you lost faith in me, my dear? Even if you had come to me earlier, it would not have been wrong for me to give armor to the Trojans, because almighty Jupiter and the fates decreed that Troy should stand, and Priam should survive, for ten more years. But now, if you are sure that war is what you want, I promise to dedicate to you the gift of my most careful workmanship. I will make you whatever I can from iron or gold or silver, and it will be as perfect as my furnace and my bellows will allow. You must trust the power of your prayers." And with that, exactly as she wished, he returned her embrace, and lay down beside her, and slipped quietly into sleep.

Vulcan's workshop

But just after midnight he awoke, and could not go back to sleep.

> It was the hour when a woman who must spend her
> life in spinning—a thankless task—rattles the embers
> in the grate and makes sure that her servant-girls are
> up and ready to card their wool by lamplight; she her-
> self has worked all day and half the night so that she
> may be a good wife to her husband and give a decent
> upbringing to her small children.

He got up out of his snug bed and flew off to his smithy on the island of Sicily, beneath mount Etna. He landed at a place where smoke curls up from a crevasse, and thunder grumbles from deep under the ground. Here the giant Cyclopes have hollowed out a cavern for their workshops: you can hear them hammering on the anvils, and the sizzling of tempered metal, and the roar of their fire-breathing furnaces. This is his home, and the country is called Vulcania after him.

The Cyclopes, stripped to the waist, were hard at work. They had almost completed work on a thunderbolt for Jupiter to throw down from heaven to earth. Already they had fitted it with triple tornadoes, triple rain-clouds, triple bursts of yellow fire and southerly gales; and—as a final touch—they were adding terrifying flashes of lightning and the crackling, clattering noise of rage and fear and flame. Some of them were attaching wheels to a chariot in which Mars might visit conflict on men and cities. Others they were making armor for Minerva: on her shield they were polishing awful patterns of golden dragons' scales, and on her breastplate they had engraved the Gorgon's severed head, with glaring eyes and snakes instead of hair.

"Cyclopes of Etna," said Vulcan, "drop your tools, and leave whatever it is that you have begun. Listen to me now: your next job is make armor for a distinguished hero. It will take all your strength and dexterity, all your experience and skill—and it must be finished very quickly."

He needed to say no more; the giants went straight to work and divided up the various operations between themselves, while streams of bronze and gold and vivid steel ran molten in their furnaces. Bellows panted in and out. Metal cooled in hissing water. They lifted the ingots onto the anvils that lay heavy on the creaking floor, turning them in the grip of their tongs, twisting them and forcing them into shape—all for a great shield in a pattern of seven concentric circles, designed to stand alone against all the weapons of the Latins.

Evander urges Aeneas to find more allies among the Etruscans

While Vulcan was giving his instructions to the Cyclopes in Sicily, Evander was woken by the light of dawn and by birds chirping under the eaves of his simple house. He put on a tunic and sandals, strapped on his sword and threw a panther-skin over his left shoulder, and the two dogs that guarded his door went ahead of him and kept their master company. Remembering their conversation and the gifts that he had promised, he went to Aeneas' room, and found that he too was up early. They greeted each other and sat down together to talk. Aeneas' companion, Achates, and young Pallas joined them.

"My dear general," began the king. "As long as you are alive, I will never think of Troy as a conquered city. But even for such a man as you, we have few resources to help you in war. On one side we're shut in by the river, and on the other Turnus is pressing us hard. From our walls we can hear the jangling of his army's weapons. However, it unexpectedly turns out that I can arrange reinforcements for you from rich and powerful friends. You are indeed here on the orders of the fates.

"Not far from here, in the hills of Etruria, is the city of Agylla, an ancient foundation, where once a people from Lydia settled. They were a famous people, magnificent warriors, and they flourished there for many years. But then a king called Mezentius came to the throne: he was arrogant, capricious and aggressive. I cannot tell you of the crimes that he committed during his reign—they are unspeakable. He's a murderer as well as a tyrant. I only wish that the gods would do to him and his children what he has done to others. His most revolting torture was to lash his victims face to face and mouth to mouth with corpses. Leaking blood and pus, the dead would infect the living and bring them to a slow and painful end. But recently his citizens rebelled: they couldn't tolerate his atrocious deeds any longer. They surrounded the palace, killed his bodyguard and set fire to his apartments. But Mezentius escaped; under cover of the fighting he slipped

away to the territory of the Rutulians, where Turnus has taken him in as an ally. That has made the people of Agylla more furious still, and now they're demanding that their king be sent back to them for punishment. There are thousands of them, and you, Aeneas, can take command of them all. I'll show you how to get there. Their ships are drawn up all along the riverbank. They are ready for war—but an omen holds them back. They have an old prophet who has brought them this word from the gods: 'You are the best young men of Etruria, better and braver than any Etruscans who have gone before you. You are right to be angry with Mezentius, and he deserves your anger. But it is ordained that no one from Italy can overcome such an enemy. You should choose a foreigner to lead you.' The Etruscans are uneasy at this warning, and their army will not move from its position. Their chief, a man called Tarchon, has sent envoys to me, offering me the crown and the scepter of Etruria; he wants me to accept them as symbols of sovereignty, and to come to their camp as their king. But I am an old man: my blood is running colder and I'm getting slower in my movements. I can't take over their kingdom; it's too late to expect great deeds from me. I would have urged my son Pallas to do it, but his mother was Italian and he takes half his lineage from her.

"But *you,* on the other hand, are favored by the fates both in your youth and in your nationality. The gods surely intend you to be a leader of Trojans and Italians together. Go to the Etruscans; and Pallas, my hope and my consolation, shall go with you. It's time that he learned to be a soldier and to take on the responsibilities of a warrior. In these earliest days of his youth, you will be an example for him, someone to look up to, a tutor. I will send two hundred Arcadian horsemen with him, the pick of our strong young men. And Pallas will give you two hundred more, as his own gift to you."

During this speech, Aeneas and the loyal Achates had kept their eyes on the ground. They were still thinking doubtfully of the difficulties ahead of them, when Venus sent them a sign from an empty heaven: a bolt of lightning quivering through the air, with a thunderclap behind it. The world tipped and slanted round them. An Etruscan trumpet call: crash after crash assaulted them, clouds had piled up in a cloudless sky, glowing like warriors in blood-red armor; and thunder clattered like the sound of battle. Everyone stood spellbound, except Aeneas; he recognized a promise that his mother had made. "Evander," he said, "do not ask me to explain this portent, but I know it is intended for me. My mother Venus told me that, if ever war threatened, she would send me this sign and that she would bring new arms from Vulcan to help me. I foresee death for the Latins, and a terrible punishment for Turnus. I see shields and helmets sinking in the Tiber, brave soldiers' bodies tumbled in the waves. So let the Latins break their agreements. And if they want war, let them have it."

Aeneas sets off for Etruria, accompanied by Evander's son

Aeneas rose from his chair. He confidently approached the shrines where he had prayed the day before, and relit the fires on Hercules' altar. Evander and the young men of Troy selected sheep for the customary sacrifice, and then Aeneas went back to his ships and gave orders to his men. A few, chosen for their courage, would accompany him to Etruria. The rest were to row easily downstream on the flat water; they were to tell Ascanius what had happened and report on his father's plans. Evander gave horses to those Trojans who were going with Aeneas; Aeneas' own horse had a lion-skin, dirty-yellow with gilded claws, spread over its back.

Meanwhile the rumor spread through Pallanteum that an expedition was about to leave for the castle of the Etruscan king, and the prospect of war loomed vividly in the anxious women's minds. The more their apprehension grew, the more desperately they prayed, while Evander seized his son's hand and wept. No one could console him.

"If only Jupiter could bring back to me those years that are now long past. In those days, I slaughtered a whole army under the walls of Praeneste and set alight a whole mountain of shields that I had taken from them. In those days, I fought singlehandedly with King Erulus. His mother was a nymph, and when he was born—it's a strange story—she had given him three lives to live. I killed him once, and stripped him of his armor. I killed him a second time, and stripped him of his armor. I killed him a third time, and stripped him of his armor, and I finally sent him down to Hades. If I were still young, you, my son, would never have to be torn from my arms, and Mezentius would never have come so insolently into my country and massacred my men and left my women widows. I beg you, Jupiter and all the gods of Olympus whom you rule: as I am king of the Arcadians, pity me; and as I am a father, hear my prayers. If you intend to keep Pallas safe, if it is my lot to see him again, then let me live, and I do not care what burden of suffering you may lay upon me. But if he is fated to be killed in action, then let me die while I still do not know his future, while I can hold out hope for him, and touch my hand to his. As long as I still have you, my dearest boy, the only joy of my old age, no calamity can harm me." As soon as he had finished his farewell, he fainted. His attendants carried him back indoors.

Meanwhile the gates had been opened for the cavalry to pass through. Aeneas rode in front, with Achates as usual at his side and the young Trojans close behind. Among them was Pallas, in an elegant cloak and breastplate; his face was as bright and eager as Venus' morning star, which dispels the darkness from the ocean and the sky. Mothers stood fearful on the walls, peering after the shimmer of dust and armor as long as they could see it. But the horsemen trotted on through the brush until they came to the place where the road ended, and then, at a shouted order, they shifted their formation. To the sound of their horses' hooves drumming on the dry bare ground, they galloped across the plain until they came to a stand of pine-trees near a cold-running stream. For generations the place had been sacred: the very earliest inhabitants of Latium had dedicated it to Silvanus, the god of fields and flocks, and used to hold feasts there in his honor. A ring of steep hills encircled it, and from the top of the ridge, Aeneas could look down on the tents of Tarchon and the Etruscan army, spreading out far over the fields. But his own men were weary: for the moment they must look to their horses, and rest themselves.

Venus delivers Aeneas' new armor

Venus too was not far off. With her pale shining aura wrapped around her, she flew down through the clouds to bring Aeneas his gifts. When she saw him encamped in the distant valley by the stream, she revealed herself to him and said: "Here are the arms that I promised you, which Vulcan has made. Now you need not hesitate to challenge Turnus, or any of the arrogant Latins." She kissed him, and placed the shining arms beneath an oak-tree. He was elated by the gifts and by her generosity; and he could not take his eyes off

them. He examined them, picking them up one by one and turning them over in his hands. There was a fiercely-plumed helmet, which shot out daggers of reflected light; a murderous sword; a bronze-plated tunic—well-fitted for a hero—shining like a cloud at evening, which first glows with the colors of sunset and then seems to burst into flame; greaves, inlaid with silver and gold; a spear. And, finally, elaborate beyond all human words, there was a shield.

Historical events in the future of Rome are illustrated on Aeneas' new shield

On the shield Vulcan—who was also skilled in prophecy—had depicted future events in Roman history, the campaigns and achievements of the race that would be descended from Ascanius. A wolf stretched out in a mossy cave sacred to

Mars; the twins, Romulus and Remus, played beside her or fed from her udders. She had turned her head to nudge them and wash them one by one with her tongue; they showed no fear as she licked them into shape. Next to them, the city of Rome herself, and the Circus: spectators sat in seats hollowed out of the hillside, ostensibly to watch the games, but in fact ready to perpetrate the wicked abduction of the Sabine women. And then, at the conclusion of a war between the sons of Romulus and the Sabine king, the kings were shown making peace in front of Jupiter's altar: they had cups in their hands, and were sealing their agreement with the sacrifice of a pig. Nearby appeared Mettius: he was a king of Alba Longa—he ought never to have broken his treaty with Rome—who for punishment had been lashed to a pair of chariots and torn in two. King Tullus of Rome was dragging the liar's body through the woods, and the thorn-bushes were wet with his blood.

Examples of heroism, treachery and virtue

When Tarquin, the last Roman king, had been expelled, Porsenna of Etruria would promise to reinstate him. The shield showed him besieging Rome, and the Romans fighting for their freedom. In one scene Porsenna was angry, in another he was threatening revenge—first on Horatius, who had broken down the last bridge over the Tiber to prevent Porsenna's army from entering the city; and then on Cloelia, who had been taken hostage but had escaped and swum across the river back to Rome. On the summit of the Capitol, you could see Manlius standing guard over the great temple that still had a thatched roof, just as it had in the days of Romulus. Among columns of gold a silver goose flapped its wings and hissed, to warn him that the Gauls' attack was imminent. And there were the Gauls as well, lurking in the thickets just below the citadel, hidden in the dark shadows of a moonless night. Their hair and clothes and weapons—their striped cloaks, the collars round their pale necks, the two spears that each of them held, their tall shields—everything was inlaid in polished gold.

Vulcan had depicted too the most ancient Roman rituals, with dancing priests and priests in woolen caps, naked revels in honor of Pan, shields that had fallen from heaven in the reign of Numa, and mothers in procession through the city, riding in padded carriages. And he had added scenes of Tartarus, including the gates of Hades and the punishment of vice—the traitor Catiline, for instance, clung to a steep cliff and trembled at the Furies' awful frowns. But those who had led blameless lives were shown sitting separate from the rest, with Cato instructing them in the virtues of piety and simplicity.

The battle of Actium: Augustus against Mark Antony and Cleopatra of Egypt

In the center of the shield was a seascape: the white spray and blue water of the ocean shimmered in gold, dolphins jumped and dived and flicked their tails in a silver circle. Soldiers lined the shore, and bronze ships sailed in a golden sea: it was the battle of Actium. From his high poop-deck Augustus Caesar commanded the forces of the senate and people of Rome. The great Roman gods watched over him, flames of good omen flickered round his temples and his father's star shone above his head. And not far away, his lieutenant, the tireless Agrippa, with the gods and the winds as always on his side, was splendid in the wreath that he had been awarded for his victories at sea. Opposite them: Mark Antony. His ships were all barbarian opulence, and his crews were drawn from all the nations he had subdued, from the countries that lie nearest to the dawn, from Egypt, from the Red Sea coast, from Bactria and Asia. And the queen of Egypt, Cleopatra—her name should not be spoken aloud—followed him. From the shelter of the shore the fleets approached each other at speed. Spray flew. The oars of triremes dipped and swung. Bows sliced the boiling sea apart. On forecastles and poops, men were so thickly clustered that you might have thought that all the Greek islands had been uprooted and were on the move, or that you were witnessing the collision of mountains.

Arrows with flaming tips and spears and javelins flew across the gap between the ships. Neptune's fields turned red with death. With her sacred rattle, the queen of Egypt encouraged her forces, apparently unaware of the two unlucky snakes be-

hind her. The jackal-headed Anubis, escorted by all manner of strange exotic creatures, was shown face to face with Neptune and Venus and Minerva. Between them raged the Furies, and iron-armored Mars. Discord grinned at them in her ragged robe; Bellona, the goddess of war, brandished a bloody whip. From his temple at Actium, Apollo observed the action, and aimed his bow: his arrows struck terror into the Egyptians and the Indians and the Arabs—and they fled. The queen herself looked as if she were calling for a shift in the wind, and ordering sails to be hoisted and sheets let fly. Vulcan had been able to indicate in her face the pallor of a woman who knows she is about to die; and he

had shown her in defeat, carried back to Egypt on a following sea and a westerly breeze. The Nile, grieving all along his length, held out his cloak to enfold her in his blue bosom, and called her home.

The triumph of Augustus

On another part of the shield was Augustus' triumphant return to Rome. True to his promise to all the gods of Italy, he had built them three hundred shrines, spaced equally through the city. Married women gathered in every temple, and before every altar bull after bull was sacrificed. Citizens lined the streets; they cheered and laughed and applauded. And there he was himself, sitting at the white marble entrance to Apollo's temple to receive the tribute of the conquered nations, which he hung upon the columns of the portico. In an endless line the prisoners of war filed past: they spoke as many languages as they had strange styles of costume or armor—Scythian archers, Africans in long loose robes, desert nomads, tribes from the north of Gaul and the banks of the Euphrates, from the Caspian sea, or the Rhine or the Araxes in Armenia—a river still indignant because Augustus had tamed it with a bridge.

Aeneas picked up the shield and settled it on his shoulder. He was delighted by his mother's gift and Vulcan's work, and intrigued by the promise of its imagery. Although he did not understand it, he sensed in it a glorious future for his family.

IX

Book IX
Death in the Dark

*Juno advises
Turnus to
seize his
opportunity
while Aeneas
is away*

While Aeneas was far away inland, Juno had sent her messenger Iris to visit Turnus, who was waiting in a valley among trees planted by his ancestor Pilumnus. "Turnus," said Iris softly, "the passing of time by itself has brought you an opportunity which no one would have dared to request of any god. Aeneas has left his ships and his men by the Tiber, and gone off to confer with Evander in Pallanteum. And that is not all: he has found allies in Etruria, and he is gathering reinforcements from the country people. So waste no more time. This is the moment to marshal your horses and chariots. You should attack the Trojan camp now, when they least expect it." She said no more, but flew at once up into the heavens, leaving her rainbow arcing across the clouds.

Turnus knew who she was, and lifted his hands in prayer to her as she vanished from his sight. "Iris, glory of heaven, who sent you through the clouds to earth to speak to me? Why this sudden light? Why are the stars whirling across a divided sky? Whoever it is that calls me to action, I will obey these omens. I am ready to go." He went down to the stream and drank from it, and prayed to the gods and filled the air with his devotions.

*Turnus leads
his army
against the
Trojan camp*

By now his entire army, footsoldiers and cavalry, was assembled on the plain in a dazzling show of gold and color, from the sons of the shepherd Tyrrhus in the

227

rear to Messapus in the van. Turnus took up his position in the center, and his forces moved steadily forward,

> like a river—the Ganges perhaps, deep and silent, fed
> by seven gentle tributaries; or the majestic Nile when
> he draws back his floods from the Egyptian fields and
> settles into his accustomed channel.

The Trojans first saw them as a distant smudge of dust, then as a shadow darkening the plain. But Caicus climbed onto high ground to get a better view, and gave the first alarm. "This is no weather-front," he called. "It's the enemy! Man the defenses! Fetch your weapons!" The Trojans came pouring back inside their camp and went straight to their posts on the ramparts, exactly as Aeneas had ordered them to do before he left. "Whatever happens," he had said, "do not venture outside onto the level ground; do not get drawn into a pitched battle. Stay inside the camp. You can rely on your fortifications to keep you safe." And so now, even when their excitement made it seem cowardly not go out and fight, they bolted the gates and did what he had told them: they armed themselves and waited for the enemy.

Turnus meanwhile had galloped ahead of his main column, which was moving too slowly for his patience. With twenty picked horsemen he arrived at the Trojan camp much sooner than the Trojans had expected; but they knew who he was from his gold helmet with its scarlet plume and his dappled gray horse from Thrace. "Who is with me?" he shouted to his companions. "Who will make the first contact with the enemy?" He sat steady on his horse, and threw a spear to show that the battle had begun. His companions yelled war cries and beat their swords on their shields, but the Trojans' inaction, they thought, was astonishing. Why would they not come out to fight? Why did they stay behind their earthworks? Turnus was puzzled. He rode around the camp, examining the defenses and looking for weak spots where he might force an entrance.

Have you ever seen a wolf, in the middle of the night, prowling up and down in the rain and wind by the gate of a sheepfold? He can hear the lambs bleating, but they are safe inside with their mothers, and for all his ferocity and determination he cannot get at them. He is snappish, because he has not eaten for a long time, and he needs the taste of blood.

Turnus' troops try to set the Trojan ships on fire

Turnus was like that wolf: the more he investigated, the more irritable he became. Frustration ran hot in his bones. How could he find a way in? How could he shake the Trojans' nerve? What would persuade them to leave their camp and come outside to meet him? But then he caught sight of their ships; they lay close beside the camp, protected on one side by the river and on the other by the ramparts. He called for fire: blazing himself with energy, he set light to a pine-branch and yelled to his companions to improvise their own torches. Encouraged by his example, they tore apart the cooking-fires. Bright yellow sparks shot up, and a trail of resinous smoke and ashes curled into the sky.

But then, a miracle. The fire was deflected, and the flames never reached the Trojan ships. Some god was responsible—but which one? The answer lies in a promise made long ago, though the tale will be told forever. It began when Aeneas, planning his escape from Troy by sea, was looking for timber in the forest near the city. And at that moment Cybele, the mother of all the gods, had sought an audience of Jupiter. "My son," she said. "Grant me this favor, that you have owed me since you became king on Olympus. Near the top of Mount Ida there used to be a shady stand of trees—pines and maples— which was always kept sacred to me; but I was happy to allow Aeneas to take from it whatever wood that he needed for his fleet. But now I am anxious and frightened, and I ask you to set my mother's mind at rest. Those trees came to maturity under my care. Now that they have been made into ships, I want you never to allow them be damaged on any of their voyages, or overcome by storms."

The ships are magically transformed

And Jupiter had replied: "What is this? Do you wish to deflect the will of the fates? Are you asking that these ships, which were built by mortal hands, should have immortal privileges? Are you asking that Aeneas should be granted certainty in an uncertain world? What god has that kind of power? But I can at least do this: when his ships have finished their voyage and come finally to rest in an Italian harbor, I will take away their material forms. Whichever of them have escaped the perils of the sea and have brought their Trojan master to Latium, I will turn into goddesses of the sea, water-nymphs who will swim on the crests of the waves." And to witness his assent he had called upon the pitch-encrusted banks and black bottomless eddies of the Styx, his brother Hades' river. All Olympus trembled.

So now the time allotted by the fates had passed, and the promised day had come. The assault warned Cybele that she must save her sacred ships from Turnus' torches. First she dazzled human eyes with a burst of light; then a cloud filled the eastern sky and the sound of singing floated all the way from Ida. And finally both the Trojans and Turnus' troops heard a terrible disembodied voice: "Trojans, put down your arms. You need not defend your ships—their timbers belong to me. Before Turnus can burn them, he will have to set fire to the ocean itself. Go, goddesses, go free; your mother commands you." And straightaway each of the ships broke away from her moorings and plunged down to the bottom bows-first, like a dolphin. And when they re-surfaced they had been magically transformed into beautiful young women, who were swept down the river to the sea.

Turnus rallies his forces and blockades the Trojan camp

The Tiber paused and checked his flow, and the wind muttered in the reeds. The Rutulians were amazed; Messapus' horses shied in terror, and even he became frightened. But Turnus was fearless: he never lost his confidence. He was the first to rally their spirits, and then to admonish them. "These portents are not meant to scare you, but the Trojans. They relied on those ships, and now Jupiter has taken them away. They won't stand up to us now. They can't escape by sea, and they have nowhere else to go. One half of the world is water, the other half is land—and we hold the land. And we outnumber them. And we are better armed. Whatever store the Trojans set by it, this gesture from the gods says nothing to me. Venus should be content that they have even made a landing on our territory. That was all that their fate ordained for them, and that should be enough.

"Well, I have my fate too—and that is to rid myself of these damnable Trojans and the man who has abducted Lavinia. Menelaus isn't the only one to have lost a wife to them. The Greeks took up arms to recover her—and now they're not alone either. You know the old saying, 'It is enough to perish once'? You would think it would have been enough for these people to have sinned once, despising women as they do. And these are the same ones who now put their trust in ditches and piles of earth to serve as a barrier between life and death. Wouldn't you think that they would remember the walls of Troy? Neptune built them, and still they collapsed in flames. Very well. Which of you—and I have chosen you all for just such a purpose—will come with me to break down this rampart and put these cowards to the sword? I don't need armor made by Vulcan, or a thousand ships, to fight against the Trojans. Let them take on the Etruscans as their allies, if they like. They need not fear that we will attack in the dark of night, or that we will hide in a wooden horse. We will encircle them openly, in full daylight. Don't let them think that we're like the Greeks: even Hector could hold off the Greeks, and he did—

for ten long years. But now the better part of the day is done.
Use what is left of it for resting and eating. So far, you have
done well. Get yourselves ready for a real battle tomorrow.
And Messapus, post lookouts; tell them not to take their eyes
off the gates. Light fires in a circle round the camp." Fourteen
Rutulian officers, each in charge of a hundred men in golden
helmets with scarlet plumes, were ordered to stand watch by
turns. But most of the men lay around on the grass drinking
wine from bronze cups, and the sentries stayed awake by gam-
bling round their fires.

The Trojans, still fully armed, kept a careful lookout from
behind their fortifications. In anxious haste they checked that
their gates were tightly closed; and they established connect-
ing passages between the watchtowers; they kept their spears
and arrows at the ready. Aeneas had left Mnestheus and Seres-
tus in charge while he was gone, in case anything should go
wrong; and they kept everyone hard at work. Along the line
of the earthworks, they all stood tense and alert, each respon-
sible for his own section, each with his own particular duty.

Nisus and Eury-
alus resolve to
inform Aeneas
of their
predicament

On watch at one of the gates was
Nisus; he had been sent by Ida, a nymph
from Crete, to be Aeneas' companion. He
was an eager soldier, a keen shot with a
javelin and an excellent archer. Next to
him was his friend Euryalus, the best-
looking of all the Trojans; he was hardly more than a boy, with
his first beard just beginning to show. The two of them loved
each other; they always fought side by side, and now they
stood sentry together.

"Is it the gods that put courage into our minds?" asked
Nisus. "Or do you think that a man's ambition is his own god?
I feel an urge for action, for some great undertaking. I'm tired
of doing nothing. Have you noticed the Rutulians' over-confi-
dence? Their watch fires are spread too far apart. And either
they're dozing or they've drunk too much, but in any case
they're making remarkably little noise. Let me tell you what's

forming in my mind. Everyone in our whole army—officers and all—is saying that word must be got to Aeneas about our situation. Well, I think I can see how I can slip across the slope of that hill and make my way to Pallanteum. I'll make certain that you get properly rewarded for anything that you do to help—all I want for myself is the credit for having done it."

Euryalus saw how eager his friend was, and he too was filled with a desire for glory. "You're not thinking of going off on such an expedition without me, are you, Nisus? Do you think I'd let you take a risk like that alone? My father was a warrior. He fought all through the siege of Troy, and he was never afraid of any Greek—and he didn't bring me up to be afraid either. I didn't come with you all this way, in the footsteps of Aeneas, to hang back from danger. I'm no lover of life for its own sake, and life is a price that I'm willing to pay for the kind of honor you're looking for."

"I would never accuse you of hanging back," said Nisus, "and it wouldn't be right if I did. And I pray that great Jupiter—or whoever else observes such enterprises—will bring me back to you in triumph. But no one's safety is guaranteed; and if anything should happen to me, I would want you to survive me. You deserve to have a long life—and if I'm captured and then ransomed, or if the fates forbid me to return, I hope that you'll give me a funeral and put up a memorial for me. And I could not bear to be the cause of any sorrow for your mother—especially since she was the only one of all the women to follow her son to Italy, the only one who did not want to stay behind in Sicily."

"You can invent as many reasons as you like to prevent my going with you," said Euryalus. "But my mind is made up; you can't change it. Let's waste no more time." He woke other sentries to take their places; and he and Nisus left their post and went off to ask permission to leave in search of Aeneas.

They obtain the approval of the Trojan leaders

Over all the earth, the animals were asleep; they had forgotten their fears and their minds were undisturbed. But the

Trojan leaders were met in a council of war: what should they do next, and who should take a message to Aeneas? They stood in the middle of the camp, holding their shields and leaning on their spears. Nisus and Euryalus begged excitedly to be heard: what they had to suggest, they said, was important, and it was worth interrupting the meeting. Ascanius was the first to agree to listen to them. "What is it, Nisus?" he said. "Speak up."

"Listen to me with open minds," said Nisus. "Don't ignore us just because we're young. The Rutulians are being sloppy—they're either asleep or drunk. We think that we can trick them. We've spotted a place that they've left unguarded, near the gate on the seaward side of the camp. The watch fires there are far apart and unattended. There are no flames to give light, only smoke. If you let us, we can take a chance and slip through to Pallanteum and Aeneas. We won't be away long; we'll just collect a few trophies and slit a few throats. We've already seen Pallanteum from a distance, when we've been out hunting. We know the whole riverbank. We won't get lost."

Aletes, old and experienced, addressed them: "It looks as if the gods of our fathers are still protecting us, and do not intend to destroy us yet, if they have excited such spirit and determination in the hearts of our young men." He put an arm round their shoulders and took them by their right hands. Tears ran down his cheeks. "How can I suggest an appropriate reward for you? Only the gods will know what you truly deserve. Aeneas will give you whatever else is owing, and young Ascanius will certainly never forget your courage."

"That's true," interrupted Ascanius. "I will not feel at peace until my father is safely back, but as soon as he returns, all will be well. Nisus, I swear by our family gods, and by the spirit of our forefather Assaracus, and by the shrine of Vesta, the goddess of our hearths and homes: if you restore him to me, I will give you the two engraved silver cups which he captured long ago from Arisba, and two tripods, and two ingots of gold and an ancient bowl which queen Dido gave him. If we capture Italy, and establish him as king, and when the time comes to distribute the plunder, then, Nisus, your prize will be Turnus' horse—you've seen it, and you've seen him riding it in his golden armor—and Turnus' shield and his helmet with its scarlet plumes. And my father will give you twelve beautiful women and many prisoners as well, and all their arms, and as much land as King Latinus owns. And you, Euryalus—you're exactly the same age as I am, and you'll always be my friend and companion—whatever glory comes to me, I'll share with you. Whatever I have, in peace or war, is yours—and that's my promise."

"The day will never come when I'm not ready to face danger," said Euryalus. "I only pray that fortune may be with us. But one favor I must ask: I have a mother, from King Priam's family. She came with me from Troy, and then from Sicily. I cannot bear to see her cry for her child, and so—you must believe me—I have told her nothing of this expedition, and I have not said good-bye to her. So if she should be left alone and destitute, comfort her and look after her. If I know that you will do this, I will go all the more confidently to meet whatever awaits me."

He touched the Trojans with his words, and Ascanius, whose heart was still filled with thoughts of his father, was particularly affected. "Anything that you have asked in return for such a great deed will be done," he said, with tears in his eyes. "Your mother is surely worthy of her son, and I will treat her as if she were my own; she only lacks the name of Creusa. But I swear to you, as my father would swear, that however your plan turns out, I will give to your mother and all your family whatever I promised you if all were to go well." He took off his sword, beautifully decorated in Crete with gold and ivory, and gave it to Euryalus. Mnestheus gave Nisus a lion-skin—he had stripped it from an enemy—and Aletes exchanged helmets with him. The two of them strapped on their armor, and then they were ready to go. The prayers of all the Trojans, young and old, followed them as they slipped through the gate, and Ascanius, bravely bearing a man's responsibilities on his boy's shoulders, called after them with many messages for Aeneas. But the breeze swept them away and floated them uselessly up to the clouds.

They cut their way through the enemy lines

They left the camp behind and crossed the ditch. Under the gloomy cover of the night they made for the enemy lines, where many were already fated to die. Everywhere they saw soldiers, drunk, sleeping, stretched out on the grass; they saw chariots tipped back, shafts in the air; they saw drivers leaning against the wheels in a muddle of harness and weapons and jugs of wine. Nisus warned Euryalus to be alert and ready for anything: "This job calls for daring, not caution. You keep a watch out behind, and I'll go ahead and cut a way through. And now—no more talk. To work."

A man of royal blood, named Rhamnes, lay on a pile of blankets, snoring. He was Turnus' favorite soothsayer, but his prescience could not ward off an assassin. Nisus stabbed him and his three attendants, while their weapons lay uselessly beside them. Close to them was the armor-bearer and charioteer of one of Turnus' officers, dozing by his horses: Nisus cut all the horses' throats, and then lopped off their master's head. His body was left to drip blood onto his blankets until it soaked through to the ground. Lamyrus and Lamus were the next to die, and then Serranus, a handsome young man who had gambled until very late and now was fast asleep. He would have had better luck if he had stayed up all night and played until morning. Nisus went at them

> like a hungry lion, driven by his empty belly to attack
> a sheepfold: he sinks his teeth into the lambs—they
> are too frightened to make a sound—and drags them
> away in his dripping jaws.

Euryalus was equally ruthless: he had worked himself into a rage, and slashed haphazardly through a crowd of soldiers whose names nobody knows. One of them, who saw him coming, cowered behind an enormous wine-jar, but he could not escape Euryalus' sword, which was thrust into his chest at close range. Blood spurted everywhere. Euryalus left him dying; and as he died, a stream of blood and wine came out of his mouth, mixed with his final breath.

On now to Messapus' contingent: his campfires were nearly out and his horses, hobbled, were grazing. But Nisus, realizing that his friend was nearly out of his mind with blood-lust, stopped him from approaching any closer: "Our way is clear and open now. There's no need for any more killing. It's nearly dawn; and we'll be spotted." They took away no trophies, ignoring armor and silver vessels and beautifully embroidered tapestries—except that Euryalus could not resist Rhamnes' breastplate and gold-buckled belt. They were spoils from a distant battle, family heirlooms. But they did not fit him, and instead he grabbed Messapus' plumed helmet and put that on.

Together they left the camp and made for safety. But meanwhile the Latins had deployed their cavalry. The main force had stayed back on the flat ground, but three hundred horsemen, with Volcens in command, were delivering dispatches to Turnus. They had nearly reached Turnus' lines when they spotted Nisus and Euryalus circling round them to their left. And it was no accident: their position was given away by the sheen on the helmet that Euryalus had stolen. He had not realized how much it would catch the light even in the deepest shadow.

From the head of his column, Volcens called on them to halt.

"What are you doing? Where are you going?"

Euryalus is captured, and Nisus tries to rescue him

No answer. Nisus and Euryalus dived into a wood, hoping that they could escape in the dark. But the Latins knew the ground well, so that they were able to block all the shortcuts and guard every exit; whereas in the tangle of undergrowth and bristling black holm-oaks and thorn bushes that seemed to go on for ever, it was not easy for a stranger to see where he was going.

Euryalus—scared, disoriented, impeded by his loot, and snagged among the brambles—was soon completely lost. But Nisus got away. He had dodged through the enemy and reached Latinus' stables (the place was later called Alba), before he stopped to look back for his missing friend.

"My poor Euryalus: where are you? How am I to find you?" He went back again into the wood where they had been hiding, retracing his steps through the underbrush—but there was no sign of him. Then out of the silence he heard horses and confused sounds of pursuit. A brief pause, and a shout. Euryalus was right in front of him. Unable to find his way out of the wood in the dark, he had been surprised by Volcens and his horsemen, and for all his efforts had been captured.

"What can I do?" thought Nisus. "I can't rescue him without reinforcements. Should I go after him myself? If I die, at least it will be a splendid death." He took a spear from his shoulder and raised it to the moon, high in the sky. "Help me, Diana, glory of the stars and guardian of the woods. Do you remember how my father brought gifts to your altars on my behalf, and how I gave you more myself when I had been hunting, and hung them up for you in your temple? Now give me a true aim and help me put my enemy to flight."

With his whole strength he threw his spear. It flew unwaveringly through the darkness and took Sulmo between the shoulder-blades. The point snapped off, and the broken shaft pierced him in the heart. Hot blood spilled out over his back as his body grew cold, and long-drawn sighs shuddered down his sides. His companions looked round, fearfully—and another spear, aimed even more accurately than the last, went straight through Tagus' head, temple to temple, and stuck quivering in his brain.

Nisus and Euryalus are killed

Volcens was furious: he did not know where the attack was coming from, and so he had no target to shoot back at. He drew his sword and turned to Euryalus. "Your blood will pay for the both of you," he said, and the words drove Nisus mad. His grief and terror were too much for him, and he could not stay any longer in his hiding place. "It was me! Kill *me,* kill *me!* I'm over here!" he shouted. "It was my plan—he could have done nothing without me. Whatever he did, it was only because he loved his friend too much. I swear it by the stars in heaven—they saw it all." He ran up as fast as he could, but he was too late to prevent Volcens from thrusting his sword between Euryalus' ribs, and through his chest. His blood spattered over his beautiful limbs and his head fell forward, like a bright-red flower, limp and fading after a plow has severed its stem, or a poppy bowing its weary neck to the rain.

Nisus counter-attacked. His only target was Volcens, and he did not pause till he found him. He fought his way through the soldiers who surrounded him, whirling his sword like a thunderbolt, and sliced it across his face while he was still speaking. Volcens died, and Nisus was mortally wounded. Calm and silent, he fell beside Euryalus, and at last he lay in peace. It was a good death for them both—and as long as this story is told, as long as the Roman Capitol stands solid on its rock and the Roman empire lasts, the two of them will surely never be forgotten.

The victorious Latins stripped them of their armor, and wept for Volcens, and carried him into their camp. And they grieved for Rhamnes when they found his body, and the bodies of so many others killed together. They crowded around to keep vigil over the dead and dying, and to stare at the trickles of blood, still warm, winding across the battlefield. They looked over the spoils: Messapus' helmet, and the armor which had cost so much effort to recover.

Their bodies are mutilated and put on show

By now Aurora, the goddess of the dawn, had left her bed to scatter the first rays of light over the earth. As the sun climbed in the sky and revealed the events of the night, Turnus strapped on his arms and called his troops to action. His officers drew up their bronze-bright ranks, and fired their men's anger with stories of what had happened, some true, some not so true. In front of them the heads of Euryalus and Nisus were held up on display, fixed to the points of spears—a dreadful sight, but they cheered it nonetheless. But the Trojans did not cheer. They had climbed up onto the right hand section of their wall—the left hand section was protected by the river—and from the guard-posts along the ditch, or from high on the towers, the blood-smudged features of their friends were clearly recognizable as they were carried by in a sad parade.

But Rumor was already flitting through the Trojan camp, and she whispered at last into the ear of Euryalus' mother. The poor woman felt suddenly faint, and dropped her shuttle and her basket of wool. She cut off locks of her hair in mourning, and then with a shriek she rushed up onto the rampart, from where she could best see Turnus' columns. She did not care about the enemy, or the risk of spears or arrows; she simply wailed her questions to the sky.

"Is that you, Euryalus? Were you not supposed to be the comfort of my old age? How could you leave me alone? How could you not even come to say good-bye to me before you left to go off into so much danger? Now you lie on unknown ground. The dogs and birds of Latium will disfigure you. Why have I not laid out your body for funeral, or closed your eyes? Why have I not washed your wounds, or wrapped you in the shroud that I have hurried to finish through so many days and nights, keeping as cheerful as an old woman can, working at my loom? How can I follow you? Where does your poor mutilated body lie? Is this to be my last memory of you, my son? Did I come all this way with you for this? It would be only right, you Rutulians, if you were to kill me next. Shoot me with your arrows, cut me down with your swords. And pity me, Jupiter, father of the gods: send me straight to Tartarus with your thunderbolt. There is no better way to end my worthless, miserable life." The Trojans wept and lamented with her; they had lost their will to fight, and could think of nothing but their grief. Ilioneus and the sobbing Ascanius ordered two soldiers to take her by the arms and escort her back to her hut.

The Latins attack the Trojan fortifications

But then they heard a distant trumpet blast—a brassy note from far away which beat painfully on their ears—and then an echoing shout. The Volscians, under cover of shields interlocked above their heads like a tortoise' shell, were threatening to fill in the ditch and tear down the rampart. Some of them, looking for a way over the top, had brought up scaling-ladders to a place where the Trojan line was thin, and there were gaps in the ring of defenders.

The Trojans poured down javelins and arrows on them, and pushed them back with poles, using their long experience of holding off a siege. They rolled down rocks to see if they could disrupt the Volscian tortoise, and though it was made to withstand almost any kind of pressure, the Trojans contrived to break it up. They brought up a gigantic boulder and, where the enemy was thickest, they heaved it over the parapet. It smashed through the tortoise' armored roof, and the Rutulians scattered. They were brave enough, but from then on they preferred to see what they were doing as they fought, and reverted to trying to drive the Trojans off the wall with missiles. Further down the line, the ferocious Mezentius brandished his spear as a signal to bring up firebrands, while Messapus hacked away at the earthworks and oversaw the placement of the ladders.

Who could write an epic long enough, or detailed enough, to describe the slaughter and destruction of that day? How many warriors did Turnus kill by himself? Who was sent down to the country of the dead? And who sent them?

The fighting was particularly fierce around one tower, solidly sited and linked to the wall by bridges. The Latins fought desperately to take it by storm and to bring it down; the Trojans defended it by standing at its loopholes and firing stones and arrows through them. Turnus threw a torch and set light to one of its sides; a wind sent the flames licking along the floorboards and eating at the beams. Inside the tower, panic: there seemed to be no way out. They huddled to one side, away from the fire; but under their uneven weight the tower collapsed with a heaven-shaking crash. The defenders fell with it. Some were crushed beneath its weight, and others badly wounded, either by their own weapons or by long pointed splinters. Only young Helenor and Lycus escaped. Helenor was the illegitimate son of a slave-girl and an Asian king, who had sent him off to the Trojan war ingloriously armed: the scabbard of his sword had not been decorated and there had been no heraldic device on his shield. He found himself surrounded by thousands of Turnus' troops, Italians whichever way he looked. Determined to die, he charged at the enemy's leveled spears, like a wild beast that is ringed by hunters and with a final desperate leap impales itself on their weapons.

Lycus was quicker on his feet; he dodged his way back to the rampart, and was just about to grab the hands of his friends stretched out to haul him over it, when Turnus, equally nimble, caught him and sneered: "Do you think you can get away from me, you poor fool?" With one movement he grabbed him and hauled him down, and a chunk of the wall with him. Turnus was an eagle with slashing, gripping talons, or, if you will, a wolf; and Lycus was a hare, or a swan, or a lamb stolen from the fold and bleating for its mother. A shout went up on all sides; the Rutulians shoveled down the rampart into the ditch and filled it up, and threw torches onto the roofs of the Trojan huts.

With javelins or with sharpshooters' arrows, the Latins felled Trojans and the Trojans Latins. Ilioneus brought down Lucetius with a rock as he tried to pass through the gate with a torch in his hand. And on the other side Turnus overwhelmed Caeneus and Itys and Clonius and many others. Privernus had foolishly dropped his shield to tend a minor scratch, and Capys' feathered arrow pinned his hand to his left side and penetrated his lung—a fatal wound. Arcens' son, from Sicily, was handsome and magnificently dressed in an embroidered tunic, had been reared beside a river on the lower slopes of Etna, and sent to war by his father. He was no match for Mezentius, who put down his spears and whirled a sling three times round his head. A ball of red-hot lead caught the boy between the eyes and split his head wide open—and down he went, full-length on the sand.

Ascanius' moment of triumph

It was at this point, they say, that Ascanius killed a man in battle for the first time. He had previously distinguished himself only in the hunting field, but now he aimed his arrow at Numanus, who had recently married Turnus' younger sister and was indecently proud of his new connections. He was striding up and down in the Latins' front line, shouting at the top of his voice all sorts of insults, some repeatable, some not.

"Aren't you ashamed to be besieged a second time? It seems to be a Trojan habit. The last time you tried to steal someone else's wife by force, you found yourselves hemmed

in behind your own battlements—and now it's happening all
over again. Did you come to Italy because some god told you
to—or were you just out of your minds? You won't find any
Menelaus or Agamemnon here—or anyone as tricky as Od-
ysseus. *We* are tough, and were brought up to be tough. We
take our babies down to the river as soon as they're born, and
harden them up by dipping them in cold water. School for
our boys is long hours in the woods without sleep: they learn
to ride hard and shoot straight. They're trained for a life of
work and hardship; they subdue the earth with mattocks, and
their enemies with battle-axes. However old we are, we live
with weapons in our hands; even if we're just beating an ox,
it's with the butt-end of a spear. Age doesn't wear us down
or diminish our energy—just because a man's hair is white it
doesn't mean he can't put on a helmet—and it's never too late
to make a living from theft or plunder. But all *you* hunt are
shellfish and crocuses, to steal their purple and yellow dyes.
You're soft and idle and effeminate. You do nothing but sing
and dance and wear tunics with fancy cuffs and funny banded
hats. Listen! Is that the sound of flutes and cymbals? It must
be Cybele, calling you all the way from Asia. Off you go then,
into the mountains, and practice your panpipes. Drop your
swords: let the real men do the fighting."

But Ascanius would not tolerate such taunting and teas-
ing. He raised his bow and flexed his muscles and drew back
its horsehair string. But first he invoked Jupiter: "Bring me suc-
cess in this endeavor, almighty king of heaven, and I will offer
gifts at your temple every year. I will bring to your altar a white
calf already as tall as its mother; it will have a gold rosette on
its forehead, and it will toss its horns and prance on the sand."
Jupiter heard his prayer. Out of a clear sky he sent thunder
rumbling on the left, exactly as Ascanius let his bowstring go.
His hissing arrow hit Numanus squarely between the eyes and
the point sank deep into his brain. "That," yelled Ascanius,
"is what happens when you mock the Trojans. They may be
under siege again—but if anyone questions their courage,

they can still send back an answer." The Trojans followed his shout with one of their own; their triumphant cheer, along with their morale, soared up beyond the stars.

By chance Apollo was looking down from the clouds in his quarter of the sky, and he observed the camp and the Italian assault. When he saw Ascanius victorious, he spoke to him. "Well done, my boy, the son of gods and destined to father them! This is how heroes reach heaven. You will not be merely a citizen of Troy: the laws made by your children's children will establish peace throughout the world." And he immediately came down from the heavens, riding the wind till he came to Ascanius' side, in the form of old Butes, who had once been Anchises' armor-bearer and bodyguard, and now, on Aeneas' instructions, served Ascanius. Apollo took on every detail of Butes' appearance—his voice, face, white hair, armor—and, as Ascanius tried to continue the fight, he checked him. "Child of Aeneas, be satisfied that you have killed Numanus without coming to any harm. Apollo says that you have done well, and that should be enough. He is not even resentful that you shoot as well as he does. But no more fighting for you now, my boy." Almost before he had finished speaking, he vanished from sight. The older Trojans realized that it was Apollo from the sound of the arrows rattling in his quiver as he flew away, and they restrained the impatient Ascanius, reminding him that these were the commands of a god. But they themselves went back into the battle, unafraid to expose themselves to danger.

Turnus penetrates the Trojan defenses

All along the defenses, a chaos of shouts, twanging bowstrings and whirling slingshot: the air was thick with missiles, which clattered endlessly against shields and helmets, or were tumbled about over the ground. The noise was like a cloudburst that hammers in from the west, or a hailstorm at sea, or thunder crashing in the clouds with pelting rain.

In charge of one of the entrances were two brothers, Pandarus and Bitias, raised by a nymph in the woods, and tall as the pine trees or even the mountains in the country where they had been born. At the word of command, they opened their gate and did not try to stop the enemy from coming in. As soon as the Rutulians saw the gate ajar, they rushed through it like a river in flood. But on either bank two oak trees stand tall, their leaves in shifting silhouette against the sky—the brothers, waiting in ambush, one hidden on each side of the gate, in their plumed helmets, with their swords in their hands. The Rutulians turned and tried to flee—some of them were killed right on the threshold—and the fighting grew fiercer and tempers were lost. The Trojans banded together for hand-to-hand combat, and even made short forays out beyond the wall.

Word was brought to Turnus—himself frantically engaged further down the line—that the enemy was fighting yet more desperately and that one of the gates was open. In haste he abandoned his own position and rode over to the gate where Pandarus and Bitias had had their triumph. The first Trojan to come to meet him was the hero Sarpedon's son. But Turnus' javelin took him in the throat, and went through to his chest, where the iron point rested, and blood, mixed with warm foam, jetted from his lungs. Three more Trojans were quickly dispatched, and then Turnus rounded on Bitias, who was fighting with gleaming eyes and blazing spirit. It was not a javelin that felled him—he could have shaken off a javelin—but a huge whistling spear of twisted wood, arriving like a thunderbolt. Neither the double layer of bull's hide stretched over his shield, or his breastplate of overlapping plates and golden scales, could stop it. Down he went in a shapeless heap. The earth groaned and his great shield clanged on top of him.

His fall might have reminded you of those times when blocks of stone are fitted together to make supports for a pier at a seaside resort. The builders push them into the shallow water with a mass of rubble dragging behind them, and the colossal splash brings up clouds of black ooze from the bottom. Nearby islands tremble—like the ones which Jupiter once placed on top of the rebel giant Typhoeus to keep him pinned on the ocean floor.

After Bitias' death, the war-god Mars was able to put more spirit into the Italian forces. He set sharp goads in their breasts to make them counter-attack wherever there was an opportunity; and to the Trojans he sent thoughts of flight and fear. When Pandarus saw the shift in the momentum of the battle, he leaned his shoulder against the gate and swung it back on its hinges. Many of his countrymen were left outside to take their chances; others managed to return before the gate was closed once more. But Pandarus made a terrible mistake: he failed to spot that, as the last of the Trojans slipped in, Turnus had slipped in with them. Like a tiger among a flock of sheep, he was inside the Trojan camp.

Now a new gleam shone in Turnus' eye, and on his armor. His blood-red helmet-crest flourished, and sparks like lightning flickered on his shield. The Trojans recognized him by his height and by the features that they had learned to hate, and everyone except Pandarus was afraid of him. But Pandarus cared for nothing except revenge for his brother's death, and he shouted angrily: "This is not Amata's palace, Turnus; Lavinia is not here. You're not tucked snugly away behind the walls of Ardea. This is the enemy camp, and you have no way out."

But Turnus stayed quite calm, and even laughed at him: "Come on then, if you're brave enough. Are you ready? If anyone thinks of himself as a second Priam, you'd better tell him that Achilles has returned." In answer Pandarus threw his spear at him—it had a rough knotty shaft with the bark still on it—as hard as he could. But Juno intervened: she had the wind divert it, and it slammed uselessly into the gatepost. "Very well—but you won't escape *my* weapon," gloated Turnus. "You'll see I aim much better than you." And with that he lifted up his sword and brought it down; and it split Pandarus' forehead right between the temples, right between his beardless cheeks. Down went Pandarus like his brother, and his weight as he fell made the ground shudder. His brains spattered all over his limbs and his armor, and his skull, divided exactly in two, flopped down sideways, half onto one shoulder and half onto the other.

Turnus has initial success inside the Trojan camp...

The Trojans turned and fled in terror. And if Turnus at that moment had done what common sense demanded, if he had tugged back the bolts on the gates and let his allies in, that would have been the end of the war and the end of the Trojans as well. But he was too excited, and too greedy for yet more blood, for anything except pursuit. He threw his spears and recovered them from their targets and then, inspired by Juno, he threw them yet again. So he hit Phaleris in the back, and severed the tendon behind Gyges' knee. Next Halys fell, and Phegeus—armed with far too light a shield—and others who were concentrating so hard on the defense of the wall that they did not even know that Turnus was behind them. Lynceus tried to warn them, but Turnus silenced him with a single swing of his sword: his head, still tight inside its helmet, rolled off the rampart. Then, in a final burst, he slaughtered Amycus, a hunter who smeared poison on the tips of his arrows, and Clytius, and Cretheus, a friend of the Muses because he used to write poems and set them to music, stories about horses and warriors and weapons and battles.

At last the news of Turnus' murderous foray within their gates came to the Trojan leaders, Mnestheus and Serestus. They conferred together, and they saw for themselves how their companions were scattering. "Where are you off to?" sneered Mnestheus. "Where else do you have to hide? Do know of any other fortifications? How is it that you have allowed one man, trapped within your ramparts, to run amok like this without resistance? How has he been able to send down so many good young men down to Hades? Why are you so feeble? Aren't you sorry for your unhappy country? Are you ashamed of Aeneas and the ancient gods of Troy?"

...but is compelled to withdraw

With jibes like that he put new heart into them, and they rallied and reformed their ranks. But Turnus began gradually to extricate himself from his difficulties and make for the river and the part of the camp that was ringed with water. The Trojans raised a shout and swarmed close round him

> like a band of hunters who have cornered a lion. The lion snarls and glares at them to mask his fear; but he gives ground little by little. His anger and his courage do not allow him to turn tail, but he is surrounded, whether he likes it or not, and there is no way out through the ring of men and weapons.

So Turnus withdrew—deliberately, without hurrying and still dangerous. Twice he counter-attacked; twice he forced the Trojans back along the wall. But at last they massed together in a united charge against him. Even Juno dared not help him at this point, because Iris had brought her clear instructions from Jupiter that Turnus must be allowed to escape from the Trojan camp. But by itself neither his sword nor his shield was strong enough to let him hold his ground against the rain of arrows, which left his ears ringing from hit after hit on his helmet. His crest was ripped off. His shield-boss was dented. His breastplate, pounded by stones, was split open. The Trojans were on him, spear after spear, and Mnestheus slashed at him like a lightning strike. He was dripping with grime and sweat. He could not catch his breath. He trembled all over, exhausted.

At last he was driven back to the edge of the Tiber, and he dived, armor and all, into the gentle river. The current washed away his blood and pain, and delivered him again, safe and sound, to his comrades.

BOOK X
Fathers and Sons

Jupiter calls for peace

Meanwhile, on impregnable Olympus, Jupiter ordered the doors of his palace to be opened wide. He seated himself on his throne, high among the stars, and called in the gods for a council; but as they assembled in the vaulted hall, he did not take his eyes off the Trojan camp and the armies far below him in Latium.

"Immortal gods," he said, "why have you gone back on your previous promises? And why are you quarreling among yourselves? I thought I had expressly forbidden this war between Italians and Trojans. Why, then—in complete disregard of my instructions—are they fighting? What are they afraid of? What has made them take up arms and provoke each other? The time for war will come soon enough, when armies from Carthage will bring catastrophe on Rome from across the Alps. Then mutual hatred and destruction will run unchecked. For now they must desist and make their peace."

Venus appeals to him to help the Trojans

What Jupiter had had to say was brief; but Venus' answer was not. "Father, you are all-powerful over men and the actions of men—and who else is there that we can pray to? Do you see how insolent the Rutulians are? Do you see the conceit of Turnus, so proudly driving his horses into action, so puffed up by his success? The Trojans are no longer safe behind their wall; there is fighting at the gates and all along the ramparts and the ditch is awash with blood. And Aeneas is away, and knows nothing of any of it. Will you never allow the siege to be lifted? And now another army threatens this second, infant Troy: Aeneas' old enemy, the Greek hero Diomedes, is on the move from his fortress at Arpi. I may even be wounded myself; though I am your daughter; an assault on me by mortals cannot be far off. If the Trojans have come to Italy without your blessing or approval, then let them pay for their disobedience. They do not deserve your help. But if they have faithfully followed the instructions that they were given by the gods above and below the earth, why would those instructions be revised? How can there be a change in the fate that has been determined for them?

"And yet I wonder, I wonder. Who was responsible for the fire that destroyed their ships in Sicily, or the storm that was raised off Libya by Aeolus the king of the winds? Who dispatched Iris on certain mysterious errands? Who was it that went down to stir up the spirits of the dead (that was a device that has never been tried before) so that suddenly Allecto emerged onto earth, to rant and rave throughout the towns of Italy? A future empire for the Trojans seemed reasonable enough while Fortune was on their side, but now I can hope for it no longer. So I give up: let them be conquered by whomsoever you wish. But if there is nowhere on the face of the entire earth where unforgiving Juno will leave them in peace, then, my father, as you remember the smoking ruins of Troy, I beg this of you at least: let my grandson Ascanius come safely through the fighting. If Aeneas is to be cast adrift once more on the open sea, then let him follow whatever path Fortune may allot to him. But give to me the power to protect Ascanius and save him from death in battle. I have temples on the mountain tops of Cyprus where he can lay down his arms and live out his life in comfortable obscurity.

"If that is what you want, let Italy be overwhelmed by the Carthaginians, and ruled by them. I will put no obstacles in their way. But what was your purpose in allowing the Trojans to avoid the horrors of war, and to escape from their city when the Greeks had torched it? Why did you let them live through so many other dangers by land and sea? What point was proved by encouraging them to make for Latium and raise their citadel again? Would it not have been better to leave them as squatters in the ashes of their native land, on the spot where Troy once stood? Give them back their home on the river Xanthus, I beg of you. Let the poor Trojans rebuild Troy, and live their history over again."

Juno accuses Venus of interference

Queen Juno interrupted her angrily. "You will force me to break my long silence, will you not? Why must I mention my unhappiness, long suppressed, and speak it out loud? Who was it—god or man?—who made Aeneas go to war and challenge king Latinus? Yes, I grant you that the fates brought him to Italy—though of course Cassandra's prophecies urged him on. But it was not I, was it, who encouraged him to leave his camp and entrust its charge to a boy? Did I make him sail up the river and make a pact with the Etruscans and disrupt their quiet lives? That was an act of deceit. Did a god drive him to it? Did I? Did I send Iris down to him? You complain because the Italians are attacking what you call 'this second, infant Troy'; you complain because Turnus—a descendant of one of the great Italian gods, and the son of an Italian nymph—is defending himself against foreigners in his own country. Well, why did the Trojans attack the Latins in the first place? Why are they occupying land that does not belong to them? Why are they plundering other people's property, and interfering with other people's wedding plans, and abducting other people's girls? They talk peace, so why do they make war? If it is right for you to rescue Aeneas from the Greeks, or save a man from danger by turning him into a swirl of mist, or transform ships into sea-goddesses, why is it so wrong for me to give the Rutulians a little help?

"'Aeneas is away,' you say, 'and knows nothing of any of it.' Very good—let him stay away, and then he will still know nothing. Perhaps you should attend to your mountain tops and your temples in Cyprus, rather than dabbling in serious

matters, like battles, that you do not understand. And now you
have the nerve to accuse me—me!—of trying to destroy the
pathetic remnants of Troy. Tell me then—who set the Trojans
against the Greeks? Why did Europe and Asia go to war? Why
did they corrupt their friendship with a rape? Was I respon-
sible for Paris' visit to Sparta? Did I give him the means or the
opportunity to steal Helen from Menelaus? That was the mo-
ment to watch out for your people. Now it is too late: you are
simply picking a silly quarrel with me, and your charges mean
absolutely nothing."

Jupiter remains neutral

Juno sat down, and all the other gods
took sides, and began to talk urgently
amongst each other, like the first stirring
of a wind: leaves rustle in the woods, and out at sea catspaws
warn sailors that a gale is coming. Then Jupiter, all-powerful
and all-controlling, spoke. At his voice, the house of the gods
fell silent. The earth below trembled; the winds dropped, the
air was still and a flat calm spread across the sea.

"Listen to what I am going to say, and carefully mark my
words. Just as your disagreements will never end, so the Ital-
ians and the Trojans will never make peace. One side may be
lucky today, the other tomorrow. They can always hope—but
they will get no help from me. I make no distinction between
them. So the Trojans are unlucky enough to be besieged? Did
they make a stupid mistake? Did they listen to poor advice?
I do not care—and I bear no responsibility for the Rutulians
either. What will happen will happen. I am the same indiffer-
ent king over all of them, and they are all in the hands of fate."
He called as his witness the whirling waters of the Styx, his
brother Hades' river; he bowed his head, and Mount Olympus
shifted. In silence he rose from his golden throne, and in si-
lence the gods escorted him to the doors.

The Trojans continue to resist the Latin attack

The armies of Turnus meanwhile still
battered at the Trojan rampart, killing or
setting fires wherever they could. But in-
side, Aeneas' troops stood their ground,

even with no hope of escape. They still kept a fruitless watch from the towers; and the harder it was to shore up the weak spots in their defenses, the more desperate they became. But they would not surrender, and every one of them, whether he fought with javelins or stones, firebrands or arrows, was a hero. Acmon, for instance, who was Clytius' son and Mnestheus' brother, wielded with a strength no less than theirs a rock as big as half a mountain. And the boy Ascanius, whom Venus loved, wearing a gold circlet rather than a helmet, with his hair curling down over the back of his neck, was as conspicuous as a jewel set in gold on a headdress or a necklace, or as ivory against the dark wood of a terebinth-tree. And no one could miss Ismarus, the archer from Maeonia, where the river Pactolus waters the fields and ripens the crops to gold: the points of his arrows were dipped in poison. And Mnestheus himself: he had already gained distinction among the gods by driving Turnus off the battlements, and still he fought steadily alongside Capys, who would later give his name to the city of Capua.

Aeneas to the rescue: he is supported by Tarchon and the Etruscans

While the siege continued, Aeneas was still far off. He was at sea, on a night passage. Following Evander's advice, he had entered the Etruscan camp and approached their leader Tarchon. He told him his name and where he was from, and what he wanted and what he would give him in return. He told him also how the rebel Mezentius had joined forces with Turnus, and how embittered Turnus had become. "Men must always trust each other," he said, "and now I am asking for your help." Tarchon did not hesitate. Immediately he made a pact with Aeneas—and at that moment the old prophecy was fulfilled, the prophecy which had insisted that the Etruscans must be commanded by a foreigner. Then, on the orders of the gods, they had assembled a fleet for him. Aeneas was in the lead: his ship had a figurehead consisting of Asian lions and Mount Ida above them—a cheering sight for homesick

Trojans. He sat pondering the twists and turns of warfare, and young Pallas, close beside him, asked him questions about the mysteries of celestial navigation, or about his adventures by land and sea.

A digression now, for a roster of the captains from Etruria who had contributed ships and joined Aeneas' expedition.

• In the lead, Massicus: he commanded the *Tiger,* with a thousand young men from Clusium and Cosae, sharp-shooters who carried their lightweight bows and arrows slung across their shoulders.

• The grim-faced Abas: his troops were magnificently armed and he had a golden image of Apollo on his poop-deck. The town of Populonia had sent with him six hundred experienced soldiers, and Ilva, an island with inexhaustible veins of iron ore, had sent three hundred.

• Asilus, a mediator between gods and men: he could interpret the omens in animal entrails, stars, birdsong or lightning. With him, a thousand men from Pisa, who marched in close order with spears held proudly upright.

• Astyr, very handsome, a horseman in multicolored armor: he led three hundred single-minded volunteers from Caere, Minio, old Pyrgi and Graviscae—an unhealthy spot.

• Cinyras, the bravest man in Liguria.

• Cupavo, with only a few followers: he was going to war in company with his friends, as the captain of the *Centaur,* whose prow was a match for any rock, and could cut cleanly through any kind of sea. The crest on his helmet was of swans' feathers, a reminder of the great passion of his father Cycnus. The story goes that Cycnus, grieving for his lover Phaethon, used to comfort himself by singing sad songs in the shade of the poplar trees which were Phaethon's sisters. When he was old, his white hair became the soft white plumage of a swan, and he flew away to sing among the stars.

• Ocnus, with a column from Mantua: the town was named after his mother, a soothsayer, and is protected by his father, an Etruscan river. His people had a long and complicated ancestry, but were tough soldiers, like all Etruscans. It was from this region that Mezentius had taken his five hundred rebels down to the sea past the gray reed-beds of the river Mincio.

• Aulestes, aboard the gigantic *Triton:* her hundred oars churned the surface into mottled foam, and her bow-wave chattered beneath a monstrous figure-head—an image of the sea-god blowing his horn to frighten the sea-green waves ahead of him, with a human's head and chest, extravagantly hairy, and, from the waist down, the tail of a fish.

Aeneas approaches the besieged Trojan camp from the sea

Altogether, the Etruscans had brought thirty ships to help the Trojans. They cut through the level seas with their bronze sheathed bows, while the day faded and the light of the kindly moon, going up the sky in her chariot, fell full on Mount Olympus. Aeneas was too worried to sleep; he sat at the tiller himself and tended the sheets. And suddenly, dancing towards him over the waves, came figures that he knew—the crowd of sea-nymphs whom Cybele had created from his own burning ships. They swam and dived beside him, as many of

them as once had been bronze-prowed ships drawn up on the bank of the Tiber. They had recognized Aeneas in the distance and come to greet him. One of them, the most elegant in her speech, followed close in his wake. With her right hand she took hold of his stern and hauled herself half out of the water, and used her left as an extra oar to move the ship on through the quiet sea. Her name was Cymodocea, though Aeneas did not know that.

"Are you asleep?" she asked. "Wake up now; slacken your sheets. We once were pine trees from the sacred mountain Ida; then we were your ships; and now we are nymphs of the sea. When the wicked Turnus attacked us and set us alight, we broke away from our moorings—though we did not wish to—and our mother pitied us: she gave us new forms and made us immortal, to live forever beneath the ocean. And now we have come to look for you, to tell you this: the Latins have Ascanius trapped behind his fortifications. They are well-armed, and excellent fighters, and they are pressing him hard. King Evander's cavalry and his Etruscan allies have mustered to relieve him, but Turnus is determined to head them off, and prevent them from joining forces with Ascanius. You must be sure that your friends are ready for battle as soon as dawn breaks, and you must arm yourself with the impregnable gold-rimmed shield which Vulcan gave you. Believe me: tomorrow's light will bring death to Turnus' men, and shine upon a mound of their corpses."

Cymodocea gave Aeneas' stern a final shove with her right hand—she knew exactly how to do it—and dropped away in his wake. His ship leaped forward, swifter than a javelin or an arrow flying on the wind; and behind him the rest of the fleet increased their speed. Aeneas, who had been unaware of Ascanius' position, was alarmed at the nymphs' news, but cheered by the omen of the their appearance. He looked up into the arching heavens and briefly prayed to Cybele: "Mother of the gods, tamer of lions and ruler of the turreted cities of Asia, I pray that you will be my guide and my companion in this war. Stand with my Trojans and protect them too."

As he finished his prayer, the daylight returned and the night faded away, and he gave the order to his allies to follow his signals and to stand ready in every respect for war. And then, from his position up on the poop-deck, he saw in the distance the Trojans and their camp on shore. He held up his shield high in his left hand; it caught the light, and from their earthworks the Trojans saw the flash. They raised a cheer to wake the stars, and a new hope ignited a new fire in their hearts. Their arrows flew more fiercely yet, as thick and dark in the sky as noisy cranes migrating to Macedonia on the south wind. Their fresh spirit surprised Turnus and the Italian commanders, until they looked out and saw the fleet headed in toward them, ship after ship, the whole sea on the move. Aeneas' helmet seemed to be burning under a crest of flame. The golden boss of his shield spat fire; it gleamed like a comet on a clear night, bloodshot and sorrowful, or like the dog-star rising across a gloomy sky, promising heat-wave, disease and drought.

Nevertheless Turnus did not lose his confidence; he was sure that he could hold the beach and drive off these reinforcements. To his men he said, "The opportunity you prayed for has arrived. This is our chance for total victory. We are only men, but the spirit of Mars himself possesses us. Think now of your wives and families; remember your forefathers, and *their* fame, which will last forever. We must meet the enemy right at the water's edge, while they're still nervous and before they have a chance to get their footing. Fortune will be with us as long as we do not hesitate." While he was speaking, he was already deciding whom he should take with him down to the shore and whom he should leave to prosecute the siege.

Aeneas' relief forces make a landing near the Trojan camp

Meanwhile Aeneas had rigged gangways and was disembarking his men. Many wanted to wait until the tide had ebbed, so that they could jump into shallow water; others vaulted ashore on their oars. Tarchon spotted a place without shoals, without breakers, where his ships could glide in smoothly on the rising tide. He urged his men to turn their bows to shore. "Lay to your oars," he shouted. "This is the job you came to do. Pull till your bows lift; put your prows right up onto the beach. Use the stems to drive a pathway through the sand; the keels can cut their own furrows. I'm not going to worry about damage, as long as we get ashore." His crews dug in their oars, pulling in a cloud of frantic spray until their bows ran up onto the dry land, and everyone was hard aground in Latium—all except Tarchon himself. For he had struck a ridge offshore, just below the surface, and for a long time he hung there—would he slide off, or not? The tide rocked him until finally his ship broke up. In a clutter of broken oars and floating thwarts, Tarchon and his men were dumped in the water, and they had to scramble to shore against the pressure of the undertow.

Fighting began at once. As the landings continued, Turnus wasted no time in detaching his forces and leading them down to defend the beach. Trumpets sounded. Aeneas charged against the Italians—they had come straight from their farms— and began to scatter them. It was an omen for the future.

Aeneas killed the first man to stand up against him. With a single stroke of his sword, he sliced through the bronze chain-mail and the gold-laced tunic, and deep into his side. And then

he cut down a man who had been taken from his mother's womb after her death, and had spent his childhood in Apollo's service. But that meant nothing to Aeneas' sword. Two brothers next: their father had been Hercules' companion during the twelve labors, and they swung their clubs with Hercules' energy but without his skill. One man was hit right in his mouth, just as he opened it to scream an insult that no one would ever hear. Another was badly wounded trying to impress his latest blond boy, and he would have died without having to worry any more about the young men he constantly pursued, if his brothers had not come to his rescue—seven of them, each letting fly a javelin. Some of them clanged off Aeneas' helmet or his shield. Venus deflected the others, so that they merely grazed him.

"Bring me more spears," called Aeneas to Achates, who was as ever at his side. "Whatever I used against the Greeks at Troy will certainly serve for Latins." He selected two and threw them at three of the advancing brothers. The first one hit Maeon—the point went straight through his shield and breastplate and finished deep in his chest—and the second tore off Antenor's arm at the shoulder as he tried to hold up Maeon. Numitor pulled it out of Antenor's side and threw it back, but it missed and instead wounded Achates slightly in the thigh.

But the Latins rallied. The young hero Clausus threw a javelin at Aeneas' companion Dryops and caught him in the throat. Dryops tried to say something, but instead of words came a gush of blood. Down he went, flat on his face, and bled to death. Then he killed six warriors from Thrace, three sons of Boreas and three of Idas. Halaesus, and Messapus, Neptune's son, came up to help, and at the very edge of their territory, the Italians tried to drive the Trojans one by one back to the sea. All along the line the two sides clashed. They stood foot to foot and eye to eye, man packed against man without an inch of ground between them.

Sometimes a battle is like a storm: the winds seem to blow from all directions at once. Sky and clouds and sea are a chaos of contradictory forces—and each element cancels out the other.

Pallas'
horsemen
run into
difficulty,
and Pallas
rallies them

Further inland, in a place where a flood had uprooted trees along the bank and left jagged rocks exposed, the ground became unsuitable for the Arcadian cavalry, and Pallas was forced to have his men dismount. But they were not used to fighting on foot, and as the Latins attacked, they began to drop back. Pallas tried to restore their spirit; but when encouragement failed, he had to resort to bitter words. "What are you doing? Running? Is this your legendary bravery? What would your king, my father Evander, think? He has never lost a war—and I hope to be as great a king as he is. What's the use of flight? Where are your swords? Use them! Where the enemy stand fiercest and thickest, that is where your country calls you—you, and me, your commander. We are in no danger from the gods, but only from mortals like ourselves. The enemy's hands and minds are no different than ours. There is no land to run away on in any case; our backs are to the sea. So—shall we go swimming? Or stand up for Troy?"

Pallas followed up his words with action, and rushed into the center of the enemy line. The first man he met was Lagus—bad luck for Lagus, who was surprised trying to dig up a heavy rock to use as a missile. Pallas' spear hit him at the point where his ribs joined his spine, and stuck there. Pallas started to recover it, and Lagus' friend came rushing up in the hope of revenge. But he did not think clearly enough, and Pallas was ready for him, and killed him too, along with Sthenius and Anchemolus, a man who had once raped his stepmother. Next he faced a pair of identical twins—it had amused their parents that they could not tell them apart, but Pallas distinguished them in their death. One of them he beheaded, and he chopped off the other's hand; still half-alive, its fingers twitched as they tried to disentangle themselves from Pallas' sword. And the rest of the Arcadians, when they witnessed the example that Pallas set, and remembered his shaming words, rejoined the fight with fresh enthusiasm. Two of them took off after Rhoeteus, who had tried to escape in his chariot, but as he fled, he got in the way of a spear that Pallas had aimed at someone else. Over the rail of his chariot he went, and as he died they heard the drumbeat of his heels on the ground.

Pallas was greatly cheered,

The bravery of Pallas and Lausus

like a shepherd who plans to clear a pasture by burning brushwood. He sets a few fires here and there and waits for the wind to get up; and just as eventually he can see with satisfaction the whole field aflame,

so Pallas saw his friends' individual acts of courage come together into a coherent whole. But the Italian Halaesus was experienced in war, and quick to recover his nerve. He killed the Trojans systematically, one after the other: he sliced a man's arm clean off to avoid having his own throat cut, and he beat in someone else's face with a rock, and splattered out his brains in a spray of skull-fragments and blood. When Halaesus was a boy, his father, a fortune-teller, had protected him from danger by hiding him in the woods. But now that his father was dead, the fates interceded and gave him over to Evander's son. Pallas caught up with him and prayed to the river Tiber: "Grant my weapon safe passage through Halaesus' heart, and I will hang his arms as a trophy on your sacred oak." The god heard him: as Halaesus was shielding a comrade, he left his side exposed to Pallas' thrust.

Now Mezentius' son Lausus was ready to play his role. He would not allow Pallas' prowess to intimidate his forces: first he struck down Abas, the stolid core of the resistance to the Latin advance, and then countless Etruscans and Arcadians and many Trojans who had safely survived the Greeks. But still the two lines, equal both in strength and tactics, stood immobile, each jammed against the other by the rear ranks moving up. On one side Pallas urged on his men, and on the other Lausus: they were the same age, both beautiful young men—and neither of them was destined to return alive to his native land. But Jupiter would not allow them to face each other in single combat. Death was waiting for them, but it would come from an enemy more powerful than either of them.

Pallas comes face to face with Turnus

Turnus meanwhile had received a message from his goddess-sister, that he should bring support to Lausus; and he came galloping up from the rear in his chariot. "It is time to stop fighting," he told his allies. "I want to deal with Pallas myself. He is mine—and I only wish his father were here to see it." And at his orders, his companions fell back and left an open space for him. Pallas was surprised at the Italian withdrawal, and at Turnus' challenge. He looked Turnus over carefully, taking in every detail of that awe-inspiring presence, and spoke up to him. "If I die, I will win honor for my splendid death in action; and if you die, I will win honor for my splendid trophies. It does not matter—in either case my father will not be disappointed in me. So there is no point in threatening me." He strode into the space that had been cleared between them, while his Arcadian friends shivered in anticipation.

> If you think of a lion, high up on a cliff above the plain, about to pounce upon a wild bull before he can make his charge, you will be able to imagine how Turnus looked as he jumped down from his chariot and got ready to fight.

As they came within spear-shot, Pallas decided to make the first move. Even if he and Turnus turned out not to be evenly matched, he thought that chance might well be on his side. "Hercules," he prayed. "My father took you in and sheltered you, when you came to him as a stranger. Stand by me now: I want Turnus to see me stripping his armor from him as my spoils of war, and I want him to realize, as he dies, how thoroughly he has been defeated." Hercules heard him, but all he could do was to heave the deepest of sighs and shed a fruitless tear. But Jupiter spoke to him affectionately: "Life is short, Hercules. I cannot change it. But every man has his day: he gains a good reputation from what he does, and good works come from a courageous heart. So many children of the gods have already fallen beneath the walls of Troy; I lost a child of my own there. And when Turnus comes to the end of the time that has been given to him, the fates will summon him too." And he turned his eyes away..

The death of Pallas

Pallas threw his spear, and immediately after that he drew his sword. The spear glanced off the armor on Turnus' shoulder, and pierced the rim of his shield and scraped by his ribs. Then Turnus aimed his own weapon, a long oak shaft with a sharp iron tip, and released it with a sneer: "So much for yours; let's see what mine will do." And he sent it plowing straight through Pallas' shield—all the layers of bulls' hides,

stretched over iron and bronze, could not slow it—and then through his breastplate, so that it opened a hole in his chest. Pallas tore it from the wound, its point still warm; but he was too late, for his spirit gushed out with his blood. He collapsed face downward—an ungainly clatter of armor, nothing more—and a red trickle found its way out of his mouth onto the ground.

Turnus stood over him. "Now, you Arcadians," he said, "remember to tell king Evander that I will give Pallas' body back to him, such as it is. I suppose he has earned the honor of a burial and the comfort of a tomb—I will not grudge him that. But he will regret that he ever gave a welcome to Aeneas." He put his left foot on Pallas' body and ripped off his sword-belt. On its gold plates were engravings of a terrible crime of sacrilege and murder—a famous work by a famous artist. Turnus was ecstatic to have it, and celebrated immoderately. He had forgotten, as so many men do, that nobody can tell what the fates will bring; and that it is not right to delight in success too much. But a time would come when he would be willing to pay to have Pallas' body back intact, unspoiled, unstripped— the body which now the Arcadians carried sadly back to their lines on a shield. Poor Pallas: on the same day that he had departed for the war, on the same day that he had left so many Rutulians dead, he would return home—a glorious victor and a much-lamented son.

Aeneas is inspired by anger

Word of his death reached Aeneas, followed by further intelligence that the situation had reached a point of crisis, and that his Trojans needed help. Straightaway he took up his sword to cut a savage path straight up to the front line, looking for Turnus, looking for blood. Images floated in front of him: images of Pallas and Evander, of the festival in honor of Hercules' festival which he had attended, of all their mutual promises. He took Sulmo's four sons alive, then Ufo's, as sacrifices; their blood would quench the flames on Pallas' pyre. His next victim would have been Magus: he aimed at him from a long way off, but Magus ducked under Aeneas' spear, and crawled up to grasp Aeneas round the knees like a suppliant in a temple.

"I beg you," he whined, "by the spirit of your father, and by your young hope Ascanius—spare me, so that I can see my child and my father again. You can have all the engraved silver and the gold artifacts, some finished, some not, which are hidden inside my house. Whether you win or lose has nothing to do with me. My life or death will have no effect on anything."

Aeneas answered him: "Keep all the gold and silver that you say you have—save it for your sons. Turnus wiped out all bargains of that sort when he killed Pallas. My father's spirit would agree, and so would Ascanius." He gripped Magus' helmet with his left hand and bent back his neck, and thrust in his sword up to the hilt. Standing beside Magus was a priest of

Apollo and Diana, conspicuous in his brilliant white robes and sacred wreath. As he tried to get away, he slipped; and then, with Aeneas' shadow lying long across him, he died like a sacrificial victim. Serestus took his armor and laid it as a trophy on Mars' altar.

The Latins continued to press. Aeneas angrily repelled Caeculus, a descendant of Vulcan, and Umbro from the mountains. He fought like Aegaeon, the giant who has, they say, a hundred arms and a hundred hands and fifty flame-spitting mouths and a flaming body; for every thunderbolt that Jupiter threw at him, he could hold it off with one weapon or another. Anxur, trying to sound braver than he was, boasted confidently that he still had a long old age in front of him, but Aeneas knocked aside his shield and cut off his left hand. When king Latinus' half-brother Tarquitus, a peacock in his carefully buffed armor, tried to stand in his way, Aeneas thrust his spear right through his shield and into his chest, and then, as he begged for his life, beheaded him in mid-sentence. Then he kicked the still warm body onto its back. "Not so magnificent now, are you?" he said. "Your dear mother isn't going to scatter earth on your body, let alone lay you in your family tomb. You'll either be left out in the open as food for the wild birds, or tipped into the river—and the fishes can nibble at your wounds." And when Antaeus and Luca, Turnus' right-hand man, came to take Tarquitus' place, Aeneas went after them too, and then Numa and Volcens' son Camers—the richest man in Latium and the king of Amyclae, a town till now untouched by history. No one was safe from Aeneas' fury or the whirling of his sword.

A Latin chariot charge: Niphaeus' team, frightened by Aeneas' approach and his muttered curses, swerved and pitched out their driver, and bolted in the direction of the beach. But another chariot, drawn by a pair of grays, stopped dead in front of him. Liger was driving, with his brother Lucagus beside him, brandishing his sword. Aeneas stood his ground, and took a step forward with his spear cocked. Liger stupidly tried to provoke him: "These aren't Diomedes' horses, you know, and this isn't Achilles' chariot. And this isn't Troy. This is Latium, the place where you're going to die." Aeneas did not bother to answer such nonsense, but simply ran him through.

Lucagus then tried to drive and fight at the same time, leaning forward to use his javelin instead of a whip, and bracing himself with his left foot. Aeneas' spear skidded off the rim of his shield and into his groin; he toppled out over the side, already nearly dead. And Aeneas spoke to him bitterly: "Lucagus, don't blame your horses: they didn't run away, they didn't shy at shadows. It was you that let them down, when you abandoned your chariot with that fancy somersault." He grabbed the horses' bridles; Liger, still lying on the bottom of the chariot, stretched out his hands in supplication.

"I beg you," he said, "by the parents who made you the generous man that you are, take pity on me and spare my life." But Aeneas replied: "This is a very different song from the one you sang just now. But in fact it's *you* are going to die—and you'll take your brother with you." And he rammed his swordpoint into Liger's chest, and released out his spirit.

From then, wherever Aeneas went, death followed him. He raged across the plain like a tornado or a tidal-wave, until at last Ascanius and the rest could emerge from the camp and break through the besieging forces' lines.

Juno pleads with Jupiter for Turnus' life, and creates a diversion

Up on Olympus, Jupiter spoke to Juno again. "My sister and my dearest wife. As you anticipated—and you were exactly right—it is not their own skill in war, nor their fierce courage, nor their readiness to face danger, that supports the Trojans. It is Venus."

Juno quietly replied: "My dearest husband, why do you say this to me? I am sick at heart and I am afraid of what you are going to say. If there were any power of persuasion in my love—which there was once, and which there still ought to be—you would have allowed me to rescue Turnus from battle and bring him safe home to his father. If not, then let him die, and let him pay with his blood whatever debt he owes to the Trojans. But remember that he reveres the gods—and there is a god in his own lineage, four generations back—and he has often brought generous offerings to your altars."

"So you think that I can arrange for this doomed young man's death to be postponed?" answered Jupiter. "Is that it? Very well. You may extricate him from the fighting, and snatch him away from the fates which are hovering over him. To that point I can indulge you. But if there is some deeper motive lying beneath your request, if what you are really trying to do is to change the whole course of the war, your efforts will be for nothing."

Juno's reply was muffled by tears. "Of course you will deny it—but secretly you know that you could still let Turnus live. You could, if you only would. But as things stand—I wish my fears were groundless, but I think not—an innocent man will die a horrible death."

Without another word, Juno wrapped herself in mist so that she could go down through the air to the earth like a rainstorm falling on the Trojan army and the Latin camp. Then from the hollow of a cloud she made an image in Aeneas' form—an extraordinary phenomenon. It was a body without substance—an uncast shadow. She gave it Aeneas' way of walking and talking—though the words meant nothing, just sound without thought—and Aeneas' weapons and shield and his own plumed helmet, but it was only one of those figures that men say flit about after death, in dreams that deceive the dreamer. And the ghost leaped laughing into the line of battle; it teased the Latins and derided them. Turnus faced it, but as soon as he threw a spear at it, it turned its back and moved away from him. Then of course Turnus thought that Aeneas was withdrawing. He was surprised, but his mind was filled with hope.

Turnus is extracted from the action

"What are you running from, Aeneas?" he called. "Surely not from the marriage agreement that you have made? Do you want me to make you a present of the land that you crossed the sea to find?" And he pursued the ghost towards the shore, shouting and waving his sword about. He never realized that his excitement was as fragile as a puff of wind.

With Turnus hot behind him, the ghost, still in apparent flight, ran down to the rocks by the shore, where by chance an Etruscan ship was moored, with ladders propped against her side and gangways rigged. And so it turned out that at the

exact moment when, back on the battlefield, the real Aeneas was looking for Turnus, who seemed to have mysteriously vanished, Turnus was chasing Aeneas' ghost along the pier and up a gangway and onto the ship. As soon as they were both on board, Juno snapped the mooring-ropes and shoved the ship off into the current. The ghost, no longer needing a place to hide, was at once transformed into a black cloud and floated into the sky, while a sudden squall blew up and carried Turnus out to sea.

He had no idea what had happened, least of all that he had been saved from death. He lifted his hands and spoke to Jupiter. "Have you found me guilty of some crime? Is this a punishment? Where are you taking me? If this is flight, what is there for me to flee from? Shall I ever see Latium again? What will become of my companions, who followed me into the war? Am I to believe that I have abandoned them to an unspeakable fate—either to wander leaderless or die in groaning agony. Is there is a chasm deep enough to cover me? Perhaps at least the winds will feel some sorrow for me. If I pray to them, perhaps they will throw me up on a reef or strand me on some sandbank, where neither my people nor my reputation can follow me." Indecision tore him apart: should he avoid disgrace by running on his own sword? or should he attempt the long swim ashore, to rejoin the battle with the Trojans? Three times he made up his mind, and changed it; three times Juno held him back and out of pity comforted him. At last with a following wind and sea he came smoothly to land and returned to his father's capital.

King Mezentius enters the battle Jupiter meanwhile had advised Mezentius to attack the Trojans while they were still celebrating the disappearance of Turnus. The Trojans' allies confronted Mezentius' advance with leveled weapons, their ranks closed tight in common hatred against him and him alone. But Mezentius withstood them, like a rock which sticks up above the surface of the sea, exposed to all the fury of the wind and waves, unmoved and unmovable. He killed Hebrus and Latagus and Palmus, smashing Latagus in the face with a rock and slicing the tendons behind Palmus' knees as he tried to get away. He took his armor and the crested helmet and gave them to his son Lausus to wear. He killed Evanthes and Mimas, who had been born on the same night that Hecuba, dreaming that she was pregnant with a firebrand, had given birth to Paris. Paris is buried now in a tomb in Troy, but Mimas would lie unrecognized on a beach in Italy.

Have you ever seen a wild boar driven from his lair by hounds? For years he may have lain low under the pine-trees on a mountainside, or among the reeds of a marsh; but now he has been entangled in a net. He stands his snarling ground, afraid of nothing; the hair along his back stands on end, and he moves slowly from side to side, shaking off the hunters' spears and making sure that they can see his tusks. They form a

cautious circle round him at a safe distance, so safe
that their spears, if they hit at all, are harmless.

Mezentius was just like that boar: however righteously angry
the Trojans were, no one had the courage to approach close
enough to fight with him hand-to-hand. They simply irritated
him by shooting arrows at him from long range and yelling
threats.

In the Trojan army there was a Greek called Acron. He had
joined Aeneas because something had gone awry with his mar-
riage, but in battle he still wore the colors of his wife, and so
he attracted Mezentius' attention. Mezentius pounced on him

like a lion—a lion whose hunger has made him bold,
who prowls about the woods in wait for a straying kid
or a young stag: with slavering pleasure he crouches
over the entrails of his kill, and his mane frames a
mask of fresh blood.

Acron went down in a heap, hammering the ground with his
heels as he died with a splintered spear in his belly. And Oro-
des fell close by him: his back had been turned, but Mezentius'
honor would not let him take him by surprise. He met him
face to face and man to man, and overcame him not by stealth,
but because he was a better fighter.

"Here lies the great Orodes," he said, leaning on his spear
with his foot on Orodes' body. "He fought well."

Mezentius' men cheered, but Orodes muttered: "You won't
be cheering for long. My death won't go unavenged. Whoever
you are, the fates await you too, and on this field you too will
find your resting place."

Half laughing, half insulted, Mezentius replied: "*Your* time
has come already—but I will wait until Jupiter has decided
what is to become of *me.*" He pulled the spear out of Orodes'
body, but Orodes' eyes were closed forever, in silent and un-
relenting sleep.

Caedicus killed Alcathous, Sacrator killed Hydaspes; Rapo killed Parthenius and Orses who once had seemed invincible; Messapus killed Clonius, a footsoldier, and Erichaetes, a horseman who had been thrown when his bridle had broken; Valerus, skilled and brave like his father, killed Agis. Salius killed Thronius; and Nealces, shooting from long range, killed Salius.

The gods—Venus on one side of the hall, and Juno on the other—gathered in Jupiter's palace. They were not angry like the mortals, only sorrowful; they pitied the endless struggle of both armies. Mars had no favorites: men lived and died in equal numbers. With no one a winner, no one a loser, and no thought of flight, the Furies, pale and savage, urged them on. The battle swirled around Mezentius, who shook his spear and advanced

like Orion when he wades shoulder-deep across a lake or pounds the earth with an ash-tree that he has cut in the mountains; but his head is still hidden in the clouds.

Aeneas wounds Mezentius, who is protected by his son

From the other side of the plain, Aeneas spotted him and went to meet him. Mezentius was not in the least perturbed when he saw him and stood firm, a spear's throw away from him. "Give me now a strong hand and a straight throw," he prayed. "I promise you, Lausus, that you will soon put on Aeneas' armor; I'm going to give you the spoils which I will strip from the body of this bedswerver." He lifted his spear, and threw it. It hit Aeneas' shield and ricocheted into Antores' ribs—Antores, a friend of Hercules, who had come to Italy with Evander. He had hardly expected to be wounded accidentally by a stranger; but pleasant memories of his home in Greece comforted him as he died.

Aeneas' counterattack: his spear cut through Mezentius' shield—three layers of bronze and three layers of ox-hide with linen in between—into his groin. But he was not yet dead.

Aeneas and Lausus both ran up to him: Aeneas, elated at how seriously he was wounded, stood over him with drawn sword; and Lausus wept miserably for a much-loved father—poor Lausus, whose difficult death and glorious deeds will never be forgotten. Mezentius tried to get away, dragging behind him his shield, still transfixed by Aeneas' spear.

As Aeneas raised his sword to deliver the final blow, Lausus jumped under his guard to deflect it. The Latins cheered him on, and put up a screen of missiles until such time as Mezentius could crawl away under the cover of Lausus' shield. Aeneas was forced to halt and protect himself.

> If you can think of a hailstorm or a downpour lashing
> a valley, as farmworkers run for shelter, and travelers
> crouch beneath high river-banks or rocky overhangs,
> waiting for the sun to come out again, you will be able
> to imagine Aeneas' position.

Unable to do anything till the thundercloud of battle should rumble away, he had to be content with shouting taunts at Lausus. "What are you up to? You're going to die anyway—what more can your courage do for you? You can't save your father with love alone." But the less Lausus listened to him, the angrier Aeneas became—while the Fates gathered into their hands the last threads of Lausus' short life.

The death of Lausus

At last Aeneas buried his sword deep in Lausus' body: the point went through his shield and through his breastplate—if only his armor had been as strong as his determination!—and through the tunic which his mother had woven for him with strands of gold. His lungs filled with blood, and his sad spirit left his body, wafted away by the breeze to the world below. But as Aeneas looked at the strange deathly pallor on his face, he remembered his own devotion to Anchises. And he sighed and took pity on him and stretched out his hand to him: "My poor boy, you have lived nobly—what can I do for you that would be worthy of the way that you have died? I will not take your arms as spoils—I know how proud you were of them. But as I release you to the ashes and the spirits of your ancestors, perhaps it will bring you some comfort—if there is any comfort to be had—that only the great Aeneas could bring you down." And he called on Lausus' companions, who were hesitating to come forward, to help him lift his body and wipe away the blood which had clotted in his hair.

By this time Mezentius had made his way to the river. He had stanched his wounds and washed them, and now he was leaning against a tree, with his beard straggled over his chest. His helmet was hung on a branch, and his weapons lay quietly on the grass. He tried to clear his throat so that he could breathe more easily, and his attendants gathered round him. Again and again he asked after Lausus, and sent out messengers to summon him to his anxious father's side. But as they returned, Mezentius heard them lamenting even before they came into sight, and foresaw what their news would be. They carried Lausus up to him, lying on his shield: a gallant young man, killed in a gallant fight.

Mezentius rubbed dust into his white hair, and raised his hands to heaven; then he laid them on his son's body. "Why did I desire to live so much that I would allow you, my boy, to go into battle instead of me, your father? Am I unharmed because of your wounds? Am I alive because you are dead? Now I understand at last what pain and a miserable death really mean. Lausus, your good name is stained because of my crimes: my people hated me, and they drove me from my throne, and exiled me. And it was all deserved; and long ago I should have admitted my guilt—and died. But here I am, still alive, among my fellow men. I have not yet closed my eyes to the light of day. But soon I will, Lausus, soon I will."

He hauled himself to his feet, ignoring the pain of the wound in his leg, although it slowed his step. With his old imperious manner he called for his horse—his pride and joy, his comfort—the horse that had carried him victoriously in so many campaigns. But the horse sensed his sorrow as he spoke to it: "We have lived a long time, you and I, if indeed 'a long time' means anything to mortals. Today, perhaps, you will carry home the bloody spoils which I will take from Aeneas, and together we will avenge the bitter end of Lausus. But, if our efforts fail, then you and I will die—because, my dear old friend, you will never take orders from a stranger, or submit to a Trojan master." Once more he settled himself on the familiar back, once more he put on his gleaming plumed helmet. Javelins in hand, he galloped back into the fight.

"Aeneas! Aeneas!" he called, his anger mixed with shame and grief. "Aeneas!"

Aeneas recognized Mezentius' voice. He was delighted to hear it, and balanced his spear in his hand. "Let our battle begin," he said. "Jupiter and Apollo have brought us together at last."

"How can you intimidate me, now that my son is dead?" asked Mezentius. "His loss is the only reason I could lose to you. I am not afraid of death, and I do not care what any of your gods may think. We will speak no more—but before I die I have these gifts for you."

The death of Mezentius

He threw a spear, and then another and another. In a long arc they flew and hit, but the golden boss of Aeneas' shield repelled them. He rode around Aeneas in three wide circles, and three times Aeneas stood firm in the center, turning always to face Mezentius' javelins and ward them off, safe behind his great bronze shelter. But at last he lost patience with inaction and defense; and he determined to change the momentum of the battle. He leaped out and threw his own spear, and hit Mezentius' horse between the eyes. The Trojans cheered, the Latins gasped; and the horse reared, lashing out with its front hoofs. Mezentius was thrown. The horse fell on top of him, and he lay underneath it, pinned. Aeneas drew his sword.

"Where are you now, Mezentius?" he asked. "Where is your famous courage?"

Mezentius drew a deep breath to clear his head. "Why do you taunt me? Will you be my enemy to the last? Why do you threaten me with death? To kill in battle is not a crime, and neither Lausus nor I ever promised that we would not kill you. But I do ask this, if you have any thought of pity for me now that you have beaten me. I know how much my own people hate me; and I beg you to protect my body from the vengeance that they would take on it. And bury me with my son beside me."

Those were his last words. He bared his throat to Aeneas' sword. Along with the blood that splashed down over his breastplate, his spirit left him.

BOOK XI
The Latins' Last Stand; A Warrior Maiden

The Trojans set up trophies and mourn Pallas

Morning—and time for the Trojans to bury their dead. Aeneas' mind was dulled by all the killing, but he remembered that he was the victor, and must first give his devotions to the goddess of the dawn. He cut down an oak-tree, trimmed its branches and planted it on a mound as a trophy in honor of Mars. And then he dressed it in Mezentius' armor: his helmet-plume still wet with blood, his broken spears, his breastplate pierced in a dozen places, his shield on the left side and, round the neck, his sword with its ivory grip.

Next Aeneas gathered his commanders and addressed them: "The main part of our work is finished, and we should have no anxiety about what remains. Here you can see the spoils of war I have taken from Mezentius, a proud and dangerous king—and here is what is left of Mezentius. His defeat has cleared the road to the Latins' king and the Latins' town. But you must remain on the alert. Hold your arms in readiness. When the gods give us the sign to move out, you must not be caught by surprise; fear or weariness can be no excuse for delay. And now we must commend to the earth our comrades who have not yet been buried—the last respect that we can show them as they go to the world below. Their brave spirits must be sent on their journey with splendid gifts: they have laid the foundations of our new country with their blood. But first," he added sadly, "we must see to poor Pallas.

283

He is dead, but he died courageously, and he must be taken back to his father."

In tears he went to the tent where Pallas' body had been laid. It was guarded by old Acoetes, who had once been Evander's armor-bearer, but had more recently—and less happily—served as companion to Evander's son. Around him stood a crowd of Trojans: soldiers, attendants and women with their hair let down in mourning. Aeneas could hear the sounds of their grief as he entered—they were wailing and beating their breasts. When he saw Pallas' head propped on its pillow, and his pale face, and the wound in his breast which Turnus' spear had made, his own tears burst out again.

"My poor boy," he said. "Does Fortune envy me? She sent you to me so willingly, but now she has turned against me. Why was she so determined that you should never see me as the ruler of Latium? Why could she not let you return gloriously to your father? When I left him, he embraced me and sent me out to found a kingdom. Yes, he was apprehensive, and he warned me that I was going to war with a tough enemy who would give me no quarter. But he trusted me to keep you safe—and I have betrayed his trust. Perhaps at this very moment, he is sacrificing and leaving offerings on the altars, filled with hope that we will bring home his son. And so we will—but his son is dead. Dead, and owing nothing to any god. Was this the triumphant return that Evander expected? So much for my promise: all that he has to welcome home is a body to be buried. But at least he will not see his son with disgraceful wounds in his back because he ran away; it is much better to die than survive as a coward. Italy has lost a tower of strength—and so have you, Ascanius."

They send Pallas' body home

He picked a thousand soldiers to escort Pallas' body and to share Evander's grief—small comfort for so much pain, but a debt that had to be paid to a sorrowing father. Others made a bier for him by weaving together branches of oak and wild strawberry, and shadowed it with a canopy of leaves. They lifted him up and laid him on it. His skin still had on it a soft sheen of youth and beauty,

> like a flower—a violet, maybe, or a drooping hyacinth—which a girl has picked and clutches in her hand: the blossoms have faded and it draws no more nourishment from the soil.

Aeneas brought out two purple robes, stiff with interwoven gold thread, which Dido had made for him with her own hands in happier times. He covered Pallas with one of them, and, as a final gesture of honor, he tucked it gently round his hair, which soon would be consumed by the flames of his funeral pyre.

Then he ordered the trophies of the war with Latium to be collected and carried past, along with the plunder and horses and weapons taken from the enemy. The prisoners were lined up, hands tied behind their backs; they would soon be offered up as a sacrifice to the gods below, and the flames of their pyres would be extinguished with their own blood. Their leaders were forced to carry tree-trunks decked out with captured armor and placards with their names on them. Then Acoetes came out of his tent—his grief had aged him even further—beating his breast with his fists and tearing at his cheeks with his fingernails, and threw himself at full length on the ground. They brought up Pallas' chariot next, still spattered with Latin blood. His horse followed behind, without its harness; tears stood in its eyes. Others carried Pallas' helmet and spear—all that was left of his armor, because Turnus had stolen the rest. And after that came all the Trojans and Etruscans and Arcadians, in massed formation, with their spears reversed.

After the long procession had passed, Aeneas had one last word for him, before he turned away through the ramparts and went back into the camp. "To us who still live," he said, "the fates will doubtless give other wars to fight and other tears to shed. But to you, Pallas, now and forever, I say: 'Hail and farewell.'"

*A truce for
the burial
of the dead*
Envoys arrived now from the Latin capital, with olive wreaths pulled low over their brows, requesting a truce. Would Aeneas, they asked, give back their dead, which lay scattered over the plain, and allow them to be buried? He would, they assumed, have no quarrel with those who had been beaten or killed. Would he not spare those who had once welcomed him, and whose king was to have been his father-in-law?

Aeneas listened to them courteously and granted them their truce. And then he asked them: "What quirk of fortune led you into such a terrible war with us? Why do you flee from us, who would have been your friends? Why do you ask me for peace with the dead, with those who have been lost in the chances of war? I would just as soon have peace with the living. I would never have come here, except that the fates allotted me this place to settle. I have no quarrel with you. Your king Latinus could have had our friendship, but he chose instead to entrust himself to Turnus and Turnus' army. It would have been fairer, then, if Turnus had been among the dead. If Turnus had wished to fight the matter out and turn the Trojans away, then he and I ought to have met in single combat. The best man would have won—or the one whom the gods loved best. Now go, and light funeral fires for your poor people." The envoys were silent, glancing at each other without expression.

Then one of them, older than the rest, a man called Drances, who disapproved of Turnus and disliked him, spoke in reply. "I have heard much about you, you Trojan. They say that in war and peace you are a good man. So should I praise you first as a lawgiver or a warrior? We will be pleased to carry back your sentiments to our own capital, and we will support, if the gods are willing, an alliance between you and our king. Let Turnus make his own arrangements. But we will gladly carry on our shoulders stones for the city that the fates have promised you, and help you to build the walls of another Troy."

A general murmur of approval followed; everyone agreed with him. They made a twelve-day truce, and the Trojans and Latins together worked through the woods and hills in peace and undisturbed, collecting fuel for the pyres. Ashes and oaks, pines and scented cedars, rowans: down they came to the ringing of axes and the hammering of wedges—and the wood was carried off in creaking wagons.

But by then Rumor was flitting about among the houses and behind the walls of Pallanteum. Earlier she had whispered in Evander's ear how excellently Pallas had fought in the battle against the Latins, but now she had brought the first terrible word of disaster. The Arcadians ran to the gates with their mourning torches, and according to a custom many years old they lined each side of the road with a colonnade of flickering lights. The Trojans came to meet them. And when the women on the rooftops saw the two sad columns joined, the whole town seemed overwhelmed with sorrow. Evander came out— his attendants tried to hold him back, but they could not—and he threw himself on Pallas' bier, clinging, groaning, lamenting. At last he managed to speak.

King Evander receives Pallas' body

"This is not what you promised me, Pallas. You said you would be careful when you went off to war; but I knew how tempting it would be for you to try to win a name for yourself in your very first battle. But the earliest actions of your youth brought sadness, and all you ever knew of war was harsh. None of the gods heard my prayers. Your mother is lucky not to have lived to see you as you are today. But I, on the other hand, have lived too long, kept alive only in order to survive my son. I was the one who should have joined the Trojan army, I was the one the Latins should have killed. I would have happily given my life, and then this procession would have carried me home, Pallas, not you. And I would not have blamed the Trojans, or any agreements that we made. This is an end that I would have expected for myself—in my old age. But if my son had to die before his time, at least it gives me some solace to know that when he fell, he had already killed many thousands of the enemy; and he died in the front line, fighting against the Latins. And I could think of no better end for you than this funeral which Aeneas has given you—he and all the Trojans and all the Etruscan leaders and the whole Etruscan army. They carry with them the spoils of those you killed, and there would be a tree-trunk hung with Turnus' arms too—if only he had been the same age as you, and with the same experience. But, Trojans, I must not delay your return to the war. Go, and take this message carefully to Aeneas: 'Pallas is gone—and now the only reason that I have to stay alive is the thought of your right arm, your sword-arm. You owe Turnus' life to me, a father, and to him, my son. I do not expect the gods to grant me any further pleasure in my life—nor should I—but when you have paid that debt, your career will be complete, and I can send the news to Pallas in the world below.'"

A truce for funerals on both sides

The goddess of the dawn by now had climbed up the sky. For poor ordinary mortals it was time to return to work. All along the curve of the shore, according to immemorial custom, Aeneas and Tarchon had catafalques constructed, and the Trojans laid out the bodies of their fallen friends. Flames flickered, and the smoke sent up a sooty haze across the sky. Three times in full armor they marched around the tombs, three times they rode wailing around the funeral fires. Earth and armor were wet with their tears, and the cries of men and the sobbing of trumpets echoed down again from heaven. Some of them threw onto the pyres what they had plundered from the fallen Latins—helmets and swords and bridles and chariot wheels. Some of them added their own familiar shields, and spears that had brought no luck to them. They stole oxen and pigs and sheep from the Italian fields; they cut their throats and sacrificed them. They stayed on the beach to watch their comrades' bodies burn, standing guard over their cooling ashes. They did not leave until nightfall, when the stars came out.

Further inland the Latins made their own sad farewells. Many of their dead they buried on the spot or in the neighboring fields, or they carried them back to the town. But the rest were piled up haphazardly, uncounted, and were cremated without ceremony. For mile after mile the countryside was dotted with bonfires. On the third day, they raked through the embers in the chill of dawn, collected up the muddled bones and, before they had lost their heat, placed them beneath a mound of earth. In Latinus' town, every household burst into lamentation, long and unrestrained. Mothers and wives and sisters, and small boys who had lost their fathers—all of them cursed the war, and Turnus' wedding plans. If he wanted honor and glory, they said, if he wanted a kingdom in Italy for himself, then he should take up his own arms and settle his own quarrels. Drances testily summed up their complaints: Turnus alone should answer the enemy's challenge, Turnus alone should go into battle. Yet at the same time there were those who spoke in Turnus' favor; they could not ignore the support he had from queen Amata, or the famous victories he had won.

The return of the Latin envoys from southern Italy

Amongst all this agitated argument, the envoys who had been sent to the Greek king Diomedes returned with a gloomy reply to their request for aid. All their trouble and energy and expense, they said, all the gold and the gifts and the entreaties, had gone for nothing. Diomedes had told them that the Latins must look for other allies, or else make peace with Aeneas. King Latinus was bitterly disappointed. He could not now deny that Aeneas had come at the command of the fates, or that the gods were angry: the evidence was right before their eyes, in all those heaps of dead. He summoned a council. His chiefs crowded in to his palace, and when they were all assembled, Latinus, who for all his age had lost none of his authority, made a sign for silence. Sitting impassively on his throne, he ordered the envoys to report exactly what they had heard, point by point. The leader of the embassy, the elderly Venulus, was the spokesman.

"We made the journey south—it was long, and far from easy—and at last we came to Diomedes' fort. He has conquered some land and founded a town there, called Argyripa after his native city. We went inside his walls and he invited us into his presence, and we actually touched the hand that had ravaged the land of Troy. We gave him gifts and told him who we were and where we came from. We explained who was making war on us, and why we had come to his town to ask for his help. He listened to all our arguments, and then, quite quietly, he answered us.

"'You are a fortunate people, you Italians, you children of Saturn. What can have happened to make you want to disturb your peaceful lives? What has led you to embark on a war whose outcome you cannot foresee? The fighting around the walls of Troy was bad enough: all the suffering, all the bodies washed away down the river; but those of us who survived have been unspeakably punished for destroying the city. We are a sorry lot, that even Priam might pity. Both gods and men had vengeance on us, and we were scattered all over the world. Menelaus finished up in the mountains of Carpathia, and Ulysses among the Cyclopes of Mount Etna. Achilles' son Pyrrhus never arrived home, and nor did Idomeneus. The Locrians had to settle in Libya. Even Agamemnon, the commander-in-chief of all the Greek forces, was murdered by his wife as soon as he entered his own house—the conqueror of Asia supplanted by an adulterer.

"'And as for me—the gods would not let me return to my beautiful country, to see the wife that I loved or the temples put up by my ancestors. Horrible visions haunt me to this day, and my lost companions have been transformed into seagulls, which soar and swim and scream among the cliffs—a dreadful punishment. But what else could I have expected? I had, after all, attacked the gods and wounded Venus. But this is why you must not call on me to fight another war. Troy has fallen, and I will not go to war with the Trojans again. What's past is past—and I get no pleasure from recalling it. Take the gifts which you have brought me from your country and give them to Aeneas. I have faced his weapons; I have fought hand-to-hand with him. You must believe me when I tell you that he is a mighty warrior: his shield is sure and his spear is like a storm of wind. If Troy had had two like him, the course of history would have been reversed: the Trojans would have invaded Greece, and it would be defeated Greeks who would be weeping today. The Trojan war lasted for ten years—and it lasted as long as it did because of Hector and Aeneas. Both of them were distinguished for their courage and their skill in arms—and Aeneas showed the most deference to the gods. If you have the chance to ally yourselves with him, then take it. But at all costs avoid a war.' That, my lord, is what he said to us. That was his advice."

Latinus makes a peace proposal

The Latins received this report with a babble of different opinions, like a stream whose smooth and rapid flow, held in check by a scatter of rocks, swirls and splashes and chatters between its banks. But as soon as they were calmer and their first burst of panic was quieted, Latinus offered a prayer and then spoke to them from his throne.

"I would prefer to make decisions of this importance before the event. It certainly would have been better not to have called a council like this at a moment of crisis, when the enemy are encamped beneath our walls. We are fighting a war which we did not foresee, against a race of gods and against men who can never be defeated, never be worn down by battle—and even if they are beaten, they will not stop fighting. If you ever had any hope for an alliance with Diomedes, abandon it. Each man's hope—and that a fragile one—should rest in himself. Our situation is desperate—you can feel it and see it for yourselves—but it is no one's fault. Whatever courage could do, we have achieved. Everyone has played his part. It has not been easy to make up my mind on a course of action, but now I will tell you what I have decided. Listen closely.

"Far to the west there is a tract of land near the Tuscan river. It is farmed by Italian tribes: they grow their crops where they can on the slopes of the hills, and put their flocks out to pasture on the roughest places. All this region, and the pine forests that go with it, we will give to the Trojans as a gesture of our friendship; and we will make a treaty with them and make them partners in our kingdom. If they wish, they may settle there and build themselves walls. On the other hand, if they decide they want to find another land or approach another people, they are free to depart. We will build twenty ships for them of good Italian oak; if they need more, there is timber by the shore. They can decide on how many ships they want, and they can design them as they will; we will provide fittings and rope and carpenters. Further, it is my will that a hundred envoys from the noblest Latin families go to offer them the olive branches of peace, and take them gifts: gold and ivory and, as emblems of my sovereignty, a throne and a robe. If anyone has anything to add, let him come forward. Our weary state needs whatever help it can find."

Turnus' arrogance and belligerence is criticized

Then Drances, always critical and always consumed with envy and hatred of Turnus, stood up. He was a man of property and a good speaker, but a reluctant soldier; a clever debater, though devious and not always to be trusted. His noble lineage came from his mother's side; his father was a nobody. As the members of the council listened to him, they became even more fractious.

"This is not a difficult matter, my lord; it hardly requires suggestions from us. Everyone clearly understands our danger, yet all we hear is disgruntled muttering. Turnus should stop his bombast and boasting. It was Turnus who misread the future—no: I am going to speak out, and he can threaten me as much as he wants—and it was Turnus whose wicked purposes have caused the lives of so many good men to be snuffed out, and all our citizens to mourn, while he tried his hand at his own private Trojan war. I'm sure he terrifies the gods—yet he knows that he can run away at the first sign of trouble. Now, sir: you have already ordered many gifts to be sent and many offers made to the Trojans. You must ignore any protests and add one more: you must give your daughter in formal marriage to the excellent Aeneas, and you must make a peace treaty which will stand forever. If such a plan makes you nervous, all that is left is for us to throw ourselves on Aeneas' mercy, and beg him to give up his claims and go away.

"And as for you, Turnus—don't you see how miserable we have all become? We live surrounded by danger and trouble; and you are the cause of everything that has gone wrong in Latium. In wartime no one feels safe—so all that we ask of you, Turnus, is peace, and a pact that you will promise never to break. You say that I hate you—and I will not deny it—but still I approach you as a suppliant. Take pity on your people. Put your anger aside, admit that you have been beaten—and go away. We have had enough of corpses and abandoned farms and refugees. But if you are still moved by thoughts of honor, if you must engage in a trial of strength in order to marry Lavinia, then pluck up your courage and challenge Aeneas to a single combat. Why should *we* die on the battlefield, poor useless creatures that we are, with no one to mourn us or bury us, just so that *you* may have a wife of royal blood? If you want to demonstrate the prowess that you inherited from your war-god ancestor, then go out and face your rival. He is calling you."

Turnus defends himself

Turnus' temper flared when he heard what Drances said. He snarled and spat out his answer. "I notice that you're always the first to attend a conference, where all that is needed is words—but words never won a battle. War is no time to talk—something you do very well. But then there is not much risk in making speeches, is there, as long as there is a barrier between you and the enemy, and no one is bleeding to death in the ditches? You can fulminate as fiercely as you like—as is your habit—but you cannot charge me with cowardice until you have killed your share of Trojans and hung up trophies as far as the eye can see. It is not too late to prove yourself. The enemy are not hard to find: they're all around our walls. *I* am going out to meet them—are *you?* Or will Mars only find a job for your windy tongue and flying feet?

"Admit myself beaten? I don't think that anyone who has seen the Tiber running with Trojan blood, and Evander's family wiped out, and the Arcadians stripped of their arms, would suggest that I have been beaten. And nor would Bitias or Pandarus, or anyone else of the thousand men I sent down to Tartarus when I was trapped inside the enemy's walls. 'In wartime no one feels safe'? What a silly thing to say—though I suppose it might mean something to Aeneas, or to yourself. Go on then: spread despondency and alarm; praise the troops of a twice-defeated nation; sneer at Latinus' army. The Trojans never frightened anyone—you would have seen rivers turn round and flow back to their sources before they impressed Achilles. And now you have the gall to pretend to be scared of me. Oh yes, your nervousness certainly makes your accusations hit home harder. Don't worry, Drances—I'm not going to touch you; you can keep that brave spirit of yours safe inside your manly chest.

"Now, King Latinus—I will address your proposal. If you have no further confidence in our army, if you think that our allies have deserted us, and if you truly believe, just because we have been turned back once, that we are lost and have no hope of recovery—then, by all means, let us sue for peace and admit our futility.

"But what of our old tradition of fortitude? I would like to think that we still have heroes who would rather be trampled face down in the mud than witness such a surrender. Look: many of our resources remain untouched, and many young men remain unharmed. We have reserves. The Italian towns survive. We still have friends. The Trojans have had some success of course, but it has come at a cost—they have suffered losses as great as ours, and they have been battered just as fiercely as we have. Why then do we falter so ingloriously on the threshold of victory? Why does our blood run cold even before the trumpets have sounded?

"Things change, and over time they will get better. Fortune often mocks us, and then she shows us her other face and plants us on solid ground. Very well—so Diomedes will not send us help. But there is still Messapus. And there is Tolumnius—the gods are on his side—and countless others who have been sent out to lead us. There are troops picked not just from Latium but from all over Italy—and all of them destined for glory. And there is Camilla—she's one of the distinguished Volscian people, and she commands a whole column of cavalry, bright in burnished bronze.

"But I would not wish to oppose the common good. If the Trojans should ever demand me to face Aeneas alone, and if that is your will too—then so be it. I am no stranger to Victory, and she certainly does not think so little of me that I should refuse to try anything in such a noble cause. And so I dedicate my life to you, my people, and to you, Latinus. I will go out to meet him. He may be more fearsome than the great Achilles, and he may be wearing armor made by Vulcan—but I am Turnus, and I am wrapped in the courage of my ancestors. Aeneas is calling me, you say, and me alone. Well, let him call. And Drances, remember this: if the gods are angry, it will be my death, not yours, that will appease them; and if there is a prize of honor to be won, you cannot take it away from me."

Fighting breaks out again

While the debate was continuing, a messenger arrived, bringing the terrifying news that Aeneas had left his camp and formed his battle-line. The Trojans were drawn up with the Tiber at their backs, he said, and Etruscan reinforcements were coming down to the plain to join them. The Latins milled about in confusion and shock and sudden anger. Even in their fear they demanded action. The young men noisily put on their armor, but the members of the council sat with tears in their eyes. Gloomily they muttered among themselves, or shouted each other down: they sounded like flocks of birds chattering in the tree-tops, or swans hoarsely calling to each other across a lake.

But Turnus cut them short. "You are happy," he said, "to sit in conference and praise the virtues of peace, but you seem to forget that we are already under attack." After that, he had no more to say to them, and left the meeting to give orders to his commanders. "Volusus: have the Volscians prepare for battle. Bring up my Rutulians. Messapus, Coras: deploy the cavalry across the plain. Secure the approaches to the town. Man the towers. Everyone else: come with me."

So while the citizens ran to and fro throughout the town, Latinus abandoned his plans and dissolved the council. He was gravely perturbed by the new turn of events, and upbraided himself because he had not of his own accord accepted Aeneas' terms and recognized him as his son-in-law. Earthworks were thrown up in front of the gates, and the ground was sown with rocks and stakes. Trumpets sounded the call for action. The women and children stood in a ring around the walls: they knew that the final crisis had arrived. Queen Amata with her retinue brought gifts to the temple on the hill that was dedicated to Minerva, and at her side, eyes fixed on the ground, was the girl who had begun it all, her daughter Lavinia. Married women crowded behind her, filling the temple with incense, and their desperate voices floated out through the doors. "Minerva, mighty in arms and a present help in battle, break the spear of the Trojan invader; strike him down onto the ground before our gates."

But meanwhile Turnus, in furious exhilaration, was putting on his breastplate with its bronze scales, and his glittering golden greaves, and his sword. Still bareheaded, but ready for the fight, he came down from the citadel

> as carelessly as a stallion that has escaped from his tether and broken out of his paddock: he neighs and tosses his head, so that his mane blows free over his neck and shoulders. Will he make his way to the field where the mares are pastured, or will he canter down to the river to swim?

Camilla and her cavalry enter the battle; Turnus lies in ambush for Aeneas

Camilla, with her Volscian horsemen beside her, met him outside the gates. She dismounted neatly, and all her companions after her. "Turnus," she said, "if my confidence is a measure of my courage, there is nothing I will not dare to do today. I give you my word: I will lead the charge against Aeneas and the Etruscan cavalry. Let me face danger first, while you stay on foot and go up to guard the town."

Turnus looked her straight in the eye. "Is there a braver warrior than you in Italy? Yours is the fieriest spirit of them all. How shall I repay you? It is hard enough to find the words to thank you. But I cannot let you undertake this mission alone. We must share it. Rumor has it—and it's confirmed by spies— that Aeneas has sent forward the Etruscan cavalry across the flat ground, while he himself is moving through deserted mountain passes to come down on the town from the opposite direction. But I am preparing a trap for him: I'm going to post soldiers to lie in wait for him up in the woods. Meanwhile the Etruscan advance must be checked. You're in command, and Messapus and Tiburtus will be in support." He gave similar instructions and encouragement to Messapus and the other chiefs, and then he left them to carry out his own plan.

There was a valley winding between dark wooded precipices, and along its floor a zig-zag path became ever more narrow and treacherous: it was a perfect place for an ambush. From the top of the cliffs there was a clear view of the path far below, and there was a ledge where anyone who wanted to launch a surprise attack from either side, or to make a stand and roll down boulders into the bottom of the valley, would be invisible. Turnus was very familiar with this terrain: he chose his position carefully and settled down in the dense thicket to wait.

The story of Camilla

High up on Olympus, Diana looked over her band of attendant nymphs and called the quick-winged Opis. "Do you see Camilla?" she asked, gloomily. "She is arming herself for war—though fruitlessly, I fear. She is particularly dear to me, and I have loved her and watched over her for a long time. Her father was Metabus; long ago there was a civil war in his kingdom and he was expelled for capricious cruelty. So he fought his way out, and took with him, for company in his exile, his baby daughter Camilla—named after her mother Casmilla, but with one letter dropped. He escaped through the woods into the hills, constantly attacked by snipers, and hounded by Volscian soldiers. All the way he carried Camilla clutched in the fold of his tunic.

"In front of him was a river, in full flood because of torrential rain. How should he get across? He dared not try to swim carrying the baby—that would be too dangerous for her—but all at once a plan came to him. He had with him his enormous spear, whose shaft was solid oak, knotted and hardened by fire. He lashed his daughter to the shaft with strips of bark, and as he held it poised above his head, he prayed to me: 'Diana, mother-goddess of the woods, I dedicate my daughter to you as your servant. This spear is yours—but she has it now; as a suppliant she will flee from her enemies through the air. Take her to be yours. I commit her to the random winds.'

"Metabus drew back his arm, and let the spear go. Along with the poor baby it went whirring across the furious river. But then, with a band of his pursuers close behind him, he dived into the water himself, swam across, and triumphantly pulled out the spear from the turf on the other side; Camilla, his gift to me, was still attached to it. Still no one would shelter him, no town would allow him inside its walls—but he had no intention of giving himself up. He lived the life of a shepherd alone in the mountains. The country was rough, and he brought up his daughter in the thickets, feeding her on wild mares' milk by holding her lips against their nipples.

"As soon as she learned to walk, he put a sharp javelin into her hand and a bow and a quiver over her shoulder. She did not wear any golden pins in her hair, or a long robe. Instead a tiger-skin hung down her back as a cloak. She threw spears as big as her little hand could hold, and she could bring down cranes or swans with a sling. Many of the mothers of Etruria would have liked her to marry their sons, but she was entirely devoted to me, and like me she preferred a life of hunting and virginity. I wish she had not been caught up in this war, and would not try to challenge the Trojans. I love her, and I wish that she had stayed as one of my companions. So that, Opis, is why I want you to fly down to her, wherever she may be. Go to the land of the Latins, where the battle is already beginning. Nothing good can come of it, I know. Take my quiver; take out an avenging arrow; and if anyone—Trojan or Italian—should wound her, make sure he pays the price with his own blood. And if she should die, I will let no one will steal her arms as trophies. I will carry her away inside a cloud and lay her in a tomb in her native country."

A cavalry engagement

Obediently Opis flew down from heaven to earth, in a swath of thunder and black wind. By this time the Trojans were close to Latinus' walls, and the Etruscan cavalry-commanders were moving out ahead of their well-ordered squadrons. Their horses, on a tight rein, tossed their heads to and fro, prancing and dancing until the earth seemed to shake. Spears bristled all across the plain, and swords and shields and helmets sparkled wherever they caught the light. The Italian cavalry was drawn up facing them, lances tucked under their arms or held cocked, ready to throw, and excited by the whinnying of the horses and the rhythm of cantering hooves. Now they were within range. They broke into a gallop—Messapus and his brother Coras, and Camilla on the wing—shouting to their horses and to each other. From both sides, a burst of weapons like a snow-squall. The sky went dark. Tyrrhenus and Aconteus clashed first: their leveled spears shattered, their horses thudded together breast to breast. Aconteus fell as if he had been struck by lightning, or a rock from a catapult; he skidded across the ground, the wind and the life knocked out of him.

The discipline in the Latin ranks did not last long, however. They slung their shields over their backs and turned their horses away. The Trojans came after them, with Asilas in the lead. But in front of their gates the Latins wheeled round again, screaming their war cries—and now the Trojans fled, giving free rein to their horses.

> Imagine breakers crashing onto rocks: spray flies in sheets and waves pound onto the beach. But after each advance, retreat: the rattling backwash sucks pebbles out to sea and slides away and smoothes the sand behind it.

So twice the Etruscans drove the Latins against up their own walls, and twice the Latins shifted their shields to protect their backs; but at the third attack the lines became completely entangled. Each man picked out his own opponent, and they fought face to face, bitterly back and forth. In their blood-spattered armor, they groaned and died—and among them writhed the mortally wounded horses.

Orsilochus threw his spear at Remulus' horse—he did not dare challenge the rider—and left it stuck behind its ear.

In agony and shock it reared up, lashing out with its front hooves, and Remulus slid off and rolled onto the ground. Catillus pulled down Iollas and then Herminius, a big man with a big spirit. He wore no helmet, so that his fair hair fell down to his unarmored shoulders. He was not afraid of wounds, and he let his enemies strike him if they could. But Catillus' spear went right through him from armpit to armpit and the pain bent him double.

The gallantry of Camilla   Blood was everywhere: blood and wounds and the hope for a noble death. But in the middle of the slaughter Camilla was actually happy: she was fighting with one breast bare and a quiver slung over her shoulder. Sometimes she threw javelins, sometimes she wielded a battle-axe. She never tired. Her bow clanged against the golden armor that Diana had given her, and if ever she was forced to give ground, she turned round and fired arrows over her horse's croup. Her companions rode beside her, Italian girls that Camilla had chosen to surround her like the acolytes of a goddess, her ministers in peace and war—Larina and Tulla and Tarpeia waving a bronze axe over her head. They were exactly like the Amazons of Thrace, who live beside the river Thermodon. They are warriors, ruled by warrior-queens: you must have heard of Hippolyta, or Penthesilea, the daughter of Mars? As they march, they howl their war cries—regiments of women in painted armor, carrying shields which are shaped like crescent moons.

It would not be easy to name all the men Camilla killed that day, or how many she left to die. There was, for instance, Euneus: she ran him through with her long spear when he dropped his guard. Blood poured from his mouth, and he pitched face down on the ground and lay dying on his own wound. Or Liris and Pagasus: they died together—one trying to steady his horse after it had been wounded, and the other after putting down his sword to help his friend. And many others: for every spear she threw, a Trojan fell. Ornytus was one: she saw him from a long way off, because he was a full head

taller than everyone else, and all the more conspicuous be-
cause of his odd armor. He was a hunter in peacetime, and he
had skinned a bull and used its hide as a cloak. Instead of a hel-
met he wore a wolf's head with gaping jaws and dazzling white
teeth; and he carried a short hunting-spear. Camilla caught up
with him without trouble and as she ran him through, she
teased him: "Do you think that you are chasing animals in
the woods? But today you are the game, and the hunter is a
woman, and the woman has killed you. Her name—and this
will be something that you can boast of to the shades of your
ancestors—is Camilla."

Next came Orsilochus and Butes: they had the most
powerful frames of all the Trojans. She stabbed Butes from
behind, in the nape of his neck where it shone palely just
below his helmet; the fingers of his left hand went limp, and
he dropped his shield. She avoided Orsilochus' attack by rid-
ing away in a wide circle and then suddenly cutting back—so
that the pursuer became the pursued. He was on foot, so she
was able to bring down her axe upon him from a height. He
begged for mercy, but she had none. One slicing blow, and
then another—the first through his helmet, the next through
the bones of his skull—and his warm brains dripped wet
down his cheeks.

Then the son of Aunus met her: he lived far away in the
mountains, a Ligurian—and, like all Ligurians, he could not be
trusted. Terrified by the expression on her face, he hesitated.
It was too late to run away, and she was too close in any case;
so he decided to see if he could trick her. "What is so wonder-
ful," he said, "about a woman warrior, if she has to rely on
a horse? Don't try to avoid me. Why don't we fight hand-to-
hand, on foot? Then you will know whether or not your talk
of glory is all air."

She was insulted and offended. She gave her horse to a
companion to hold and stood on foot facing him, armed ex-
actly as he was, with a sword and an undecorated shield. And
he, thinking that he had fooled her, jumped without hesitation

onto her horse, snatched at the reins and kicked his heels into its side. "You cheating Ligurian," she cried. "You're too clever for your own good. But you have tried one trick too many. Your lies will not get you back to your lying father."

Quick as a flying spark, she jumped in front of her horse before it could move off, and seized its bridle. With a single slash of her sword she had paid back Aunus' son for his deceit,

> as effortlessly as a hawk which stoops onto a dove.
> One raking mid-air stroke with its talons, and the
> dove is gone—nothing left but a splash of blood, and
> a few feathers floating down to earth.

From his throne on Olympus, Jupiter was watching the battle intently. He put fire into the heart of Tarchon, the Etruscan general, mercilessly chiding him, goading him, needling him: "Will you withdraw? Will you allow a retreat?" So Tarchon rode up and down among his horsemen, calling them by name, and if they gave ground, he turned them back into the fight.

"Are you afraid? Why have you become so feeble? You're scattered and put to flight by a woman—that looks like cowardice to me. What's happened to your swords and your spears? Are they all of a sudden useless? You're not so slow when it comes to matters of love and coupling in the dark. You're always ready for dancing to flute-music and eating and drinking, and you move fast enough whenever a priest summons you into the woods for a festival. Is this all you want, all you can get excited about?"

Tarchon was certainly prepared to die in action himself, and he spurred his horse urgently forward till he came up to Venulus, and grabbed him round the waist, and picked him up straight out of his saddle. The Latins shouted in protest, and everyone paused to look at him as he raced away like a fire through a forest, with Venulus, armor and all, hugged against his chest. He broke off the point of Venulus' spear, and using it as a dagger, held it to his throat, looking for the right spot to press it home and kill him. But Venulus struggled back, forcing the point away as hard as Tarchon pushed it in.

> You could suppose that Tarchon was an eagle, and Venulus a snake that it has caught. The snake has twisted its wounded coils about the eagle's claws; the eagle can only keep its grip by flapping its golden wings. The snake hisses and puffs its scales erect, ready to strike if it can find an opening; the eagle plunges the hook of its beak into a target that never stays still.

And so they left the battle, Tarchon rejoicing over his prey and cheering the rest of the Etruscans by his example.

The death of Camilla

At this same moment Arruns, already doomed by the fates, was riding round Camilla in wide circles. His spear was poised; he was trying for any opening that his skill or his luck would allow. Wherever she advanced, or wherever she retired after a victory, he followed unobtrusively behind her, a secret and silent pursuer. He approached her from one direction and then from another, always waiting for his chance, for a clear shot at her. But Camilla was in pursuit of a Trojan called Chloreus. At one time he had been a priest of Cybele, and he stood out because of his armor, bright with touches of purple and crimson. His horse's saddlecloth was of leather sewn with bronze and gold scales arranged to look like feathers, and everything about him was foreign or exotic. His arrows came from Lycia; his helmet and his bow, from Crete, were made of gold. He wore a yellow linen cloak whose folds were caught up with a golden pin, an embroidered tunic and leggings of a strange design. In her excitement, Camilla grew careless. Perhaps she wanted to dedicate his armor in a temple, or she fancied herself in his golden ornaments when she went hunting—she was a woman, after all. In any case, she was distracted by a blind desire for plunder.

Arruns, still circling, saw his chance. He prayed to Apollo: "Greatest of gods, and guardian of Mount Soracte: am I not your most ardent worshipper? Have I not lit fires of pinewood in your honor, and danced for you on the hot embers? Give me the power to destroy this girl. She's shaming us. I don't want spoils or trophies. My past actions will bring me glory enough. As long as I can get rid of this pestilence, I am happy to return home in disgrace." And he threw his javelin.

Apollo heard the prayer, and decided to grant half of it, but he let the other half blow away on the breeze: he would let Camilla die, but Arruns would never see his home again. As Arruns' javelin left his hand and went whistling through the air, the Volscians' eyes and attention were all turned to their princess. But she did not hear it coming, and she did not feel its wind, until the point sank into her just below her bared right breast, and remained there and drank deeply of her blood. Her comrades ran to her and held her up, but Arruns fled. He had lost his nerve, and his excitement was now overlaid with fear; he did not trust his own weapons any more, and he did not dare to face a counter-attack. Now he only wanted to hide, and to lose himself in the general melee. He ran

> like a wolf with a guilty conscience because he has killed a cowherd or a bullock; he knows that retribution is close behind, and with his tail tucked tightly between his legs, he plunges straight down the steep mountainside, ignoring the path in his panic, and dives into the cover of the woods.

Camilla was dying. She tugged at the spear-shaft, but the iron point was firmly lodged, deep between her ribs. She had lost a great deal of blood. Her eyes were dull and her cheeks were drained of all the color that had once glowed there so brightly. Her strength was nearly gone, and she turned her head to Acca, the companion that she trusted the most, who shared her most secret cares.

"I have done all I can," she whispered. "But this wound, this bitter wound...the shadows are darkening all round me... run now, and take my final word to Turnus: he must take my place, and push back the Trojans from the town...good-bye."

She let the reins go slack; she dropped her sword. She shivered, her neck drooped; her head fell forward. She slipped to the ground, and there was nothing left of her. But as her spirit, with one last protesting sigh, fluttered away into the shadows, the Trojans let out a shout of triumph, which echoed up to the stars. Now that Camilla was gone, they fought with greater energy. They reformed their ranks and charged—Trojans and Etruscans and Evander's Arcadian cavalry all together.

Camilla's death is avenged

Diana's watcher Opis still sat high up in the mountains, calmly observing the fighting. But when in the distance she saw Camilla dead, and the young men shouting and celebrating, she groaned to herself and said, "You have paid too high a price, you poor girl, for your challenge to the Trojans. What good has it done you to worship Diana in the woods, or to wear her quiver on your shoulder? And yet your queen has not let you end your life without distinction. You will not go unremembered among the peoples of the earth, and you will be avenged. Death, well-deserved, awaits the man who wounded you and marred your perfection."

She flew quickly down to a huge mound of earth, shaded with oaks, which lay at the foot of the mountain; it was the tomb of an ancient Latin king. From its summit she looked for Arruns, and she found him still wearing his bright armor, full of empty boasts about what he had done.

"What are you doing, so far away?" she asked. "Come here. Come here to die, so that you may win a prize worthy of Camilla—death from Diana's arrows." From her golden quiver she selected an arrow, and bent the bow until it formed a semicircle, and aimed. Her left hand, pushed forward, held the iron tip, and her right hand, pulled far back, held the string against her breast. All at the same time, Arruns heard the twang as she let go, he sensed her arrow as it flew, he felt the pain as he was hit. He gasped and collapsed in the dust, and while his companions left him to die, alone and forgotten on the plain, Opis flew back to Mount Olympus.

Turnus abandons his ambush; he and Aeneas are kept apart by nightfall

With their commander gone, Camilla's cavalry was the first to turn tail, and after them all the Rutulians. There was no one left now to resist the Trojans' steady advance. The Latins retreated in disorder, with bows unstrung across their exhausted shoulders. Leaderless and dispirited, they thought of nothing but saving themselves behind the shelter of their walls. Their horses' hooves, drumming on the bare dry ground, marked their flight, and the dust that they kicked up rolled in a murky cloud toward the town, where women on the watchtowers wailed and beat their breasts. Under heavy attack, the first of the fugitives tried to break through the gates before they were properly opened. Many of them died in a chaotic struggle on the threshold, or even inside the fortifications, and some were killed right in front of their own houses. Attackers were spitted on defenders' swords: the slaughter was terrible. A few of the townspeople managed to close the gates again, and dared not re-open them even to their friends who begged to be let in. Weeping parents watched as their sons pitched themselves in despair headfirst into the ditches, or gave their horses their heads and threw themselves like blind battering rams against the gates. Some mothers were inspired by Camilla's example to a fresh show of patriotism. If they had spears, they threw them; if not, they made do with wooden clubs and fire-hardened stakes, eager to be the first to die.

Acca brought the news to Turnus, who was still lying in wait for Aeneas in the woods. She told him the details of the battle: how the Volscians were defeated, Camilla was dead, the enemy was triumphant everywhere and there was panic in the town. In frustrated rage (but it was the will of Jupiter)

Turnus abandoned his hiding-place. He had no sooner left the pass than Aeneas entered it. It was now unguarded, and Aeneas was able to proceed without incident across the ridge, and eventually to emerge from the cover of the trees. Both of them made for the town as fast as they could. The routes they chose were parallel, and close enough to one another for Aeneas to see the clouds of dust rising behind Turnus' column, and for Turnus to hear the jangling equipment, tramping feet and snorting horses of Aeneas' troops. They would have attacked each other there and then, but it was already sunset. The sky in the west turned red, and as daylight faded into dusk, both armies pitched their tents and dug themselves in behind a rampart and a ditch.

Book XII
Decision and Revenge

Turnus proposes to Latinus that he and Aeneas should meet in single combat

When Turnus realized that the Latins' spirit was shattered, and saw how completely they had depended on his promises of victory, his indignation boiled over. Rage and violence flooded through him. He was like an African lion, wounded by hunters, who shakes his thick mane, and takes a bitter pleasure in biting at the spear lodged in his chest, while his mouth foams with blood. Turnus approached the king and spoke to him angrily: "I can wait no longer, Latinus. There is no reason for the Trojans to take back what they have said to you, or not to make a truce—they are all cowards. I will meet with Aeneas. Prepare the sacrifices, and let our people sit down to watch us fight. Either I dispatch him to the underworld with my sword—and why not? he is no more than an Asian refugee—and singlehandedly repay his insults to our people, or we are all defeated, and he can be our master, and Lavinia shall be his wife."

Latinus' answer was quite calm. "You are a very brave young man. But I must be as cautious as you are reckless, and as careful in my counsel as you are impetuous in your action. You have our own kingdom, inherited from your father, and many towns that you have captured; but I, besides my riches, have a wise heart. Listen to me: I am going to speak to you quite bluntly, and you must give me your careful attention.

"In Latium, or somewhere else in Italy, there are other women, daughters of noble families, that you might marry.

311

Both gods and prophets have made it clear to me that it was only *my* daughter who could not be given to a suitor from this country. But I made an exception of you, my dear boy, because I loved you, and you were a relative of mine—and my wife wept and pleaded with me. And then I had to take her away from you, though she had been promised to you—and a godless war was forced upon me. You can see very clearly, Turnus, what disasters have happened since—you yourself have been the first to suffer from them. We have already been beaten twice, and now we see all the hopes of Italy resting on this small town. The Tiber flows hot with our blood, the plain is white with our bones. So why am I still undecided? What madness is it that will not let me make up my mind, once and for all? If I am ready to make peace with them as soon as you are dead, why can I not stop fighting while you are still alive? What will your countrymen have to say (and for that matter, the rest of Italy), if I let you go out and be—I can hardly say the word—*butchered,* just because you wanted to marry my daughter? Consider how easily things can go wrong in war; and have pity on your old father, who is anxiously waiting for you at home."

Turnus will not be deterred

But words could not divert Turnus from his purposes. Latinus' efforts to deter him only made him more stubborn. To begin with he could not reply at all, but at last he said, "You are the kindest of men—but if you care for me, now is the time to put your feelings aside. I would rather die than live a dishonorable life. I can shoot an arrow and throw a spear; my arm is far from feeble. When I strike, I draw blood. But this time Aeneas' mother Venus will not be there to hide him behind a cloud when he runs away—a woman's tactic—and then take cover herself in a drift of mist."

Queen Amata was in tears. The prospect of more fighting terrified her, and she embraced Turnus as though she was about to die herself. "Turnus, you are my only hope now, the only comfort for my old age. You are the glory and the power of Latium, and our whole family leans on you even while it falls apart. If my tears move you, and if ever you thought well of me, I beg this one last favor of you: do not go back into battle with the Trojans. Whatever may happen to you will happen to me as well. The day that I am taken prisoner, and Aeneas is married to my daughter, will be my last—I could not bear to see it."

Lavinia heard her mother's words, and she too began to cry. The tears trickled down her burning cheeks, and a flush spread hotly over her face, as though someone had stained a piece of ivory with crimson dye or had mixed roses into a bunch of white lilies. When Turnus saw her, his heart turned over. He was more eager than ever to fight for her, but his reply to Amata was brief. "Do not send me off with tears or despondent words. War is cruel: I cannot choose the moment of my death." He turned to an attendant. "Go to Aeneas and tell him this, though he may not wish to hear it. Tomorrow, at the first glimmer of dawn, our armies will stand down. For them, the war will be over—but not for him and me. We will fight to the death in single combat, and the winner will take Lavinia as his wife."

Turnus and Aeneas prepare to fight

He went quickly back to his tent and called for his horses. They had once belonged to the god Pilumnus; they were whiter than the whitest snow, and galloped faster then the wind, and it raised his spirits to see them. While the grooms fussed round them, patting them on the shoulders and combing their manes, Turnus put on his own armor: a cuirass of pale copper and gold; a sword which Vulcan had made for his father, and had tempered in the river Styx; a shield; and a helmet with a scarlet crest. Lastly, he took up a spear which he had propped against a column: he had captured it earlier as a spoil of war. He gripped it firmly and hefted it, and spoke urgently to it. "Once you belonged to my enemy, but now you are mine. You have always done everything I asked you. This Trojan is no better than a girl—so let me bring him to his knees, and with my own hands batter in

his breastplate and rub dust into his curled and scented hair."
His face was wildly flushed, and his eyes crackled; he was like
a bull before his first battle, that snorts or butts trees or gores
the empty air or kicks up clouds of dust—but only for effect.

At the same time Aeneas, looking equally imposing in the
armor that his mother had given him, prepared himself for his
meeting with Turnus and worked up his own indignation. But he
was relieved that a truce was to be struck and that there would
be no more war. He spoke to his companions and soothed As-
canius' fears. He explained that everything that would happen
was the work of fate. And then he sent word to king Latinus
that he was ready to discuss the terms of the peace.

Already the mountaintops were edged with a line of light;
the horses of the sun had risen from the ocean and from their
flared nostrils they were breathing the glow of day. Under
the walls Latins and Trojans collaborated in measuring out a
space for the combat, and preparing fires and raising mounds
of grass to serve as altars for the gods which were common
to both sides. Some of them, wearing purple sashes and olive
wreaths on their foreheads, brought water and torches. The
Latin troops came out first, marching out of the gates in close
order with their spears on their shoulders. Opposite them, the
Trojans and Etruscans, each in their distinctive armor, were
drawn up as though they themselves were going into battle.
Between the ranks the commanders flitted to and fro, flaunt-
ing their gold and scarlet: Mnestheus and Asilas and Neptune's
son Messapus. At a signal, both armies retired to their own
side of the cleared space; they stuck their spears in the ground
and propped their shields against them. On the towers and
rooftops and high above the gates were crowds of excited
women and those who were too young or too old to fight.

Juno sends Turnus' divine sister to help him

From a hill which is now the site of
Alba Longa, but was then without name
or distinction, Juno was watching both
the armies and Latinus' town. She spoke
to Turnus' sister, a goddess who presides

over pools and streams—a responsibility given to her by Jupiter after he had seduced her. "Juturna, dear and glorious nymph," she said. "You know that of all the Latin girls that found their way into Jupiter's bed and then were turned away, you are my favorite; and you know how I gladly made a place for you among the gods. Now listen: I am giving you due warning of sorrow in your future, so that you will not think that it was my fault. As long as Fortune allowed the war to go Latium's way, I protected Turnus and your town. But now I see Turnus' luck running out; the day is approaching when a hostile fate will strike him down. I cannot bear to contemplate this truce or this single combat. But you must do whatever you dare to assist your brother—and it is right that you should. However miserable we are today, tomorrow will be better."

Juturna wept at these words; three and four times she beat her breast in grief. But Juno told her: "This is no time for tears. Hurry—go to save your brother's life in any way you can. Stir up the war again—the peace must not hold. And I will give you the courage that you need." And so she vanished, leaving Juturna bewildered and full of a sad foreboding.

A truce is struck

Below her, the kings came forward. Latinus was magnificent in a four-horsed chariot, wearing a crown with twelve golden rays, the symbol of his ancestor, the sun. Turnus followed him, drawn by his two white horses, with two broad-bladed spears in his hand. To meet them rode the first father of the Roman people, Aeneas, carrying his star-bright shield and wearing the armor that Vulcan had made for him, and beside him Ascanius, the other hope for the splendid future of Rome. Fires flickered on the altars, where a young boar and an unshorn lamb were held ready for them by a priest in a white robe. With knives they marked the animals' foreheads, and turned toward the rising sun to scatter grain and salt, and pour libations.

The dutiful Aeneas unsheathed his sword and prayed: "Let the Sun witness what I am about to say, as well as this land for which I have suffered so much; let Jupiter witness my words, and his consort Juno—who is now, I trust, better disposed toward me—and glorious Mars, who governs the course of all campaigns. I call on the springs and rivers of Italy to hear me, and on all the spirits of the heavens and the deep blue sea. If Turnus is fated to defeat me, we will withdraw to Pallanteum, and Ascanius will leave the country. No son of mine will ever return here under arms or declare war upon you again. But if the victory should fall to me—and I believe that this is the will of the gods—I will never require Italy to be subservient to Troy, and I will not seek to rule this kingdom by myself. Rather let both nations, undefeated, be united by a treaty, under conditions agreed upon by both. Our gods will be your gods. Latinus, soon to be my father-in-law, will keep his army and his kingdom; and my Trojans will build a new city for me—and I will name it after my future wife Lavinia."

Latinus followed, looking up into the heavens and raising his right hand. "I swear," he said, "by the land of Latium and the sea and the stars. I swear by Apollo and Diana and two-headed Janus. I swear by the gods who have power below and all that is holy in the country of the dead. Now I lay my hand on the altars: the flames will be my witnesses; and Jupiter, who confirms treaties by his thunderbolts, will hear my oath. The day when this pact will be cancelled will never come; no circumstance whatever will be allowed to break this peace. My mind is made up, and I will never alter it—not if the earth is overwhelmed by the sea, or heaven collapses into hell. My decision is unchangeable." He held up his scepter. "Once this was part of a tree, but it will never sprout a single leaf or give a scrap of shade. A forester lopped it off the trunk with his axe and trimmed off its branches and foliage; and then an artist imprisoned it in bronze and made it into this scepter, which the kings of Latium always wield."

With these oaths they made their covenant before all their nobles; and they cut the victims' throats over the fires, and tore out their entrails while they were still alive, and piled them up on the altars.

*Dissatisfaction
among the
Latins*
But all was not yet well: the Rutulians began to wonder if the odds for the single combat were in their favor after all, and misgivings moved in their hearts: the closer they looked, the more the balance seemed to tip. They were uneasy at Turnus' appearance as he came up to bow before the altars. His step had lost its spring, his eyes were lowered and his face was gaunt and pale. His sister Juturna saw that the people had begun to mutter among themselves, and that their confidence was slipping. So she went down to them in the form of Camers, a man of long and distinguished family history, and a fearsome warrior. She moved along the lines and whispered various suggestions in their ears, knowing exactly what their effect would be. "Aren't you ashamed, Rutulians, to send up one man to represent us all? Are we not equal to them, in numbers and in strength?" Or: "Look at them: Trojans, Arcadians and Etruscans, haphazardly thrown together. Yes, they hate Turnus; but if we only sent out half our army, most of our soldiers would find no one to fight against." Or: "No doubt Aeneas will one day become one of the gods whom he so devotedly cultivates, and of course his name will live for ever. But does that mean that we must lose our country to him, and be compelled to bow to the arrogance of petty tyrants? Why do we sit here in complete indifference?"

In this way she fanned the young men's discontent. Murmurs of complaint slithered up and down the ranks, and one by one all the Italian tribes, and finally the Latins, changed their minds. Those who before had hoped for peace and quiet and security now wanted to arm again. The treaty, they said, was flawed: Turnus had been placed in an unfair and unfortunate situation. And for confirmation Juturna sent them a sign from heaven, which perturbed the Italians more than anything that she had done before, and deceived them completely: one of Jupiter's golden eagles swooped down out of the morning sky and sent a flock of water-birds squawking off along the shore. In a flash of its talons, it seized a swan. The water-birds fled, but then, as the Italians watched intently, they turned miraculously back, the whole chattering cloud of them, enough to darken the sky. They mobbed the eagle until, overcome by their numbers, it could no longer manage the weight of its prey, and was forced to let go of the swan and drop it back into the river. Then it soared up and away, until they could see it no longer.

The truce is broken

The Rutulians greeted the omen with delight, and the tension left them. "This is what I have prayed for," said Tolumnius, who could foretell the future from bird behavior, "and what I had expected. I understand what the gods are telling us. I am ready for another fight, and you, you misbegotten people, should follow me. This stranger is terrifying you now, as though you were a flock of helpless waterfowl. He has driven you from your homes along the shore, but if you stand together against him, he will withdraw. He will set his sails and depart across the sea. For a moment it seemed your king was lost. Now you see that you can still defend him."

Tolumnius took a step forward and launched his spear at the enemy; it was well-aimed, and its wooden shaft hummed through the air. Excitement flickered through the Latin troops: they broke their formations to cheer. In the path of the spear stood nine handsome brothers, sons of an Arcadian father and an Etruscan mother. It hit the first of them square in the stomach, by his belt-buckle, just below his ribs; he crumpled onto the sand. But his brothers, unthinking in their grief, charged forward, with their swords drawn or spears at the ready. The Latins resisted them, and that drew in the Trojans and Arcadians. Both sides were united in their determination to settle the matter with the sword. Altars were torn up, fires extinguished and sacrifices abandoned. Latinus hastily retired and took with him the images of his rejected gods, with the negotiations unfinished. A storm raged across the sky, but the wind was a wind of weapons, and rain was a rain of iron.

Both sides whipped on their chariot teams or leaped onto their horses; they entered the battle with their swords already in hand. Messapus, eager to play his part in breaking of the agreement, rode up to the Etruscan chief Aulestes—he had recognized him by the emblem on his shield—and took him by surprise. Aulestes' horse stumbled, and Aulestes was thrown headfirst onto the remains of an altar. He begged for his life, but Messapus thrust downwards at him from his horse with an enormous pike. "You will make a better victim for the gods than any lamb," he said, and the Italians ran up to strip his body while it was still warm. Ebysus came to help, but Corynaeus grabbed a brand and pushed it into Ebysus' face until his beard was singed and smoking; and then he took his hair with his left hand and held him down with a knee in his back and stabbed him below the ribs. Alsus, a shepherd, was caught by Podalirius; Podalirius stood over him about to strike; but Alsus swung back at him with an axe, and split his head apart from hairline to chin. Blood splattered over his armor. His eyes were closed in silence and unrelenting sleep, looking out for ever into darkness.

Aeneas is wounded by a sniper

But Aeneas did not move. Still trying to honor the gods, he stood bareheaded and unarmed.

"What has possessed you?" he shouted to his men. "Why have you ripped the pact apart? Your anger is pointless—the treaty has already been struck. New laws have been laid down. Only I have the right to go to war—so trust me. Do not be nervous about the terms of the agreement—they are clear: Turnus is mine to fight and mine to..."

But he did not finish: an arrow had hit him—but who had shot it? Was it one of Turnus' men? An accident? An act of god? No one ever knew; and no one ever took the credit, or boasted that he had been the one to wound Aeneas. But when Turnus saw Aeneas fall back from the front line, and his commanders worrying round him, he was fired by a sudden hope.

"Bring me my horses and my arms," he ordered. He jumped exuberantly into his chariot and flicked the reins.

Turnus returns to action

His assault left many dead, and many nearly dead—trampled or crushed or, if they tried to avoid him, transfixed by his spear. He lashed his horses to a sweat, and under their hooves the blood of the fallen spurted like scarlet dew and stained the sand. He was as swift and fierce

as Mars himself, when he stirs up war along the icy Hebrus river, sounding his shield like a gong. His signal sends his horses galloping like a wind across an open plain, until the farthest borders of Thrace quake under their tread; and close beside him are his companions, Fear and Rage and Treachery.

Turnus closed with Sthenelus and killed him; from farther off he shot Thamyrus and Pholus, and the brothers Glaucus and Lades—their father had given them their arms, either to fight their enemies at close quarters or to outride the wind on horseback. And at extreme long range he let fly at Eumedes, who had his name from his grandfather, and his courage from his famous father Dolon. During the Trojan war Dolon had slipped behind the Greek lines to spy out their intentions; he had been captured, and when he gave them information about the Trojan dispositions, he cheekily asked for Achilles' chariot-team as a reward. But Diomedes gave him a quite different reward—death—and after that he had no interest in Achilles' horses. When Eumedes was hit and lying on the ground, Turnus stopped his chariot and jumped down. He put his foot on his neck and disarmed him, and used his own sword to cut his throat. "You came looking for Italian land—now lie on it," he said. "Those who come here to dig foundations for a city will only dig their graves." So Eumedes died, and after him all his companions, pierced by spears or pulled down from their horses.

Wherever Turnus went, he was like a gale roaring in from the Aegean; the breakers shatter on the rocks and the clouds are chased across the sky. His own impetus carried him along and his crest streamed out behind him on the wind: the enemy columns yielded, and the lines fell back. Phegeus tried to check his wild progress by throwing himself in front of his chariot and wrenching aside the heads of his foam-snorting horses. He hung from the ridgepole, and was dragged along until Turnus' spear-blade found him and pierced his armored tunic and wounded him. But Phegeus would not give in; he managed to get his shield between himself and Turnus so that he could fight back. But at last he became entangled between the wheel and the axle and could hold on no longer. Turnus leaned over and slipped his sword into the gap where his helmet met his cuirass, and cut off his head and left his body on the sand.

Aeneas looks for medical assistance

Aeneas saw nothing of Turnus' victories, because Mnestheus and the loyal Achates and Ascanius had taken him back to the camp. He was bleeding, and had to use his spear as a crutch in order to walk at all. He was angrily trying to pull out the broken shaft of the arrow, and at the same time he called for help from whoever was willing to give it: "Open up the wound with a sword. Cut the arrowhead out—I don't care how deep it is. I have to get back to the battle." But then old Iapyx hurried up. A long time ago Apollo had been in love with him and had offered to teach him various skills—how to tell the future, play the lyre, or shoot arrows; but Iapyx, in an effort to postpone the death of his father, had preferred to learn the properties of herbs and the silent, inconspicuous art of healing.

Now, with his robe tucked up in the manner of Paeon, the doctor of the gods, he fussed over Aeneas, palpating him, dosing him with herbs, futilely trying to loosen the arrowhead or pull it out with pincers. Aeneas grumbled to himself and leant on his spear, ignoring Ascanius, who waited anxiously at his side with a crowd of young men behind him. Nothing worked—and Apollo offered no assistance. But the sounds of the battlefield, in ever-louder horror, were coming closer: the sunlight was dimmed with dust, and already horsemen were circling the camp and javelins were falling inside it. All around them they could hear the screams and groans of young men who were compelled to fight and die according to the harsh rhythms of war.

His wound is miraculously cured

Greatly alarmed by her son's wound, Venus, picked a sprig of dittany—a purple-flowering herb with hairy leaves on its stalk, which the wild goats chew if they are injured by hunters. She wrapped herself in a dark cloud, and brought it from a mountainside in Crete to Italy, where she steeped it in fresh water and into it—her secret prescription—she sprinkled drops of ambrosia and fragrant panacea. Iapyx, all unknowing, found it in his hand, and bathed Aeneas' wound: the pain vanished, and the bleeding stopped. He touched the arrowhead once. It fell out of its own accord, and Aeneas was as vigorous as ever.

"Quick! Bring Aeneas his arms," cried Iapyx, rousing the Trojans out of their inaction. "Why are you standing doing nothing? This has not happened by human skill or a doctor's art. It was not my hand that saved you, Aeneas. A greater power has revived you for greater deeds."

Aeneas was eager to get back into the fight, and would wait for no assistance. One by one he put on his greaves, and then his cuirass; he slung his shield by his side, and hefted his spear. Fully armed, he embraced Ascanius, and tipped back his helmet to kiss him. "Other people can teach you how to win by luck. But from me, my dear boy, you can learn courage and the virtue of hard work. For now, I will defend you, and show you where there are prizes to be won. But if ever you want guidance when you are a man, you need only think of this: your uncle was Hector, and Aeneas was your father."

He is ready to fight once more

He hurled himself out of the gate, brandishing his spear, with Antheus and Mnestheus right behind him, and then the rest of his army. The camp was left empty, but the plain was filled with a blinding dust from the tread of the soldiers' feet. Turnus and the Italians spotted them, and Turnus felt cold shivering through his bones. But Juturna had heard the columns even before they came into sight; she had recognized the sound and fled in terror. The Trojans advanced across the open ground, dark and threatening, wave after wave of them, massed in close formation like a line of squalls approaching from the sea, at first so distant that inland the farmers feel no more than an uneasy stirring of trouble; but then they hear the gusting of the wind that soon will topple trees and flatten all their crops.

The armies met in close formation. The Trojans killed Osiris, Arcetius, Epulo, Ufens. They killed Tolumnius, the soothsayer who had thrown the spear that broke the truce; and then it was the Rutulians' turn to flee across the parched fields. But Aeneas took no notice of them: he was too proud to strike a fugitive in the back, and anyone who faced him he ignored. He was in search of one opponent only—but in the haze of blowing sand he could not find him. Where was he? Where was Turnus?

Aeneas goes in search of Turnus, but Turnus' sister keeps him out of reach

This was Juturna's moment: though she was still alarmed, she summoned up the strength to knock Metiscus, Turnus' driver, out of his chariot, and leave him behind. She took his place at the reins, and at the same time she assumed Metiscus' voice and form and armor.

Imagine a swallow flying about in a rich man's house: her chicks are squawking hungrily in their nest, and she darts to and fro to pick up scraps for them under the high ceilings of the hall or in the empty colonnades or by the fishponds.

In the same way, in Turnus' chariot, Juturna turned and twisted: she let Aeneas catch a glimpse of Turnus and then spirited him away, keeping him always just too far away to fight. Meanwhile Aeneas moved in frustrated circles, tracking him, losing him and vainly challenging him. But as often as he set eyes on Turnus and tried to get within range, Juturna would jerk at the reins and be off in the opposite direction. Tossed and distracted on the tide of battle, Aeneas was left with no coherent plan—and vulnerable as well, for Messapus, with two iron-tipped spears in his left hand, came up silently behind him. He threw one of them, excellently aimed, but Aeneas ducked down on one knee and crouched behind his shield. The spear hit him on the helmet, but did no more than slice off the plume. But he was irritated that he had been taken by surprise, and could not keep Messapus' chariot in sight. He called many times on Jupiter, recalling the altars where the pact had been made and broken; and now he turned to Mars, no longer bothering to contain his anger, and began a terrible slaughter of anyone who crossed his path.

The fog of war   No exact record remains of what Aeneas did that day, or what Turnus brought about. There is no means of detailing the carnage, no way to count the great men dead. Was it the will of Jupiter that Trojans and Italians, once destined to live in peace, should now clash so savagely together? And if Turnus and Aeneas thought at all, it was of blood and fury, but never of defeat.

Sucro was the first to delay the Trojan advance, but not for long; Aeneas drove his sword-blade through his ribs and killed him quickly, stabbing him in the heart. Turnus pulled Amycus from his horse, along with his brother Diores; one came at him with a long spear, the other with a sword. But Turnus climbed down to meet them both on foot, and decapitated them, and then drove away with their dripping heads suspended from his chariot. Talo and Tanais and Cethegus came three against one at Aeneas, but they went down, and the gloomy Onites as well. Turnus in his turn killed two brothers, acolytes from Apollo's oracle in Lycia, and young Menoetes: he was an Arcadian who hated war—for all the good that did him—and had grown up a fisherman, poor and untouched by ambition, on his father's rented farm. No fire howling through a stand of parched laurel bushes, no flash-flood carving its own path of destruction as it thunders out of the mountains down to the sea, could consume a landscape with the violence of this battle.

Aeneas flung a rock at Murranus and sent him spinning from his chariot. Once he was on the ground, the wheels went over him and his horses trampled him without a break in the rhythm of their hooves; they did not care that he was their master, or that he used to boast of his ancestors, counting back through generations of Latin kings. When the foolhardy Hyllus charged at Turnus, he was met with a spear between the eyes, below his gold circlet; his helmet gave no resistance, and the blade stuck deep inside his brain. Neither his gods nor his shield protected Cupencus from a fatal wound when he came face to face with Aeneas, and Cretheus' sword could not ward off Turnus. And Turnus cut down Aeolus too, and he died where he fell. He had fought unscathed against all the Greeks, and even against Achilles. Once he had had a proud house in Lyrnesus, and an estate on the slopes of Ida—but his tomb was on the empty plain of Latium. All along the line the armies were fully engaged: Trojans and Latins, Etruscan footsoldiers and Arcadian horsemen, Mnestheus and Serestus and Messapus and Asilas—every one of them straining to the limit of his strength. No respite, no pause, a vast unending struggle.

Aeneas changes his tactics, and attacks the Latins' capital

But at last Venus suggested to Aeneas how he might break the deadlock: why did he not divert a column to the town and make a surprise attack on it? And sure enough, as he ranged back and forth looking for Turnus, he found the town lying undefended and untouched in the middle of the turmoil. At once his imagination showed him a broader stratagem, and so he summoned Mnestheus and Sergestus and Serestus, and stood on a mound to address the Trojan forces. They clustered around him, still holding their javelins and shields, and listened carefully.

"We must act quickly," he said, "while Jupiter is on our side. I know this is a change of plan, but surprise is the key. This town, the center of Latinus' kingdom, was the cause of the war, and today I will destroy it. Unless they agree to accept the bit that we will put in their mouths, unless they admit themselves defeated and surrender without condition, I will turn every tower into a pile of smoking ashes. How long am I supposed to wait, while Turnus decides whether or not he will fight me—never mind that he is already beaten? This moment is the crux of our entire campaign, the climax of the war that never should have happened in the first place. So—bring me torches. The next treaty will be negotiated with fire."

Immediately the Trojans went to work: they made a contest of it, to see who could first form a wedge and reach the walls. They put up ladders, and from nowhere flames flickered up. All resistance at the gates was cut down; the sky was dark with spears and arrows. Aeneas stood beneath the walls, shaking his fist and railing at Latinus. "How can you have forced me into war a second time? The gods themselves are witnesses that your people have attacked me twice, and twice you have made promises and then broken them."

The despair of Amata and Latinus

The citizens began to argue among themselves: should they unlock the gates and let the Trojans in? Should they drag king Latinus onto the battlements to answer Aeneas' charges? Or should they take up arms and defend the walls?

You may have seen a shepherd trying to dislodge a swarm of bees which has gathered in the cleft of a rock; he lights a fire and fills their shelter with pungent smoke. The bees are agitated: black poison rolls into every cell, and they complain with an impotent, ill-tempered buzzing. But for all their noise only smoke emerges into the air.

But far worse than apprehension and indecision was coming to the weary Latins. When Queen Amata saw the enemy first approaching, and then attacking the walls and setting fire to them, but no sign of Turnus' forces or of Turnus himself, she supposed that he had been killed. In a sudden fit of grief she insisted that the war was all her fault, and that her stubbornness had been its only cause. And then guilt drove her out of her wits: her mourning changed to a determination to die, and she took a rope and threw it over a beam and hanged herself. When her women heard what she had done, they ran wailing through the palace, and Lavinia ran with them, tearing her hair and cheeks; and the terrible news spread from them into the rest of the town. Wandering among his despondent subjects, Latinus could only tear his clothes and pour handfuls of dust over his white hair; his wife's suicide and the catastrophe lowering over his kingdom had broken him.

But at the far end of the plain, Turnus in fact was still in action: he was pursuing the few remaining stragglers, but his heart was not in the chase, and his confidence in his own cavalry was quickly fading. And on the breeze came the faint vague sounds of voices from the town: he could hear nothing clearly, but surely there was confusion in those cries, and dreadful pain.

"What is it?" he asked. "Has something also happened? All this shouting—what does it mean?"

Turnus comes to the defense of the town

Unable to think clearly, he stopped; and his sister Juturna, still in the form of his driver Metiscus, still in control of his horses and his chariot, answered him: "This is the moment to press the Trojans harder, Turnus. The way to victory lies open. Go after Aeneas now—the defense of the town can be left to others, but he is still out there in the field, routing the Italians. In return we must bring death and destruction onto the Trojans. Your numbers are no less than theirs, and neither is your honor."

"You are Juturna, not Metiscus," said Turnus. "I've been aware of that for a long time, just as I know that it was mainly because of you that the treaty was broken and the war started up again. You're a goddess, but you can't deceive me. But which of the Olympians wanted you to send you down to do what you have done? Or were you sent to witness the cruel death of your poor brother? What can I do now? Will Fortune guarantee my safety? She didn't save Murranus: he was my closest friend and a great warrior, and it took a great wound to bring him down. But he died right there in front of me, calling my name. She didn't save Ufens: poor fellow—the Trojans took his body and his armor, but at least he did not see me dishonored. Shall I let our homes be destroyed—at least that hasn't happened yet—or counter Drances' words with action? Shall I retreat, and allow my countrymen to say they saw me running away? Surely death would be better than that. Perhaps the spirits of the underworld will receive me kindly; I certainly feel rejected by the gods above. I have lived a life to be proud of: I have never turned my back on an enemy, and I have never disgraced my ancestors."

At that moment a courier came galloping through the enemy ranks; his horse was in a lather, and he had been wounded in the face by an arrow, but he managed to gasp out: "Turnus! You're our last hope. Take pity on us. Aeneas has descended on us like a lightning bolt; he's threatening to devastate every citadel in Italy and kill us all. Already he's set torches to Latinus' walls. The Latins have no one to look to except you. The king has gone mad; he can only mumble crazily about sons-in-law and treaties. The queen has killed herself. Even though she loved you, her terror would let her live no longer. Only Messapus and Atinas are left to hold the line, and the Trojan army is thick around them. The ground before the town has sprouted an iron crop—every blade of wheat a naked sword—while you are out here careering about in an empty meadow."

Turnus had nothing to say. His mind could barely grasp the picture that the messenger had drawn, while shame and fury mingled with sorrow in his heart. Yet his duty was clear. As soon as the clouds receded from his brain, he fixed all his energy and attention on the walls. Even from his chariot he could see a spiral jet of flame working its way up among the houses from story to story. Already one of the towers was completely involved, a tower that he had built himself: he had lashed its beams together and wheeled it into position, and he had linked it to the wall by bridges.

Turnus resolves to fight Aeneas face to face after all

"Very well," he said. "The fates have had their say. I've made up my mind. I will follow wherever the unrelenting gods and my fortune lead me, to my meeting with Aeneas. If I must die, then I will die; but you will never again see me trying to avoid my destiny. Let me go mad, Juturna, before madness overruns us all."

He jumped down from his chariot and charged into the midst of the enemy, thinking nothing of the danger from their weapons, thinking nothing of his sister, who was left to mourn his going.

He ran with the energy of a fall of rocks dislodged from the top of a mountain in a windstorm: perhaps a downpour has washed away the ground beneath them, or the passage of time has worked them loose. Nothing can slow them or withstand them as they crash straight down the cliff-face, carrying trees and flocks and men before them in a jumbled mass.

With no less force Turnus smashed through the Trojan columns, and the spears that whistled around him, until he stopped on the blood-soaked ground beneath the walls.

He held up his hand. "Hold your fire now, Rutulians," he yelled. "Latins, cease fire. Leave the end of this business to me. I am the one who would not abide by the treaty, and I must pay for it. The matter must be settled by my sword, not by yours."

The champions meet

When he heard them calling Turnus' name, Aeneas left the towers, and came down from the walls. No one tried to

stand in his way; he was too fierce in his joy, and too fearsome
in his armor. He seemed taller than Mount Athos, or even Eryx
in Sicily; he seemed

> as grand as the grandest of the Apennines when the
> wind keens through its feathery holm-oaks and its
> snowy crest is outlined against the sky.

The eyes of every Rutulian and every Trojan and every Italian
were fixed on him in admiration. They all laid down their arms,
whether they were guarding the parapet above or pounding in
the battering-ram below. Even Latinus was amazed at the sight
of these two heroes, who had come together from the oppo-
site ends of the earth and were about to decide their quarrel
with the force of iron.

A space was cleared. They advanced at a steady speed.
Each threw a spear, and each spear glanced off the other's
shield. The earth shook. Still they came on, each of them con-
fident in his courage and in his fate and in his sword,

> like two bulls battling on an Italian mountainside.
> Their foreheads thud together, and the herdsmen
> stand back warily. The rest of the herd keep a re-
> spectful silence, but the heifers are alert: which one
> of the bulls will be dominant, which one will they
> have to follow? Horns rip into necks and bloodied
> shoulders. Bellowing echoes off the trunks of the
> surrounding trees.

So Aeneas and Turnus were joined at close quarters, shield
against sky-shattering shield, while Jupiter held their futures
equally balanced in his scales. Neither of them knew which
side was weighted down with death.

Turnus at last found an opening, and put the whole weight
of his body behind his descending sword; a well-struck blow,
he thought, and the Trojans and the Latins cried out in alarm

and anticipation. But his sword betrayed him. It snapped in mid-swing, and he would have been left defenseless if he had not ducked away, and then run off faster than the wind, puzzling at his right hand still grasping a bladeless hilt. Today they say that, when he jumped down from his chariot, he had left behind the sword his father had given him, and grabbed instead the sword of his charioteer. As long as the Trojans had been in retreat, this had been enough; but when it came up against the armor made by Vulcan, the mortal blade shattered at the first stroke as though it were made of ice, and lay in bright slivers on the sand.

Turnus in flight; Aeneas in vain pursuit Turnus dodged across the plain in a series of futile arcs, blocked in one direction by the Trojans, in another by a waste of marshland, and in a third by the blank-faced walls. Stride for stride Aeneas followed him, even though his pursuit was slow: his wound had left him weak and limping, but his passion was undiminished.

He was like a hound close on the heels of a stag, who is hemmed in on one side by a steep riverbank, and on the other spooked by a scarecrow made of scarlet feathers. Whichever one of a thousand paths the stag may take, the eager dog is always just behind, yapping or baring his teeth. Now he has him—or he thinks he does, but he snaps at empty air—and all along the water's edge the racket fades and then returns.

At length Turnus' circles carried him back to his Rutulians; he called to them by name and asked who had his proper sword. And Aeneas called to them too, threatening every kind of death to anyone who should come near him, as well as destruction for the town—and still, despite his wound, he stayed right behind Turnus. Five times they ran around the walls, and turned and ran back again—and for no slight or trivial stakes: they raced for Turnus' blood and Turnus' life.

By chance they passed by a spot where an olive tree had recently stood: it had had bitter leaves, and had been sacred to Faunus. For many years sailors saved from shipwrecks had brought gifts to it and hung their clothes on it as offerings to the country gods. But the Trojans, who cared nothing about its history, had cut it down so that they could have a clear field of fire when they attacked the town. The stump was still there, however, and Aeneas' spear was stuck in it, held deep and fast among the roots. Now he tried to pull it out. If he could not catch up with Turnus on foot, he thought, at least a spear might overtake him. But Turnus, mad with fear, cried out: "Faunus, I have always worshipped you. Earth, oldest and holiest of all goddesses, I have always honored you. But the Trojans have insulted you with their war. So pity me, and hold his spear in place." His prayer was answered; for however much he tugged and twisted it, Aeneas could not pull out the spear from the wood's clenched fist. But while he was still struggling with it, Juturna, again disguised as the charioteer Metiscus, dashed forward and gave her brother back his sword; and in return Venus, angry at Juturna's interference, wrenched Aeneas' spear from the olive root. So both of them were elated—one reunited with his faithful sword, the other with his spear. Panting, but with lifting spirits, they stood face to face a second time.

Jupiter persuades Juno to stop harassing the Trojans: the Trojans and Latins must join together and become a single people

Wrapped in fog, Jupiter was watching the battle from a mist. He spoke to Juno: "What will be the end of all this, my dear wife? What else is there left to do? You know—of course you know—that Aeneas is already a hero, already worshipped as a god. He has his place reserved for him in heaven and the fates will take him up among the stars. So what are you still planning for him? What do you hope for, lingering there in the chilly clouds? Was it right that a god should be wounded by a mortal? Was it right to give Turnus back his sword—Juturna could not have done it without your aid—and put new strength into the Latins when they had already been defeated? Stop whatever you are doing, and listen to me: I do not want to see you pining away in silent sorrow, but on the other hand I do not want to hear you asking, however persuasively, for help in any of your troubles. Your campaign has gone far enough: you have harassed the Trojans on land and sea, you have stirred up wars beyond all reason, you have disrupted Latinus' family and undermined what would have been a happy marriage. You are to do no more. I forbid it."

"I have left the earth," answered Juno, with downcast eyes, "and I have deserted Turnus, not because I wanted to, but because I knew that that was what you wanted. If I had not, you would not see me up here on my throne alone, enduring without complaint what is unfair along with what is fair. I would be standing at the forefront of the fighting, a fiery vision, luring the Trojans into the grasp of the enemy. Yes, I admit it, I sent Juturna to help her poor brother, and I allowed her to run great risks to save his life; but I did not allow her actually to throw a spear or bend a bow. By the indomitable Styx, the river that makes even the gods afraid, I swear that this is true. But still I yield to your command: much as I hate the Trojans, I will leave the battle. But there is no law of fate to forbid my asking you one favor on behalf of Latium and your people's future greatness. When—as I suppose they must—the two sides make peace, and Aeneas has his marriage, and when they are linked by laws and treaties, do not have the Latins change their original name, or their traditional dress, or their language. Let Latium last for centuries, and the kings of Alba Longa; and in the future let the strength of Rome be reinforced by Italian courage. Troy is gone—so let her name go too."

Jupiter smiled. "You must indeed be my sister as well as my wife," he said. "Nothing will change your mind once it is made up. But do not be angry any longer—it will do you no good. But you have convinced me, and I am happy to do what you ask. The Italians shall keep their language, and their customs, and their name shall remain as it is. The Trojans shall be mingled with them, and no one will recognize any difference. The religion of both peoples—beliefs and practices—will become as one, and everyone will speak the same language: Latin. From them will spring a race of Trojans and Italians inextricably intermixed—a race that you will see outdo all other men, and perhaps even the gods, in their service to humanity. And certainly no one else will worship you with greater fervor then they will." Juno was content. She bowed her head in acquiescence, and turned away, and left her vantage-point among the clouds.

Jupiter sends a message to warn off Turnus' sister

But although Juno was appeased, Jupiter's plans were not yet complete. He now prepared to separate Juturna from her brother's army, and he turned to the Furies who crouch at the foot of his throne. There are three of them—or so they say: the twin daughters of Night, and Megaera whose father is Hades. They writhe like snakes and fly like birds, and whenever Jupiter decides it is time to make mortals suffer, it is their task to strike them with the fear of plague or death or war.

He chose one of them now, and sent her down as a warning to Juturna. She flew as swiftly as a whirlwind or a poisoned arrow shot by a barbarian, which hums so faintly through the darkness that no one is aware of its coming. When she had reached the earth and found the two armies, she turned herself into a small bird, one of those that sometimes sits on tombs or on the roofs of deserted houses, insistently shrieking late into the night. In this form she fluttered again and again into Turnus' face and beat threateningly at his shield with her wings. He felt an awful apprehension creeping over him: his hair stood on end and his voice stuck in his throat.

But Juturna heard the calls and the pulsing wings from a long way off, and she knew exactly who it was. In despair she pulled at her hair and tore her cheeks and beat her breast with her fists. "I cannot help you any more, my dearest brother. I must leave the battlefield at once. My strength is worn out, and I can keep you safe no longer. How can I overcome a Fury? I am already afraid, but must you terrify me still more, you disgusting bird? I know the sound of your deadly wings—and I know that great Jupiter's commands cannot be ignored. But is this how he repays me for letting him seduce me? He gave me eternal life—for this? Why did he take away my right to die? I could now be done with pain and go with you, my poor brother, to the underworld. Immortality is hardly a delight if I have to live forever without you. I only wish that earth could open wide enough to swallow me and drag me down—a goddess though I am—among the grimmest spirits of the dead." She could speak no more for weeping; she wrapped her head in a veil of watery gray and dived into the depths of her pool.

To Turnus, Aeneas' spear now seemed as big as a tree-trunk; and Aeneas' voice was full of savage scorn. "Turnus, why do you hesitate? Why do you hang back? Our contest is not supposed to be a footrace; it is a fight. Change your shape if you will; but this is first and foremost a matter of courage and skill. So make your choice: will you soar among the stars or burrow below the earth?"

Turnus is left alone and unsupported

"Your words are full of heat," replied Turnus, shaking his head, "but they do not burn me. I can be touched only by the gods, or by Jupiter, who is my real enemy." He looked around, and saw an enormous stone, which had lain on the plain for countless years to serve as a boundary marker. It was so heavy that twelve men of normal size, the sort of men that earth produces nowadays, could not have carried it on their shoulders. But Turnus did not realize that he had become as tall as a hero, with a hero's speed: he ran to the stone and scooped it up and lifted it over his head and threw it at Aeneas. But as soon as he let go of it, his knees went weak and his blood went cold: the stone flew through the air—far, but not far enough. It never reached its target.

We can all remember the terror of a nightmare:
our eyes are pressed shut, and whatever we want to
do, we cannot achieve it. For all our attempts to run,
our feet are stuck. We try to scream, but not a single
word, not even a squeak, comes out.

So wherever Turnus' courage urged him into action, the Fury
barred his way, and all kinds of visions tilted and slid in his
head. There were the Latins; there was the Latins' town; and
there was himself, sluggish in his panic. With death tower-
ing over him, he was unable to attack, unable to retreat. And
where was his chariot? Where was his sister who had been
driving it?

Turnus' last appeal to Aeneas...

In that moment of his hesitation, Ae-
neas saw his chance. He raised his spear,
and his arm flashed forward with all his
body-weight behind it. A catapult never
hurled a rock against a rampart with greater force, nor did such
thunder ever follow lightning. As fast and deadly as a black
tornado, the spear passed underneath the rim of Turnus' seven-
layered shield, nicked his cuirass, and stuck shuddering in his
thigh. His knees gave way. The Rutulians leaned forward; their
cries echoed and re-echoed across the mountains and the dis-
tant woods, but Turnus was crouching on the ground. Humbly
he lifted up his eyes and stretched out his hand to Aeneas.

"Whatever happens to me, I have deserved it. I will not
beg for my life—you must do what you must do. But if you
have any feeling for a parent's loss, I implore you to take pity
on Daunus, my old father—I know how much Anchises meant
to you—and if you kill me, send my body back to my own
people. You have defeated me, and humbled me in front of all
the Italian tribes. Lavinia will be your wife, not mine. You and
I must not hate each other any longer."

...and Aeneas' decision

Aeneas frowned, and stood over
him with sword raised, but he checked
his hand. The mention of Anchises had

touched him, and he was on the verge, the very edge, of changing his mind. But then, across Turnus' shoulder, he saw the belt that Turnus had taken as a trophy and still was pleased to wear, the belt that he recognized from the designs engraved in gold upon it, the belt that had once belonged to Pallas. And just that glimpse of it was enough to remind Aeneas of how much he had grieved for Pallas, and his compassion was driven out by a burst of terrible rage.

"Did you hope to escape me, still dressed up in what you have stolen from my friend? But now it is Pallas—not I—who offers you up for sacrifice. It is Pallas who gives you this final wound, and Pallas who makes you pay your debt at last—with your own degenerate blood."

His sword drove hot and deep into Turnus' heart. And Turnus' limbs became chilled and slack, and his protesting spirit fluttered away into the shadows.

APPENDIX I
Outline of the Plot of the Aeneid

Book I

The Trojan War has come to an end, and a band of Trojans, both men and women, led by Aeneas, have escaped from the city just before it is completely destroyed by the Greeks. Aeneas is destined to found a new Troy, which is eventually to become the city of Rome; and when the story begins, his Trojans—harried wherever they go by the goddess Juno—are on the last leg of their voyage from Troy to Italy. But they are driven ashore by a storm on the coast of Africa, and Aeneas' mother Venus, in disguise, guides him to the court of Dido, the queen of Carthage. Dido welcomes the Trojans and asks Aeneas to tell her about his previous adventures.

Books II and III

A flashback: Aeneas recounts how the Trojans were tricked by the wooden horse into opening their gates to the enemy; how he fought desperately to save the city; and how the gods ordered him to gather together his family and the companions with whom he must depart from the city. Where he is supposed to go is not immediately clear to him, and he tries to settle on various islands of the Aegean, before he realizes that the gods intend him to make for Italy. After many difficulties he reaches Sicily, where his father dies, and as soon as they leave Sicily the storm arises with which Book I began.

Book IV

Dido is fascinated by Aeneas' heroics and falls in love with him. He lingers for a whole winter with her in Carthage before Jupiter sternly reminds him that he must press on to Italy. He abandons Dido, and in despair she commits suicide.

Books V and VI

The Trojans set sail once more, and digress only to hold funeral games in Sicily in honor of Aeneas' dead father. Before they make their final landfall in Italy, Aeneas, acting as usual on divine advice, visits the underworld where he witnesses the punishment of the wicked and the rewards of the just. He meets the spirits of famous Romans yet to be born, and confers with the ghost of his father.

Book VII

The Trojans come to shore in the territory of the Latins, at the mouth of the river Tiber, and are encouraged by omens that they have arrived at the right spot for their new foundation. Aeneas is warmly received by king Latinus, who remembers an old prophecy that his daughter Lavinia is destined to marry a stranger from a strange land. But Lavinia is already engaged to a local chieftain Turnus, who therefore violently resents the Trojans' arrival, and with Juno's help foments a war against them.

Book VIII

Fighting breaks out at once. While the rest of the Trojans are besieged by Turnus in their camp, Aeneas travels up the river to look for help. He is welcomed by king Evander, who shows him round his town, intimating that this will one day be the site of Rome. Evander sends Aeneas off to Etruria, where he can find allies in his war against the Latins, and sends along his own young son Pallas, entrusted to Aeneas' care. On the way, Venus gives Aeneas a wonderful new shield whose decorations mysteriously illustrate the future greatness of Rome.

Book IX

Meanwhile, the battle rages around the Trojan camp, as Turnus' forces try to break down its defensive earthworks. Two young Trojans make an attempt to break through the Latin lines in order to tell Aeneas of the crisis, but their eagerness for glory makes them careless. Their expedition is a disaster and only serves to make Turnus more determined.

Book X

Aeneas and his new allies arrive by sea to relieve the Trojan camp. In the ensuing battle, individual acts of great and often futile courage, interrupted by all manner of unexpected twists in the flow of the action, culminate in horrendous casualties on both sides, including Evander's son Pallas, who is killed by Turnus.

Book XI

A truce is struck, so that the dead can be buried, and Pallas' body is sadly escorted home. Peace feelers include the suggestion that Aeneas and Turnus should meet in single combat; but the negotiations do not go smoothly, and the truce does not hold. Fighting breaks out once more, as Turnus becomes more and more frustrated with his failure to break the Trojans. He is encouraged by the gallantry of Camilla, a young woman who leads the Volscian cavalry, but she is killed in action.

Book XII

It appears that neither side is capable of overcoming the other. But after much discussion the gods agree that the Trojan and Latin races should merge as one, and that the Latin customs and language should be preserved forever: whatever happens, the future of Rome must be assured. So the single combat is arranged once more. With both armies cheering them on, Aeneas and Turnus fight it out alone, until Aeneas in his victory avenges the death of Pallas.

APPENDIX II

Significant Events in Roman History

1180 BCE   (traditional) Fall of Troy

753   Founding of Rome by Romulus and Remus

509   Fall of the Roman Monarchy. Establishment of the Republic

509–280   Rome gains control over Etruscans, Latins and central Italy

390   Gauls invade Italy and temporarily occupy Rome

280–275   Rome gains control over Greek cities of southern Italy

264–241   First Punic War. Sicily becomes first Roman province

218–202   Second Punic War

146   Third Punic War. Destruction of Carthage

Sack of Corinth. Greece comes under Roman control

100   Birth of Julius Caesar

70   Birth of Vergil

63   Birth of Octavian (later Augustus Caesar)

49–46   Civil War: Julius Caesar v. Pompey

46   Julius Caesar becomes dictator

44   Julius Caesar assassinated

31   Battle of Actium. Establishment of Roman Empire

19   Death of Vergil

14 CE   Death of Augustus Caesar

465 CE   Empire in Decline: Rome sacked by the Vandals

476 CE   Last Roman Emperor deposed

APPENDIX III
Family Trees

(the equal sign signifies a mating)

1. The Gods:

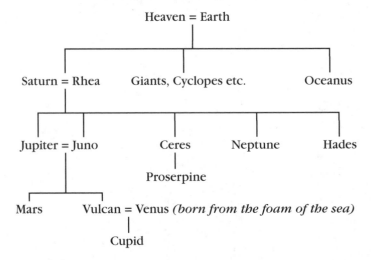

Heaven = Earth

Saturn = Rhea   Giants, Cyclopes etc.   Oceanus

Jupiter = Juno   Ceres   Neptune   Hades

Proserpine

Mars   Vulcan = Venus *(born from the foam of the sea)*

Cupid

Gods who were by one means or another also the offspring
of Jupiter:

Apollo
Bacchus
Diana
Hercules
Mercury
Minerva *(born fully formed from Jupiter's head)*

2. Priam's family:

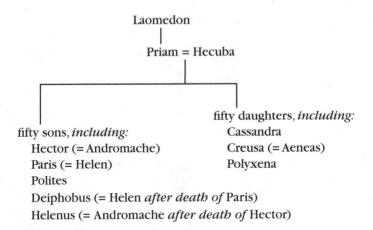

Laomedon
|
Priam = Hecuba

fifty sons, *including:*
   Hector (= Andromache)
   Paris (= Helen)
   Polites
   Deiphobus (= Helen *after death of* Paris)
   Helenus (= Andromache *after death of* Hector)

fifty daughters, *including:*
   Cassandra
   Creusa (= Aeneas)
   Polyxena

3. Aeneas' family:

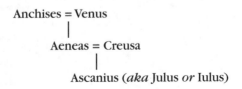

Anchises = Venus
|
Aeneas = Creusa
|
Ascanius (*aka* Julus *or* Iulus)

4. Dido's family:

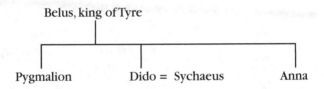

Belus, king of Tyre

Pygmalion   Dido = Sychaeus   Anna

5. Latinus' family:

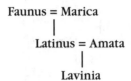

APPENDIX IV
Discussion Questions

1. What is an epic poem? In what ways does the *Aeneid* adhere to and depart from the traditional definition?

2. Can we say that the *Aeneid* is a "timeless" piece of literature, or is it merely a historical curiosity? Does the unfamiliar setting make the main characters seem more or less accessible or sympathetic?

3. In the original Latin, Aeneas is routinely described as *pius* (lit. *pious*). Is Aeneas' piety an attractive characteristic, or does he come off as a bit of a prig? Do his actions at the very end of the story seem consistent with everything else that he does?

4. Is it fair to suggest that Turnus is more fully depicted and more interesting than Aeneas? In what ways might Turnus be considered a more sympathetic character?

5. What does Vergil mean when he says at the beginning of Book 7 that he plans to introduce "a more serious tone" and "a more universal theme"? What are the differences in tone and theme between the two halves of the *Aeneid?*

6. As is normal in an ancient epic, the main characters in the *Aeneid* are larger than life heroic figures—gods, kings, mighty warriors. Does the work suffer from a lack of "ordinary people"?

7.   What is the function of the gods and other supernatural beings, who are very active throughout?

8.   Does the persistent presence of gods and supernatural beings make the story more or less satisfactory?

9.   What was the role of women in the Roman society of Vergil's time? How does Vergil treat women (e.g. Helen, Hecuba, Creusa, Andromache, Dido, Amata, Camilla) in the *Aeneid*? Is it true, as one critic has suggested, that the *Aeneid* celebrates "macho" behavior as no other work of literature?

10. Much is made in the *Aeneid* of father-son relationships. How much do the relationships that Vergil describes have in common with contemporary father-son relationships? Do Vergil's fathers and sons set a good example?

11. Are we supposed to sympathize with Dido or with Aeneas in their meetings in Books IV and VI? Is Dido's fury reasonable? Is Aeneas a cad? What other possible actions could Aeneas have taken? What other possible actions could Dido have taken?

12. The *Aeneid* is full of similes. What do the similes have in common? Do they have any other function beyond the simple comparison of one action/person to another?

13. What were the historical, political and cultural relationships between the Romans and the Greeks? How does Vergil differentiate between the Greeks and the Trojans (soon to be Romans), or between the Trojans and the Italians?

14. Is all the violence necessary? How much of it is gratuitous? How much of the *Aeneid* can be seen as an anti-war tract?

15. Does Vergil (or his hero Aeneas) have a sense of humor? Are there any moments of comic relief or lightness in the work?

16. Is the *Aeneid* a work of propaganda? If it is, does this get in the way of our appreciation of the narrative?

17. How are patriotic themes dealt with? Does Vergil's patriotism differ in any way from contemporary definitions?

18. There is a tradition that when Vergil died, he requested (unsuccessfully) that the manuscript of the *Aeneid* should be destroyed because it needed so much revision and polishing. What changes do you think he might have made himself? What changes would you have suggested to him?

19. How would you set about making the *Aeneid* into a movie?

20. What would be the effect of retelling Books I to VI from the point of view of Ascanius and Books VII to XII from the point of view of Turnus?

The Main Characters of the Aeneid

(names in parentheses with equal sign preceding are Greek equivalents for Roman names)

Characters in the Narrative

Acestes [Uh-KESS-teez]: king of Drepanon in Sicily. An old ally of Priam and the Trojans.

Achaemenides [Ahk-eye-MEN-id-eez]: one of Ulysses' sailors, left behind in Sicily among the Cyclopes.

Achates [Uh-KATE-eez]: a Trojan warrior and Aeneas' closest companion; he usually accompanies Aeneas on dangerous or delicate missions.

Achilles [Uh-KILL-eez]: the most effective warrior in the Greek army. The protagonist of Homer's *Iliad.*

Aeneas [Eye-NEE-us]: son of the goddess Venus and the mortal Anchises, chosen by Jupiter to establish a new Troy in Italy. The protagonist of the *Aeneid.*

Aeolus [EE-oh-lus]: god of the winds.

Agamemnon [Ag-uh-MEM-non]: king of Mycenae in Argos, and with his brother Menelaus the joint leader of the Greek expedition against Troy. On his return from the war he was murdered by his wife, who had taken up with a lover in his absence. However, her ostensible reason was that he had sacrificed their daughter Iphigeneia in order to gain a fair wind for Troy.

Allecto [Ah-LEK-toe]: one of the Furies (see below), sent by Juno to stir up opposition to Aeneas.

Amata [Uh-MAH-tuh]: wife of king Latinus of Latium, and mother of Lavinia.

Anchises [Ann-KAI-seez]: Aeneas' father, whom Aeneas rescues from the ruins of Troy.

Andromache [Ann-DRAH-mah-kee]: wife of Hector and the mother of Astyanax. She was taken to Greece as a slave after the fall of Troy, where she eventually married Helenus.

Anna [ANN-uh]: sister and confidante of queen Dido of Carthage.

Apollo [Uh-POLL-low]: god of prophecy, poetical inspiration and the sun. Though his most famous oracle is at Delphi in central Greece, he also had an important temple and oracle near Cumae, on the west coast of Italy.

Ascanius [Uh-SKAY-nee-us]: the son of Aeneas and Creusa. Also known as Julus or Iulus. The future founder of Alba Longa.

Astyanax [Uh-STY-uh-nax]: the infant son of Hector and Andromache, murdered by the Greeks after the fall of Troy.

Atlas [AT-lus]: one of the old gods who preceded Jupiter. He rebelled against Jupiter and was condemned to stand as a mountain in northwest Africa and carry the world on his shoulders. The Atlas Mountains and the Atlantic Ocean are named after him.

Bacchus [BACK-us] or **Dionysus** [Die-oh-NIGH-sus]: god of all vegetation and especially of the vine. His worship is often accompanied by wild ritual dances carried out by his women followers, known as Bacchantes, who are said to be inspired or possessed by him.

Calchas [KALL-kuss]: a prophet who accompanied the Greek army to Troy. It was he who advised Agamemnon to sacrifice Iphigeneia.

Camilla [Kuh-MILL-uh]: a young woman of the Volscians who fights in support of Turnus.

Cassandra [Kuh-SAND-ruh]: a daughter of Priam. Apollo had once fallen in love with her, and when she rejected him he gave her the power of making true prophecies which no one would ever believe.

Celaeno [Sell-EYE-no]: leader of the Harpies, winged monsters who harass the Trojans.

Cerberus [SIRB-urr-us]: the three-headed watchdog of the underworld.

Ceres [SEAR-eez] or Demeter [De-MEAT-er]: goddess of the earth and crops. Mother of Proserpina.

Charon [CARE-ohn]: the ferryman who escorts the spirits of the dead across the river Styx to the underworld.

Charybdis [Car-IB-diss]: a dangerous whirlpool on the southern side of the straits of Messina, which separate Italy and Sicily. On the other side is the monster Scylla.

Circe [SIR-see]: a witch who lives on the island of Aeea, off the west coast of Italy. She captures travelers and turns them into animals.

Creusa [Kray-OOH-suh]: a daughter of Priam. The wife of Aeneas and mother of Ascanius.

Cupid [KEW-pid]: son of Venus. Usually depicted as a small child with a bow from which he fires the arrows of love.

Cybele [SIB-bull-ee]: goddess of the earth, or Earth-mother, associated or identified with Ceres. Often described as riding in a chariot designed to look like a wheeled turret.

Cyclopes [Sigh-CLO-peez]: man-eating giants who have one eye in the middle of their foreheads. They live in Sicily, either as shepherds or workers in Vulcan's smithy under Mount Etna.

Daedalus [DEE-duh-lus]: designer of the doors of the temple at Cumae, and before that, of the famous maze in Crete which served as a prison for the Minotaur, the offspring of King Minos' wife and a bull.

Deiphobus [Day-IF-uh-bus]: a son of Priam, who married Helen after the death of Paris. Later murdered by Menelaus.

Diana [Die-ANN-uh] (= Artemis [ART-emm-iss]): goddess of hunting, childbirth and chastity, and (under her other name of Hecate) queen of the underworld. Also associated with Proserpina.

Dido [DYE-doh]: the founder and queen of Carthage, who fled from Tyre in Phoenicia after her husband Sychaeus was murdered.

Diomedes [Die-oh-MEED-eez]: a Greek warrior in the war against Troy, famous for his beautiful horses. He lived in retirement at Arpi in southern Italy.

Drances [DRANK-eez]: a Latin politician, opposed to Turnus.

Eryx [ER-iks]: son of Venus and half-brother to Aeneas. Killed in a boxing match with Hercules. A mountain in Sicily was named after him.

Euryalus [Yoo-rih-AY-lus]: a young man, one of Aeneas' companions, in love with Nisus.

Evander [E-VAN-dur]: king of Pallanteum (later to be the site of Rome), who came to Italy from Arcadia in Greece. The father of Pallas, and an ally of Aeneas.

Furies [FYUR-eez): winged women who carry out the vengeance of the gods. They have snakes for hair, and carry whips and torches.

Hades [HAY-deez]: brother of Jupiter and king of the underworld (which is also known as Tartarus or Avernus).

Hecate [HECK-uh-tee]: see Diana

Hector [HEK-tur]: a son of Priam, and the most successful fighter in the Trojan army. Killed in single combat by Achilles.

Hecuba [HEK-oo-bah]: the wife of Priam, and the mother of all his children.

Helen [HELL-en]: the wife of Menelaus, king of Sparta. The most beautiful woman in the world, she possessed, in Christopher Marlowe's phrase, "the face that launched a thousand ships". Her abduction by Paris was the occasion of the Trojan war.

Helenus [HELL-en-us]: a son of Priam, and, like his sister Cassandra, a prophet. Taken to Greece as a slave after the fall of Troy, and subsequently married to Andromache.

Hercules [HER-kyew-leez] (= Heracles [HARE-uh-kleez]): son of Jupiter and a mortal, but promoted to immortality after his death. He was required by Jupiter to perform the famous twelve labors for king Eurystheus of Argos, the last of which was to steal the watchdog Cerberus from the underworld. He traditionally appears wearing a lion-skin and carrying a club.

Iarbas [Ee-AR-bass]: an African king whose kingdom borders Carthage.

Ilioneus [Il-ee-ON-yoos]: one of Aeneas' companions, often used as an envoy on diplomatic missions.

Iris [EYE-riss]: a messenger of the gods, especially of Juno. Usually appears as a rainbow.

Ixion [IKS-ee-on]: a Greek king who once attempted to rape Juno. As his punishment, he is lashed to a wheel which turns for ever in the underworld.

Julus (or Iulus) [YOO-lus]: alternative name of Ascanius.

Juno [JEW-noh] (= Hera [HARE-uh]): queen of the gods. Jupiter's husband and sister. She hates Venus, Aeneas and all the Trojans.

Jupiter [JEW-pit-er] (= Zeus [ZYOOS]): king of the gods, whom he rules from his palace on Mount Olympus in northeast Greece. Husband and sister of Juno. He punishes mortals with thunderbolts that he has made for him by the Cyclopes.

Juturna [Jew-TURN-uh]: a water-nymph, once seduced by Jupiter. Sister to Turnus.

Laocoon [Lay-O-koh-own]: the priest of Neptune in Troy, who warns the Trojans about the wooden horse.

Latinus [Lah-TEE-nus]: king of the Latins of Latium. He wants his daughter Lavinia to marry Aeneas rather than Turnus.

Lausus [LAUS-us]: son of Mezentius, king of the Etruscans.

Lavinia [Luh-VEEN-ee-uh]: daughter of Latinus and Amata, engaged to be married to Turnus.

Mars [MARZ](= Ares [AIR-eez]): god of war.

Menelaus [Men-uh-LAY-us]: king of Sparta and with his brother Agamemnon the joint leader of the Greek expedition to Troy. The husband of Helen.

Mercury [MURR-cure-ee] (= **Hermes** [HER-meez]): god of travel, trade and trickery, and Jupiter's messenger of Jupiter. Usually depicted wearing winged sandals.

Messapus [Mes-SAH-pus]: one of Turnus' chief lieutenants.

Mezentius [Me-ZEN-tee-us]: exiled king of the Etruscans. He is hostile to Evander and an ally of Turnus in the war against Aeneas.

Minerva [Min-UR-vuh] (= **Athena** [Uh-THEEN-uh]): goddess of wisdom and the arts. She is usually depicted in full armor, often with the head of a Gorgon (a snake-haired monster) on her shield.

Minos [MEE-nos]: (1) the first king of Crete, and later one of the judges in the underworld. (2) son (or grandson) of Minos 1; the king of Crete whose wife fell in love with a bull. Their offspring, the Minotaur, was kept in a maze beneath his palace which was designed by Daedalus.

Misenus [My-SEE-nus]: a trumpeter in the Trojan army.

Mnestheus [MNEES-thyoos]: one of Aeneas' most trusted companions

Neptune [NEP-tyoon] (= **Poseidon** [Po-SIDE-un]): god of the sea. Brother of Hades and Jupiter. With Apollo he had built the original walls of Troy, but he had punished the Trojans when their king refused to pay him for his work.

Nisus [NEES-us]: a young man, one of Aeneas' companions, in love with Euryalus.

Opis [OH-pis]: messenger of Diana.

Orion [Oh-RYE-un]: a giant, famous for his skill at hunting and metalwork, who at his death was changed into a constellation.

Orpheus [ORF-yoos]: legendary Greek poet and lyre-player whose music could charm rivers into pausing in their flow and the birds in the trees to stop singing.

Palinurus [Pal-een-YOUR-us]: Aeneas' steersman and navigator.

Pallas [PALL-as]: son of Evander, king of Pallanteum..

Paris [PAIR-is]: one of Priam's sons. He was chosen by Jupiter to judge the beauty contest between Juno, Minerva and Venus, and as a reward for choosing Venus he was allowed to abduct Helen, the wife of Menelaus.

Pirithous [Pi-ri-THOW-us]: Theseus' companion in many of his adventures.

Polites [Puh-LIE-teez]: a son of Priam, killed by Pyrrhus.

Polyphemus [Poll-ih-FEE-mus]: the largest and fiercest of the Cyclopes (see above), blinded by Ulysses.

Priam [PRY-am]: king of Troy, husband of Hecuba, and the father of fifty sons and fifty daughters.

Proserpina [Pro-SIR-pin-uh] (= **Persephone** [Purr-SEFF-uh-nee]): wife of Hades, who abducted her to the underworld. She was allowed to spend the spring and summer on earth with her mother Ceres. Associated with Diana/Hecate.

Pygmalion [Pig-MAY-lee-uhn]: king of Tyre and Dido's wicked brother, who murdered her husband Sychaeus.

Pyrrhus [PIRR-us]: a Greek warrior, the son of Achilles.

Saturn [SAT-urn] (= **Cronos** [CROW-nus]): one of the old gods who preceded Jupiter. He became one of the earliest Italian kings and taught the inhabitants the art of agriculture. The period of his reign is often looked back upon as a Golden Age.

Scylla [SILL-uh]: a dangerous monster who lives on the northern (Italian) side of the straits of Messina, opposite the whirlpool Charybdis.

Sinon [SEE-nohn]: a Greek double agent who tricks the Trojans into bringing the wooden horse inside their city.

Sibyl [SIB-buhl], the: priestess of Apollo at Cumae, who serves as Aeneas' guide through the underworld.

Sychaeus [Sik-EYE-us]: Dido's husband, murdered by Pygmalion.

Tarchon [TARK-ohn]: an Etruscan chieftain, and an ally to Aeneas.

Theseus [THEES-yoos]: a legendary king of Athens, who as a young man killed the Minotaur of Crete and later went to the underworld with his friend Pirithous to try to kidnap Proserpina.

Turnus [TURN-us]: chief of the Rutulians, an Italian tribe, whose capital is Ardea. Engaged to Lavinia, and the leader of the effort to expel Aeneas from Italy.

Ulysses [You-LISS-eez] (= Odysseus [Oh-DISS-yus]): a Greek warrior from Ithaca, famous for his cunning and the instigator of the trick involving the wooden horse. Under his Greek name, Odysseus, the protagonist of Homer's *Odyssey*.

Venus [VEE-nus] (= Aphrodite [Af-roh-DIE-tee]): goddess of love. The mother of Aeneas, and, among the gods, the most enthusiastic supporter of the Trojans. The winner of the beauty contest which was judged by Paris.

Vesta [VEST-uh]: goddess of the domestic hearth.

Vulcan [VULL-kin] (= Hephaistos [Heff-EYE-stus]): god of metallurgy and blacksmiths; a husband of Venus. He has his workshop under Mount Etna in Sicily and his workers are the one-eyed giants, the Cyclopes.

Characters in Roman Legend and History
(as foretold to Aeneas mainly in Books VI and VIII)

Agrippa [A-GRIP-uh]: in command of Augustus' fleet at the battle of Actium.

Alba Longa [ALB-uh LONG-uh]: city twelve miles from the site of Rome, founded by Ascanius, son of Aeneas.

Ancus Martius [ANK-us MART-ee-us]: the fourth king of Rome.

Antony (Mark Antony, anglicized from Marcus Antonius [MARK-us Ant-OH-nee-us]): after Caesar's assassination, he became one of the pretenders to the supreme power in Rome. He was defeated by Augustus at the battle of Actium, and committed suicide.

Augustus [Ow-GUST-us]: also referred to as Augustus Caesar. Born as Octavian, he was the great-nephew of Julius Caesar. He was a student in Athens at the moment of Julius Caesar's assassination, and as Caesar's heir he returned to Rome to assume Caesar's dictatorial power. In more than ten years of fighting and political wrangling, he systematically overcame all opposition, and at the battle of Actium (31 BCE), he defeated Antony, his last rival. He then became the first Roman emperor, and in 27 BCE the Senate granted him the title of Augustus (Latin: honored, revered).

Brutus [BROOT-us]: one of the first two Roman consuls (elected heads of state). He led the movement to drive out the kings from Rome and establish the republic in 509 BCE. He executed his two sons, who had conspired with the Etruscans to reinstate the monarchy. An ancestor of the Brutus who led the conspiracy to assassinate Julius Caesar.

Caesar [SEEZ-er]: Julius Caesar, the distinguished Roman general and statesman. He conquered Gaul, and fought a civil war against his son-in-law and chief political rival,

Pompey, after which he became dictator. He was assassinated on the Ides (15th) of March in 44 BCE by a group of senators who feared that he wanted to make himself king. Caesar is also used as a generic name for all the Roman emperors.

Camillus [Cuh-MILL-us]: a famous general of the early Roman republic.

Catiline [CAT-ill-ine]: conspired unsuccessfully to overthrow the republic in 63 BCE.

Cato [KAY-toh]: a much-admired example of the traditional Roman virtues of old-fashioned plain living and sober seriousness.

Cincinnatus [Sin-sin-AT-us]: appointed by the Senate, for a term of six months, to lead the Roman forces in a war against a neighboring Italian tribe. When senators came to bring him the news of his appointment he was found working on his small farm.

Cleopatra [Clee-oh-PAT-ruh]: queen of Egypt. She was the ally and lover of Antony, who deserted him at the battle of Actium and later committed suicide.

Cloelia [Cloh-EE-lee-a]: a young woman who, having been taken hostage by the Etruscan king Porsenna, escaped by swimming back to Rome across the Tiber.

Cossus [KOSS-us]: in the early wars of Rome, he won special distinction by killing an enemy commander in single combat.

Fabius [FAYB-ee-us]: Quintus Fabius Maximus was appointed dictator in the second Punic war (218–201 BCE), after Hannibal, the Carthaginian general, had invaded Italy and won two easy victories. By ingenious maneuvering, Fabius refused to give Hannibal an opportunity to engage the Romans in a further pitched battle, until

Hannibal's lines of communication became seriously overextended. Fabius was given the nickname of Cunctator, the Delayer.

Fabricius [Fab-REE-cee-us]: general in the war in southern Italy (279 BCE) against king Pyrrhus of Epirus. Pyrrhus' doctor had approached Fabricius with an offer to poison his royal patient, but Fabricius refused to gain any advantage from treachery.

Forum [FOR-um]: the open space in the middle of Rome, first used as a market place and later as a center for all political and judicial activity.

Gauls [GAWLS]: Celtic tribes living in the northwest of Italy and what is now France.

Gracchi [GRACK-eye], the (Tiberius Gracchus and his brother Gaius Gracchus): aristocrats whose well-intended, though unorthodox or even illegal, attempts to solve social problems and introduce democratic reforms caused serious constitutional crises in 133 and 123 BCE.

Hannibal [HAN-ni-buhl]: the Carthaginian general in the Second Punic war (218–202 BCE), who crossed the Alps in order to invade Italy. Eventually he was compelled to return to Carthage, where he was defeated by Scipio.

Horatius [Ho-RAY-tee-us]: in the war against king Porsenna, he saved Rome by single-handedly preventing the Etruscan army from crossing the last bridge across the Tiber.

Julius Caesar [JEWL-ee-us SEEZ-er]: see Caesar

Manlius [MAN-lee-us]: during the Gauls' occupation of Rome (380 BCE), he was commander of the garrison on the Capitol. When the Gauls made a night assault, the sacred geese who were kept in the temple gave the alarm, and Capitol was saved.

Marcellus [Mar-SELL-us]: (1) a famous Roman general. He served with great distinction in the first and second Punic wars, and in a campaign against the Gauls (222 BCE) defeated the enemy chieftain in single combat. (2) a descendant of Marcellus 1, and the nephew of the emperor Augustus. He was an extremely promising and popular young man, and was designated by Augustus to be his heir. However, he died unexpectedly of fever at the age of 18.

Mark Antony: see Antony

Mettius [METT-ee-us]: a king of Alba Longa before it was absorbed by Rome.

Numa Pompilius (NYOOM-ah Pomp-EE-lee-us): the second king of Rome.

Pompey (anglicized form of Pompeius [Pom-PAY-us]): the main political rival and son-in-law of Julius Caesar.

Porsenna [Por-SENN-uh]: Etruscan king who attacked Rome in an attempt to restore the Tarquin family to the throne of Rome after the expulsion of the kings.

Quintus Fabius Maximus: see Fabius.

Remus [REEM-us]: Romulus' twin brother, and with him joint founder of Rome.

Rhea Silvia [REE-a SEELV-ee-a]: mother of Romulus and Remus.

Romulus [ROM-yoo-lus]: son of Mars and Rhea Silvia, and with his twin brother Remus joint founder of Rome. As babies, the twins were set adrift down the Tiber by their wicked uncle, who had usurped the throne of Alba Longa, and wanted to prevent them from succeeding to the throne. According to legend, they were cast ashore and rescued by a wolf. They decided to found a city of their own, but Romulus quarreled with Remus and killed him. He then became the first king of Rome.

Sabines [SAYB-eyenz]: an Italian tribe. According to legend, Romulus, in the very early days of Rome, realized that his city needed women in order to maintain its population. He therefore invited the neighboring Sabines to a festival; at a signal, the Romans leapt upon the Sabine women and abducted them.

Scipio [SIP-ee-oh]: (1) Roman general who defeated Carthaginian forces in Spain and Africa in the final stages of the second Punic war, and won the nickname Africanus for his final defeat of Hannibal at the battle of Zama just outside Carthage (202 BCE). (2) Grandson of Scipio 1, who destroyed Carthage in 146 BCE.

Silvius [SILV-ee-us]: son of Aeneas and Lavinia, and Ascanius' successor as king of Alba Longa. His name means "born in the woods."

Silvius Aeneas [SILV-ee-us Uh-NEE-us]: descendant of Ascanius, and a later king of Alba Longa.

Tarquins [TAR-kwinz]: the last two kings of Rome. They were Etruscans from the Tarquin family. The seventh and last king, Tarquin the Proud, was expelled in 509 BCE. He fled to Etruria and persuaded king Porsenna to try to reinstate him.

Torquatus [Tor-KWAH-tus]: a Roman general in the wars against the Etruscans. He executed his son when the latter attacked the enemy without permission.

Tullus Hostilius [TULL-us Host-EEL-ee-us]: the third king of Rome.

Why Vergil?
A Collection of Interpretations
Stephanie Quinn, ed.

xv + 452 pp. (2000)
Paperback, ISBN 978-0-86516-418-5
Hardcover, ISBN 978-0-86516-435-2

The more than 40 essays contained in *Why Vergil?* cover a wide range of topics and include many well known names, e.g., Bernard Knox, Adam Parry, George Duckworth, Herbert Benario, Meyer Reinhold, Marilyn Skinner, and Charles Segal. The collection contains essays on Vergilian criticism and Vergil's place in literary tradition, as well as a selection of 20th century literature works influenced by Vergil.

> We lack automatic and simple answers to the question "Why Vergil?" —or many similar questions for that matter: why literature, why art, especially why old literature—and at that—why literature in an old language? Yet even after 2,000 years, the voice of Vergil still resonates with the universal human cry.
>
> **–Stephanie Quinn,** from the Introduction

The Labors of Aeneas
What A Pain It Was to Found the Roman Race
Rose Williams

vi + 108 pp. (2003) Paperback
ISBN 978-0-86516-556-4

This paperback book retells the story of Vergil's *Aeneid* in a light-hearted and understandable manner with humorous insights and asides. This volume makes Books I–XII of Vergil's *Aeneid* enjoyable and easy to follow.

> This is Virgil's famous propaganda piece, the *Aeneid* cheerfully made accessible to a modern reader who wouldn't glance at a formal transla-tion. It is faithful to the story and might be used in conjunction with a high school Latin class. Beyond that, it was fun for this long-ago Latin student to peruse a cheeky retelling.
>
> **–Juliet Waldron,** *The Historical Novels Review,* Issue 27, Feb 2004

The Art of the *Aeneid*
2ⁿᵈ Edition

William S. Anderson

vi + 138 pp. (2005, 2nd Ed., 1989 reprint of the 1969
Prentice-Hall edition) Paperback
ISBN 978-0-86516-598-4

Anderson's narrative in *The Art of the Aeneid* provides the modern reader fresh
insights into Vergil, into the *Aeneid*. His analysis illuminates the literary and his-
torical context and covers each of the twelve books of one of the greatest and most
enduring works of Latin literature.

Features:
• Notes • Chronology of Vergil's historical context • List of sources for further
reading • Index • Map of the wanderings of Aeneas

Poet and Artist
*Imaging the *Aeneid**

Henry V. Bender and David Califf

xvi + 88 pp. (2004) Paperback + CD-ROM
ISBN 978-0-86516-585-4

Poet and Artist is a winning combination of a CD that features the Ogilby plates
(included by John Dryden in his translation of the *Aeneid*) and a student edition
of selected lines of Vergil's epic, complete with questions about Vergil's Latin
masterpiece. By juxtaposing the images on the plates, the text of Vergil, and the
useful questions to be used as guidelines, the authors have enabled students to
increase their comprehension of the Latin passage and its textual details and to
reflect more critically upon the text and the artist's canvas.

Poet and Artist includes the unadapted Latin text (1857 lines) of all of the following
lines from Vergil's *Aeneid*: I.1–519, II.1–56, 199–297, 469–566, 735–804, IV.1–449,
642–705, VI.1–211, 450–476, 847–901, X.420–509, XII.791–842, 887–952

LEGAMUS TRANSITIONAL READERS

The LEGAMUS Transitional Readers are designed for students moving from a textbook to reading authentic Latin authors. Each text includes pre-reading materials, grammatical exercises, complete vocabulary, notes designed for reading comprehension, and other reading aids.

— Teacher's Guides are available for all these titles —

Catullus: *A LEGAMUS Transitional Reader*

Sean Smith and Kenneth F. Kitchell, Jr.

xxx + 160 pp. (2006) Paperback
ISBN 978-0-86516-634-9

Cicero: *A LEGAMUS Transitional Reader*

Mark Haynes and Judith Sebesta

xxii + 226 pp. (2010) Paperback
ISBN 978-0-86516-656-1

Horace: *A LEGAMUS Transitional Reader*

Ronnie Ancona and David J. Murphy

xxiv + 189 pp. (2008) Paperback
ISBN 978-0-86516-676-9

Ovid: *A LEGAMUS Transitional Reader*

Caroline Perkins and Denise Davis-Henry

xxv + 127 pp. (2007) Paperback
ISBN 978-0-86516-604-2

Vergil: *A LEGAMUS Transitional Reader*

Thomas J. Sienkewicz and LeaAnn A. Osburn

xxiv + 135 pp. (2004) Paperback
ISBN 978-0-86516-578-6

Caesar: *A LEGAMUS Transitional Reader*

Hans Mueller and Rose Williams

Forthcoming (2012) Paperback
ISBN 978-0-86516-733-9

WWW.BOLCHAZY.COM